PRACTICE
MAKES
PERFECT®

Spanish
Sentence Builder

SECOND EDITION

PRACTICE MAKES PERFECT®

Spanish
Sentence Builder

SECOND EDITION

Gilda Nissenberg

Mc
Graw
Hill
Education

New York   Chicago   San Francisco   Athens   London   Madrid
Mexico City   Milan   New Dehli   Singapore   Sydney   Toronto

1 2 3 4 5 6 7 8 9   LHS   22 21 20 19 18 17

ISBN   978-1-260-01925-4
MHID   1-260-01925-X

e-ISBN 978-1-260-01926-1
e-MHID   1-260-01926-8

Interior design by Village Typographers, Inc.

McGraw-Hill Education products are available at special quantity discounts to use as premiums and sales promotions or for use in corporate training programs. To contact a representative, please visit the Contact Us pages at www.mhprofessional.com.

Contents

Introduction

A short paragraph that communicates an idea, a letter, or a written request to grab the attention of a reader are examples of what you want to be able write in Spanish. But in order to write each of these you have to learn how to build effective sentences to communicate your ideas clearly. Writing is a skill that presents challenges to those who want to communicate effectively in a foreign language.

This book will help you build your writing skills in Spanish. You will find the elements that you need: clear explanations of how different grammatical structures in the Spanish language must be combined to create sentences and abundant examples that illustrate how to combine the structures to build the sentences. You will start with the least complex sentences and move gradually to more complex structures.

The only way to acquire and improve writing skills is to practice writing. This book includes different types of exercises for you to practice as you learn. Some exercises ask for a variation of a model; others require that you use a series of words in the appropriate order to build a sentence, choose the most appropriate answer among multiple choices, or use the required punctuation to communicate the correct message.

You will find ample opportunities to write your own original sentences in a given context. As a result, your writing skills will improve. An answer key is provided at the end of the book with the correct answers and sample sentences for all but the most personalized exercises.

Sentence writing may be challenging at times. Paying close attention to instructions, practicing regularly, and applying the rules of sentence building consistently will make you a better writer. With this book you will discover ways to build your sentences and build your confidence as a writer in Spanish.

¡A escribir!

Declarative sentences and word order

Sentences and phrases are different in nature and serve different purposes to communicate ideas and thoughts.

What is a phrase?

A phrase consists of more than one word. It does not have the *subject + predicate* organization of a sentence.

one or more words → phrase

Some phrases are formulas used frequently in social situations. Note that they do not have a subject and a verb:

Buenos días.	*Good morning.*
Hasta luego.	*Bye for now.*

Other phrases may be clichés or proverbs that apply to specific situations. They are rarely translated word for word.

La niña de sus ojos.	*The apple of his eye.*
El alma de la fiesta.	*The life of the party.*

Other types of phrases are classified as *prepositional phrases*, **con su hermano** (*with his brother*), or *adverbial phrases*, **a través de los años** (*throughout the years*), that add information to your sentences. In later units you will study these phrases and incorporate them into your writing practice.

What is a sentence?

Unlike a phrase, a *sentence* is defined as a grammatical unit:

subject + predicate → sentence

To build this unit in Spanish you need nouns, a verb, object pronouns, adverbs, etc., elements you have previously learned. Think of these elements as the blocks that help you build a structure. A Spanish sentence includes a *subject*, a word or a group of words that tell you what or whom the sentence is about, and a *predicate*, a word or words that tell us something about the subject. A capital letter is required to start a sentence and a period indicates the end of the message.

Declarative sentences

A *declarative sentence* (from the Latin **declarare**) makes a statement. A statement communicates information; it does not ask a question, it does not express exclamations or give a command. A declarative sentence consists of the following elements:

subject + predicate

El piloto + aterriza el avión.
El piloto **aterriza** el avión.   *The pilot **lands (is landing)** the plane.*
El piloto **aterrizó** el avión.   *The pilot **landed** the plane.*
El piloto **aterrizará** el avión.   *The pilot **will land** the plane.*

The verb in each of the three previous examples is in the *indicative* mode. The verb can be in the present, **aterriza**; the past, **aterrizó**; the future, **aterrizará**; or in compound tenses such as **ha aterrizado**, *has arrived*.

EJERCICIO 1·1

¿Es una oración o es una frase? *Indica* **O** *si es una oración;* **F** *si es una frase.*

1. _____ Luisa y yo.

2. _____ La mesa está servida.

3. _____ Leemos el periódico.

4. _____ Buenas noches.

5. _____ De nada.

6. _____ Esto es cierto.

EJERCICIO 1·2

Práctica y repaso. *Escribe cada oración en el tiempo verbal indicado.*

1. Mi hermano Marcos está en Buenos Aires.

   PRETÉRITO _____

   FUTURO _____

2. Él vive en Argentina.

   PRETÉRITO _____

   FUTURO _____

3. Tiene un apartamento en el centro de la ciudad.

   PRETÉRITO _____

   FUTURO _____

4. Trabaja en una oficina del gobierno.

PRETÉRITO _____

FUTURO _____

5. Marcos viaja a Santiago también.

PRETÉRITO _____

FUTURO _____

Word order in declarative sentences

In English, the natural word order of the parts of a sentence is: *subject + verb + object*. This is also the most frequent word order in Spanish:

> **subject + verb + object**
>
> Mario contestó el teléfono.   *Mario answered the phone.*

Unlike English, Spanish allows a bit more flexibility in word order. Here are other possibilities:

> **verb + subject + object or other elements**
>
> Vino un hombre con Lucía.   *A man came with Lucia.*
> Se aproximan los coches.   *The cars are getting closer.*

There are other possibilities in the word order:

> **Anoche** cenamos en "Casa Paco".   ***Last night*** *we dined at "Casa Paco."*
> **A Luisa la** vimos en el restaurante.   *We saw **Luisa** at the restaurant.*
> **Con mucho entusiasmo**, el músico toca   *The musician plays the piano **with a lot of***
>   el piano.   ***enthusiasm**.*

In the previous examples, the Spanish sentences begin with an adverb (**Anoche**), a direct object (**A Luisa**), or a phrase (**Con mucho entusiasmo**). Note the comma between the phrase and the rest of the sentence in the third example.

Remember that in Spanish the subject is not always explicit. Verb endings indicate *who* does the action. Let's look at some examples where the subject is implicit or understood:

> Encontr**amos** los zapatos.   ***We** found the shoes.*
> Viv**o** en Argentina.   ***I** live in Argentina.*
> Sal**ieron** a las cuatro y media.   ***They** left at four-thirty.*
> Escrib**es** una lista larga.   ***You** write a long list.*

EJERCICIO
1·3

Coloca (place) las palabras en el orden siguiente: sujeto + verbo + otros elementos. Usa la puntuación apropiada.

1. vive / Pedro Gómez / en ese edificio _____

2. es / Lucía / la esposa / de Pedro _____

3. la noticia / leímos / de su boda / en el periódico _____

4. tienen / en la playa / una casa _____

5. salieron / Lucía y su esposo / de luna de miel _____

6. en Barcelona / nacieron / Pedro y Lucía _____

7. estudiaron / mis hermanos / con ellos _____

8. anoche / de Pedro / recibimos / un email _____

EJERCICIO

1·4

Mi rutina. *Elige una de las frases o palabras para terminar las oraciones.*

día tras día / cuando necesito comunicarme / en la piscina olímpica / con sólo un billete / en diez minutos / en el autobús camino a casa / cuando hago mucho ejercicio / con frecuencia

1. Escribo cartas en español _____.

2. Voy a mi oficina _____.

3. Tengo hambre _____.

4. Practico la natación _____.

5. Corro casi una milla _____.

6. Voy a ganar la lotería _____.

7. Visito la biblioteca _____.

8. Leo el periódico _____.

Sentences with direct and indirect objects

To express ideas clearly in your sentences, you must arrange the words in a proper and logical order in Spanish. A sequence of words cannot always be translated word for word. Let's consider sentences that contain direct and/or indirect objects.

Direct object nouns

In Spanish, the direct object (**complemento directo**) usually follows the verb:

subject + verb + direct object

El juez dictó **la sentencia**. *The judge pronounced **the sentence**.*

In the previous sentence, these syntactical elements can be identified:

- **El juez** is the *subject* of the verb, in this case a person who does the action of the verb.
- **Dictó** is the *verb*. It is in the past tense and tells what the subject did.
- **La sentencia** is the *direct object*. The direct object receives the action of the verb.

¿Hay un complemento directo? *Si hay un complemento directo, subráyalo.*

1. Celebramos el cumpleaños de Laura.

2. Sus amigos hicieron una fiesta en la casa de Dora.

3. A las seis, llegaron los invitados.

4. Todos felicitaron a Laura en el día de su cumpleaños.

5. Sirvieron la cena en la terraza de Dora.

6. Luego saqué mi guitarra.

7. Canté dos rancheras a mis amigos.

8. Entró una chica encantadora.

9. Ahora sé su nombre.

El complemento directo. *Escoge el sustantivo (noun) apropiado para completar cada oración de manera apropiada.*

un presidente / una reacción / un recuento / una solución / un problema / una pregunta / una campaña / un proyecto

1. La noticia provoca _____ favorable para el candidato.

2. Todos los ciudadanos (*citizens*) quieren _____ honesto.

3. La campaña presidencial crea _____ para el partido de la oposición.

4. Una candidata exige (*demands*) _____ de los votos electorales.

5. El periodista hace _____ difícil a los dos candidatos.

6. Los expertos predicen _____ larga y dura.

7. Muchos jóvenes prefieren _____ rápida a sus problemas económicos.

The personal a with direct object nouns

This is a quick review of the use of the *personal* **a.** This preposition is placed before the *direct object* if the direct object is a definite or specific person or persons. The contraction **al** (**a** + **el** = **al**) is used if the masculine article **el** (*the*) follows the preposition.

subject + verb + personal a + direct object

Recibimos **a** Roberto.	*We greeted Roberto.*
Vimos **a** tu hermana.	*We saw your sister.*
Reconocimos **al** tío de Ana.	*We recognized Ana's uncle.*

The *personal* **a** is also used with the following direct objects:

◆ Domestic animals and pets. This shows emotions or attachment for these animals:

Luisa quiere **a su perro** con locura.	*Luisa loves **her dog** to death.*
La niña baña **a su gatito**.	*The girl bathes **her kitten**.*

◆ Objects or entities that involve a degree of emotional attachment:

Amo **a mi patria**.	*I love **my country**.*
La niña adora **a su osito de peluche**.	*The girl adores **her teddy bear**.*

◆ Indefinite pronouns that refer to a person: **alguien** (*someone*), **alguno/a** (*someone*), **nadie** (*no one*), **ninguno/a** (*no, no one*):

Vieron **a alguien** en el teatro.	*They saw **someone** in the theater.*

◆ Countries, cities, and geographical names *not* preceded by a definite article *may* sometimes have the *personal* **a**:

Extraño **a Barcelona**.	*I miss **Barcelona**.*
Extraño **Barcelona**.	*I miss **Barcelona**.*

Note that the personal **a** is *not* used when the direct object is a person following a form of the verb **tener**:

Tenemos dos tíos.	*We **have** two uncles.*
Juanita **tiene** amigos en Perú.	*Juanita **has** friends in Peru.*

EJERCICIO
1·7

*Si es necesario, escribe la preposición **a** en cada oración. Si no es necesario, escribe una **X**.*

1. Mis hijos tienen _____ paciencia.

2. Las chicas saben _____ la verdad.

3. Conozco _____ tu jefe.

4. Sara tiene _____ sus amigos y su apoyo (*support*).

5. Invitamos _____ la familia García.

6. Saludamos _____ la bandera.

7. Amo _____ mi perrito y mi gata.

8. Extraño _____ Pedro.

En español.

1. Melissa works at the bookstore.

_____

2. She sees her boss (**jefe**) at the bus stop every morning.

_____

3. I know her boss.

_____

4. He drinks four cups of coffee in the morning.

_____

5. Melissa prefers tea.

_____

6. I saw her boss last week.

_____

7. He wears old clothes.

_____

8. Melissa's boss needs a new jacket.

_____

Direct and indirect object nouns in a sentence

When a sentence contains both a direct and an indirect object noun, the *direct object precedes the indirect object* in Spanish and both are placed after the verb:

> **subject + verb + direct object + indirect object**

> El chico comprará **ese libro a su padre**.　　　*The boy will buy **this book for his father**.*

- ◆ **El chico** is the subject of the verb.
- ◆ **Comprará** is the verb. It is in the future tense.
- ◆ **Ese libro** is the direct object. It receives the action of the verb.
- ◆ **A su padre** is the indirect object. It receives the action (done for him).

A few more examples follow. Note that, in these sentences, the preposition **a** is not the personal **a**; here, it introduces the *indirect object*. The English equivalent is *to*.

La Internet ofrece **oportunidades a nuestros estudiantes**.

*The Internet offers **opportunities to our students**.*

La bolsa de valores disminuyó **el capital a los inversores**.

*The stock market decreased **the wealth for the investors**.*

El doctor Benítez recetó **un antibiótico a su paciente**.

*Dr. Benítez prescribed **an antibiotic for his patient**.*

¿Entiendes el mensaje? *Coloca* (place) *las palabras en el orden apropiado. Empieza la oración con el sujeto. Usa la puntuación y la ortografía apropiadas.*

1. alquiló / Paula / a su hermana Ana / un apartamento

_____

2. ella / la llave / tiene / del apartamento

_____

3. la hermana / ayuda / necesita

_____

4. en la universidad / inglés / Ana / estudia

_____

5. un trabajo mejor / ella / encontrará

_____

6. saludos / Ana y su hermana / envían / a sus amigos

_____

7. a sus primos / invitan / a su apartamento

_____

Negative declarative sentences

Declarative sentences are not all affirmative; some are negative. Not all affirmative sentences require an affirmative word. However, negative sentences *must* include negative words. These negative words are *adverbs* that modify the action of the verb. In Spanish, a simple way to turn an affirmative sentence into a negative sentence is to place the word **no** directly before the verb:

subject + no + verb (affirmative sentence) → negative sentence

Mario trabaja en aquella oficina.
Mario works in that office.

Mario **no** trabaja en aquella oficina.
*Mario does **not** work in that office.*

Other negative adverbs may be used to build negative declarative sentences. The negative words **nunca** (*never*), **jamás** (*never*), **tampoco** (*neither, nor*), and **ni** (*neither, nor*) appear before the verb in the following examples:

Nunca salimos de noche.	We **never** go out at night.
Jamás dice mentiras.	She **never** tells lies.
Tampoco niega la verdad.	She does not deny the truth, **either**.
La secretaria **ni** terminó la carta.	The secretary did not **even** finish the letter.

EJERCICIO

1·10

Te toca a ti. *Cambia las oraciones afirmativas a negativas. Usa* **nunca, jamás, tampoco** *o* **ni** *para sustituir las palabras subrayadas.*

1. Digo mentiras <u>siempre</u>.

_____

2. Falto (*miss*) a mi trabajo <u>a menudo</u>.

_____

3. Duermo hasta tarde <u>todos los días</u>.

_____

4. <u>Casi todos los días</u> termino el desayuno.

_____

5. Ahorro (*save*) agua <u>con frecuencia</u>.

_____

6. <u>A veces</u> gasto todo mi salario en la tienda.

_____

7. <u>Casi siempre</u> recibo un bono por Navidad.

_____

Remember that in Spanish two or three negative words may be used in the same sentence. If a negative word (**nunca, jamás**) follows a verb, the verb must also be preceded by a negative.

Nunca jamás te voy a ayudar con tu tarea.	I will **never ever** help you with your homework.
Elisa **no** viaja **nunca**.	Elisa **never** travels.
Yo **no** viajaré **jamás** contigo.	I will **never** travel with you.
Lucy **no** quiere **nada**.	Lucy **does not** want **anything**.

You may use redundant negative elements in a sentence, especially in informal conversations. Note that neither the auxiliary English verb *does* nor *did* is translated if the Spanish verb is in the past tense:

Marta **no** vendrá **nunca jamás**.	Marta will **never ever** come.
Lucy **no tiene** tiempo **nunca**.	Lucy **does not ever** have time.

Escribe las oraciones de nuevo. Usa las palabras negativas en el orden sugerido en el modelo.

MODELO   Mi cuenta de ahorro aumenta.

        no... nunca   *Mi cuenta de ahorro no aumenta nunca*   .

        no... jamás   *Mi cuenta de ahorro no aumenta nunca jamás*   .

1. Los políticos mienten.

    no... nunca _____.

    no... jamás _____.

2. Los periodistas redactan noticias optimistas.

    no... nunca _____.

    no... jamás _____.

3. Los vendedores respaldan (*back up*) sus productos.

    no... nunca _____.

    no... jamás _____.

4. Los camareros sirven a los clientes con amabilidad.

    no... nunca _____.

    no... jamás _____.

5. Los maestros asignan poca tarea a sus estudiantes.

    no... nunca _____.

    no... jamás _____.

6. Los marineros tienen miedo al mar.

    no... nunca _____.

    no... jamás _____.

Negative declarative sentences with negative pronouns

Note that the subject of the following sentences is a negative pronoun: **nadie** (*no one*), **ninguno/a** (*no one*), or **nada** (*nothing*). These pronouns appear with other negative words in the same sentence:

Mañana **no** viene n**adie**.   *Tomorrow **no one** will come.*
No hay **ningún** problema.   *There is **no** problem.*
Ninguno salió de su casa.   *No one* left their homes.*

¡Más énfasis! *Añade (add) otra palabra negativa (**nadie** / **nunca** / **jamás** / **nada**) a cada oración.*

1. _____ jamás vamos a tener un año tan próspero.

2. No vemos _____ desde aquí.

3. Julia _____ invita a nadie a su casa.

4. No llames a Felipe _____ .

5. Nunca viene _____ a esta clase.

6. Nunca dice _____ a nadie.

Interrogative sentences

When you need information about a matter or a person, you use a question, that is, an *interrogative sentence*. In English and Spanish there are several ways to create questions. In the first example below, the verb form is **sabes**. Unlike Spanish, the English equivalent requires a form of the auxiliary verb *to do* to pose the question in the present tense:

<table>
<tr><td>¿Sabes la respuesta?</td><td>Do you know the answer?</td></tr>
</table>

In English an interrogative sentence with a verb in the past tense may include the past form *did* or a form of the auxiliary verb *to have*:

<table>
<tr><td>¿Salió Marcos?</td><td>Did Marcos leave?</td></tr>
<tr><td>¿Has visto a mi hermana?</td><td>Have you seen my sister?</td></tr>
</table>

Consider another question with a verb in the future tense that uses a form of the verb **ir**, *to go*:

<table>
<tr><td>¿Irás a la fiesta?</td><td>Will you go to the party?</td></tr>
</table>

A third type uses a form of the verb **estar**, *to be*, and no auxiliary in the English equivalent:

<table>
<tr><td>¿Está Juan en su casa?</td><td>Is Juan at home?</td></tr>
</table>

Interrogative sentences and declarative sentences

In Unit 1, you studied declarative sentences. One way to create an interrogative sentence in Spanish is to use a declarative sentence that ends with a rising inflection. The intonation communicates a question in spoken language. Spanish question marks precede and follow all interrogative sentences in writing.

¿ + declarative sentence + ? → interrogative sentence

The message of a declarative sentence changes when it is used to create a question:

<table>
<tr><td>La tienda está cerrada.</td><td>The store is closed.</td></tr>
<tr><td>¿La tienda está cerrada?</td><td>The store is closed?</td></tr>
</table>

Práctica fácil. *Cambia las oraciones afirmativas a preguntas. Usa los signos de interrogación.*

1. Llegas tarde.

_____

2. María ya está lista.

_____

3. Tiene poca paciencia.

_____

4. Esperamos hasta las cinco.

_____

5. Hay un taxi en la esquina.

_____

6. Hace calor en la calle.

_____

7. Lloverá esta noche.

_____

8. Llegaremos al cine a tiempo.

_____

Interrogative sentences and negative declarative sentences

If you add question marks to a negative declarative sentence you will have an interrogative sentence:

¿ + negative declarative sentence + ? → interrogative sentence

No estabas trabajando para esa compañía.	*You were not working for that company.*
¿**No estabas** trabajando para esa compañía?	*Were you not (Weren't you) working for that company?*

The type of construction described above is used when the questioner expects an affirmative answer or an affirmation. When followed by **no**, some adverbs change their meaning and can be used to build similar interrogative sentences:

ya no	*no longer*
todavía no	*not yet*
aún no	*not yet*

Add the appropriate question marks to form an interrogative sentence:

Ya no trabajan aquí.	*They do **not** work here **any longer**.*
¿**Ya no** trabajan aquí?	*They do **not** work here **any longer**?*
Todavía no has terminado.	*You have **not** finished **yet**.*
¿**Todavía no** has terminado?	*Have you **not** finished **yet**?*
No tienes la respuesta **aún**.	*You **still** do **not** have the answer.*
¿**No** tienes la respuesta **aún**?	*You **still** do **not** have the answer?*

EJERCICIO
2·2

Escribe otra oración interrogativa. Empieza (start) la oración con las palabras indicadas. Usa los signos de interrogación.

1. ¿Te gusta tu trabajo?

   No _____

2. ¿Ganas mucho dinero?

   Todavía no _____

3. ¿Estudias en una universidad?

   Ya no _____

4. ¿Estás listo/a para un ascenso (*promotion*)?

   No _____

5. ¿Tienes novio/a?

   Todavía no _____

6. ¿Estás enamorado/a?

   Ya no _____

Interrogative sentences and word order

Here is a frequently used structure to build interrogative sentences in Spanish:

¿ + verb + subject + other predicate elements + ?

¿Conoce tu hermano a María?	***Does** your brother know María?*

Consider the above English sentence. It includes the helping or auxiliary verb *does*, followed by the subject and the predicate. The Spanish sentence does not need an auxiliary verb. A form of the auxiliary, *do* or *does* in the present, *did* in the past, and *will* in the future tense, always precedes the verb in English. Remember that these words do not translate into Spanish.

¿Viven tus hermanos en Miami?	***Do** your brothers live in Miami?*
¿Veis (vosotros) este programa?	***Do** you watch this program?*
¿Recibieron los chicos el paquete?	***Did** the children receive the package?*
¿Vendrá el cartero mañana?	***Will** the mail carrier come tomorrow?*

There are exceptions to this rule in English. One is the English verb *to be*.

¿**Eres** la amiga de Ana?	*Are you Ana's friend?*
¿**Está** Julián en casa?	*Is Julián at home?*

Some constructions in English use the auxiliaries *to have* and *can*:

¿**No tienes** vergüenza?	*Have you no shame?*
¿**Puedes** ayudarme?	*Can you help me? / Are you able to help me?*

Of course in Spanish sentences, the subject may not always be explicit. The verb ending helps you identify the subject. Look at the following examples:

¿Hab**las** alemán?	*Do you speak German?*
¿Comp**raron** esa casa?	*Did they buy that house?*
¿Llove**rá** esta noche en Asturias?	*Will it rain tonight in Asturias?*

EJERCICIO
2·3

Escribe la pregunta. *Coloca las palabras en el orden apropiado. ¡Usa los signos de interrogación!*

1. profesora / es / tu / de matemáticas / ella

   _____

2. aprecian / los conocimientos de la profesora / los alumnos

   _____

3. ella / tiene / un hermano / en esta facultad

   _____

4. eres / su alumna / preferida

   _____

5. sus colegas / a / admira / disciplinas / otras / de

   _____

6. ella / responde / tus preguntas

   _____

7. explicó / la profesora / teoría / la

   _____

¡De vacaciones! *Escribe cada pregunta otra vez. Ahora, usa el orden sujeto + verbo + otros elementos del predicado.*

1. ¿Van Uds. de viaje a Barcelona?

_____

2. ¿Visitarán los chicos a sus abuelos?

_____

3. ¿Recibirán tus padres a mis amigos?

_____

4. ¿Hablas tú catalán?

_____

5. ¿Visitará tu marido a tus padres?

_____

6. ¿Regresarán todos a mi casa?

_____

Polite questions and word order

Some situations require us to be polite when making a request, particularly when we don't know the person or persons of whom we're asking the favor. The personal pronouns **Ud.** (*you*, formal singular) and **Uds.** (*you*, both familiar and formal plural) follow the verb when the circumstances require a polite tone:

¿ + verb + subject pronoun + object + ?

¿ + Desea + **Ud.** + un café + ?

¿Desea **Ud.** un café?	*Would **you** like some coffee?*
¿Sabe **Ud.** la hora de la salida?	*Do **you** know the departure time?*
¿Necesitan **Uds.** otro recibo?	*Do **you** need another receipt?*

La cortesía, en español. *Usa los pronombres personales indicados entre paréntesis.*

1. Do you (**Ud.**) need help?

_____

2. Do you (**Uds.**) see the children?

_____

3. Did you (**Uds.**) arrive yet?

_____

4. Did you (**Ud.**) give (**hacer**) a donation?

_____

5. Did you (**Uds.**) return (**entregar**) the car?

_____

6. Do you (**Ud.**) want a seat near a window?

_____

Polite phrases in interrogative sentences

Another to way to communicate a polite question is to use a phrase, such as **por favor**, or an imperative form before the question:

Con permiso	*Pardon me / Excuse me*
Por favor	*Please*
Disculpe	*Pardon me / Excuse me*
Perdón	*Pardon me / Excuse me*

Notice the punctuation:

polite phrase + , + ¿ + verb + subject pronoun + object + ?

Perdón, ¿tiene Ud. el boleto?	***Excuse me**, do you have your ticket?*
Por favor, ¿pueden Uds. abrir la puerta?	***Please**, could you open the door?*

EJERCICIO
2·6

En la tienda, en español. *Usa la forma **Ud**. para las oraciones interrogativas en español.*

1. Do you want this dress? _____

2. Do you prefer this pair of shoes? _____

3. Do you need new glasses? _____

4. Are you tired? _____

5. Are you ready to pay? _____

6. Did you pay with a credit card? _____

Alternative questions

Alternative questions are very similar in nature to the simple questions or *yes/no* interrogatives. Alternative questions offer a choice, that is, two or more alternate answers. Note the pattern and the punctuation:

¿Prefieren té **o** café?	*Do they prefer coffee **or** tea?*
¿Hoy es sábado **o** domingo?	*Is today Saturday **or** Sunday?*
¿Fueron a la playa, a la tienda **o** al cine?	*Did they go to the beach, the store, **or** the movies?*

EJERCICIO
2·7

¿Cuál es la pregunta? *Observa el ejemplo para crear una pregunta con cada lista de palabras. Usa el presente de indicativo y la ortografía y puntuación apropiadas.*

MODELO   tener (tú) favorable / un comentario / desfavorable
          ¿Tienes un comentario favorable o desfavorable?

1. preferir (tú) / un refresco de limón / una cola / una cerveza

   _____

2. llegar (vosotros) esta tarde / mañana

   _____

3. desear (ellos) / ir a la playa / nadar en la piscina

   _____

4. comprar (nosotros) la corbata / el sombrero / un libro

   _____

5. querer (Uds.) ver una película / cenar conmigo

   _____

6. dormir (Ud.) en la hamaca / en el sillón

   _____

7. vivir (él) en la ciudad / en el campo

   _____

Tag questions

Another way of forming a question, in both English and Spanish, is to add a *tag question* to the end of a declarative sentence:

declarative sentence + , + ¿ + tag + ? → tag question

Tienes dinero, **¿no?**   *You have some money, **don't you?***

Tag questions are used in informal spoken communication. Most likely, the person posing a tag question expects agreement, but a *no* answer is also possible. Here are the most common "tags" added to create these questions:

¿no?	*isn't, aren't?*
¿cierto?	*is it not?, isn't it?, are they not?, aren't they?*
¿no es cierto?	*is it not (isn't it) true?*
¿verdad?	*right?*
¿no es verdad?	*is it not (isn't it) true?*
¿no crees?	*don't you think?*
La gerente es inteligente, **¿no?**	*The manager is smart, **isn't she?***
Esta bufanda es cara, **¿verdad?**	*This scarf is expensive, **right?***
Martín nada muy bien, **¿cierto? / ¿no es cierto?**	*Martin swims very well, **doesn't he / right?***
La chica tiene talento, **¿no es verdad?**	*The girl has talent, **doesn't she / isn't it true?***

EJERCICIO
2·8

Escribe la oración otra vez. Termina (end) la oración con las palabras indicadas. Usa la puntuación y los signos de interrogación necesarios.

1. Lucía ve muchos programas dramáticos. (no)

_____

2. Pedro prefiere los documentales del canal de cable. (no es verdad)

_____

3. Carla y Marcos van a un concierto de un grupo mexicano. (no es cierto)

_____

4. En el concierto venderán copias del último CD. (verdad)

_____

5. Después del concierto irán a cenar todos juntos. (no es cierto)

_____

6. Celebran la ocasión especial del cumpleaños de Lucía. (no es verdad)

_____

Questions with short answers

Answers to *yes/no* questions frequently include phrases that stress the answers. The following phrases are used in both informal and formal situations, mostly to add emphasis. Exclamation points are added:

¡Claro, claro que sí!, ¡claro que no!	*Of course; of course not!*
¡Cómo no!	*Sure!*
¡Desde luego!	*Indeed!*

¡Naturalmente!	*Naturally!*
¡Por supuesto (que no)!	*Absolutely (not)!*
¡Qué va!	*No way!*
¡Ni modo!	*No way!*
—¿Vas a ir a la biblioteca esta tarde?	*—Are you going to the library this afternoon?*
—¡Claro que no!	***—Of course not!***
—¿Prefieres ir a ver a Ana?	*—Do you prefer to go see Ana?*
—¡Por supuesto!	***—Sure!***

Un poco de geografía. *Usa una de las siguientes expresiones para reaccionar a la pregunta:* **qué va, naturalmente, claro que sí.**

1. ¿Los Estados Unidos está en el hemisferio sur? _____

2. ¿El Río Amazonas atraviesa Canadá? _____

3. ¿La capital de Chile es Santiago? _____

4. ¿El Mar Caribe está cerca de Panamá? _____

5. ¿España es parte de Sur América? _____

Questions and answers

In the previous chapter, you saw a variety of ways to build interrogative sentences and form questions. In this chapter, you will continue practicing interrogative structures that ask for more precise information. In English, we call them *complex* or *information* questions.

¿Dónde están mis llaves?	**Where** *are my keys?*
¿Quién es este señor?	**Who** *is this gentleman?*

Specific information questions

Questions that expect more specific information than a simple choice answer or a straightforward *yes/no* response are information questions. They start with an *interrogative pronoun*, an *interrogative adverb*, or any other *interrogative word or phrase*.

Questions with interrogative words

Interrogative words are adverbs used to ask for specific information. In general, interrogative words are followed by the regular word order in interrogative sentences. Note that these are not *yes/no* questions.

**¿ + interrogative word + verb + subject + complement + ? →
complex question**

¿Qué hace Ana con su salario?   **What** *does Ana do with her salary?*

You will need one of the following interrogatives or question words to form a complex (information) question. Note that in Spanish they all have a written accent mark:

¿Adónde?	*Where to?*
¿Cómo?	*How?*
¿Cuál?, ¿Cuáles?	*Which?*
¿Cuándo?	*When?*
¿Cuánto?, ¿Cuánta?	*How much?*
¿Cuántos?, ¿Cuántas?	*How many?*
¿Dónde?	*Where?*
¿Qué?	*What?*
¿Quién?, ¿Quiénes?	*Who?*

Here are some example sentences:

¿**Qué** hora es?	**What** time is it?
¿**Quién** llegó?	**Who** has arrived?
¿**Dónde** está tu hermana?	**Where** is your sister?
¿**Cómo** trabajan ellas?	**How** do they work?

Answers to question words

Certain adverbs are used to answer the following specific questions. Here is a short list of questions and possible answers. Note that some are set or fixed expressions:

¿**Cómo?**	**How?**
más o menos	*not so great, so-so*
bien	*well*
bastante bien	*rather well*
mal	*badly*
mejor	*better*
peor	*worse*
—¿**Cómo** te sientes?	—**How** *do you feel?*
—**Más o menos.**	—**Not so great.**

¿**Cuándo?**	**When?**
anoche	*last night*
ayer	*yesterday*
después	*later*
de vez en cuando	*once in a while*
en seguida	*right away*
mañana	*tomorrow*
nunca	*never*
—¿**Cuándo** vas a la playa?	—**When** *do you go to the beach?*
—**De vez en cuando.**	—**Once in a while.**

¿**Dónde?**	**Where?**
aquí	*here*
adentro	*inside*
debajo	*under*
cerca	*near, close to*
por allí	*over there*
por acá	*over here*
—¿**Dónde** están las fotos?	—**Where** *are the pictures?*
—**Aquí** tengo las fotos.	—*I have the pictures* **here.**

In Unit 11 you will learn more about adverbs and their use.

Lee cada oración. Después, escribe una pregunta basada en la palabra subrayada en la oración.

MODELO   Mi nombre es Juan.

       ¿Cómo te llamas?

1. Se llama Nora.

   _____

2. Vive en la Avenida de los Presidentes.

   _____

3. Su cumpleaños es el cinco de mayo.

   _____

4. Nora limpia su apartamento el viernes por la tarde.

   _____

5. Nora estudia publicidad.

   _____

6. Ella quiere trabajar en una empresa en Nueva York.

   _____

7. Laura, Martina y Felipa son sus amigas.

   _____

8. Este verano, todas van de vacaciones a Punta Cana.

   _____

¿Cuál es la palabra que necesitas para iniciar la pregunta? Subraya la respuesta.

1. ¿Cuál / Qué regalo prefieres, el cuadro o la fotografía?
2. ¿Cuál / Quién es la opinión de la madre?
3. ¿Quiénes / Cuáles son los colores preferidos del cliente?
4. ¿Qué / Cuál es la fecha para terminar el trabajo?
5. ¿Qué / Cuál día es hoy, tu aniversario?
6. ¿Cuál / Qué hay en la caja?

Complex questions with prepositions + interrogative words

Certain prepositions followed by a question word are used to elicit concrete or fuller responses to a question:

¿preposition + interrogative word + verb + subject + complement(s)?

¿Desde + cuándo + vive + Ana + en San Diego?
Since when does Ana live in San Diego?

Here is a list of *prepositions* followed by a question word used to create complex questions:

¿A quién / A quiénes?	*(To) Whom?*
¿Con quién / quiénes?	*With whom?*
¿De dónde?	*From where? / Where from?*
¿Desde cuándo?	*Since when?*
¿Hacia dónde?	*Toward where?*
¿Hasta cuándo?	*Until when?*
¿Para dónde?	*To(ward) where?*
¿Para qué?	*What for?*
¿Para quién / quiénes?	*For whom?*
¿Por dónde?	*Through where?*
¿Por qué?	*Why?*
¿Por quién / quiénes?	*For whom?*
¿A quién llamaste?	***Whom** did you call?*
¿Desde cuándo eres novia de Aldo?	***Since when** are you (have you been) Aldo's girlfriend?*
¿Hasta cuándo vas a trabajar?	***Until when** will you work?*
¿Para qué compras esta maleta?	***What** are you buying this suitcase **for**?*
¿Por qué no estudias matemáticas?	***Why** don't you study math?*

EJERCICIO
3·3

En español. *Usa la persona* **tú.**

1. Where are you from?

   _____

2. Where are you going?

   _____

3. Since when do you study (have you been studying) Spanish?

   _____

4. When are you going to finish this exercise?

   _____

5. Until when are you going to wait?

   _____

6. To whom do you write most of your e-mails?

   _____

7. Who is knocking (**tocar a**) at the door?

_____

8. Where are you (**tú**)?

_____

Limiting questions

Some interrogatives are used to ask limiting or partial questions. Some elicit a specific answer about a noun: _how much?, how many?, which?_

¿Cuál? (_sing._), ¿Cuáles? (_pl._)	_Which?_
¿Cuánto? (_masc. sing._); ¿Cuánta? (_fem. sing._)	_How much?_
¿Cuántos? (_masc. pl._); ¿Cuántas? (_fem. pl._)	_How many?_
¿**Cuáles** son tus colores preferidos?	_**Which** are your favorite colors?_
¿**Cuánto** dinero necesitas?	_**How much** money do you need?_
¿**Cuántos** regalos vas a comprar?	_**How many** gifts are you going to buy?_

EJERCICIO
3·4

Entrevista. _Tienes la oportunidad de entrevistar a un(a) cantante famoso/a. Escribe una pregunta con las palabras de cada serie. Usa los signos de interrogación._

MODELO   quién / con / aprendió / guitarra / tocar / a / la
          ¿Con quién aprendió a tocar la guitarra?

1. países / ha visitado / cuántos

_____

2. decidió / que / cuándo / quería / cantante / ser

_____

3. su / será / próximo / concierto / dónde / su

_____

4. voz / cómo / la / ensaya (_rehearse_) / conciertos / para / los

_____

5. decidió / por / dedicarse / qué / música / a / la

_____

6. son / sus / cantantes / cuáles / favoritos

_____

7. quiere / hacer / futuro / qué / el / en

_____

8. vacaciones / serán / cuándo / próximas / sus

_____

Diez preguntas. _Lee el párrafo. Después, escribe una pregunta acerca de cada una de las frases subrayadas. Usa las siguientes palabras interrogativas:_

cuándo / cuántos / cómo / dónde / para qué / por qué / qué / quiénes

Abel Ruiz, a sus 19 años, es un gran atleta. Cuando era niño jugaba al fútbol y esa experiencia todavía lo inspira. Su padre lo llevaba a ver los partidos de fútbol. Abel quiere ser famoso, como sus ídolos, y jugar con un equipo profesional en los Estados Unidos. Ahora, Abel juega para el equipo de la universidad. Abel es muy disciplinado: siempre va a las prácticas y hace ejercicios para mantenerse en buena forma física. Tal vez Abel será un jugador famoso en unos cinco años.

1. a sus diecinueve años, _____

2. jugaba al fútbol _____

3. Su padre lo llevaba _____

4. Abel quiere ser famoso _____

5. en los Estados Unidos _____

6. para el equipo de la universidad _____

7. Abel es muy disciplinado _____

8. hace ejercicios para mantenerse en buena forma física _____

9. Abel será un jugador famoso _____

10. en unos cinco años _____

Responding to a question with another question

Frequently, a question is answered with another question if more information is needed or desired to answer the initial question:

—¿Dónde están los papeles?   —_Where are the papers?_
—**¿Qué papeles?**   —**_What papers?_**

In a conversation, a question that follows a previous question may express surprise, interest, or another emotion:

—¿Conoces al novio de Lupita?　　　　　—*Do you know Lupita's boyfriend?*
—**¿Lupita tiene novio?**　　　　　　　　—***Lupita has a boyfriend?***
—**¿No lo sabías?**　　　　　　　　　　　—***You did not know that?***
—**¿De veras?**　　　　　　　　　　　　　—***Really?***

EJERCICIO
3·6

Preguntas y más preguntas. *Indica la palabra interrogativa que responde con otra pregunta.*

1. —¿Recibiste mi mensaje? —¿_____ mensaje?

2. —¿No sabes que Ana está de viaje por Ecuador? —¿_____ fue Ana?

3. —Pero, ¿tú no recuerdas que hablamos de Ana? —¿_____ hablamos, ayer?

4. —¿Ayer? ¿No hablamos esta mañana? —¿A _____ hora?

5. —¿Por qué no te acuerdas?¿Tienes amnesia? —¿Amnesia yo? ¿De _____ hablas?

6. —¿Es esa una pregunta retórica? —¿A _____ de las preguntas te refieres?

7. —¿Quieres volverme loco? —¿_____ dices?

8. —¿Estás sorda (*deaf*)? —¿_____?

Exclamatory sentences

When we want to communicate strong feelings, emotions, or a sense of urgency, we need exclamatory sentences (**oraciones exclamativas o admirativas**). These sentences are common in informal speech; the speaker adds facial expressions and voice modulation to stress his or her emotions. An exclamatory sentence can also be defined as a more forceful version of a declarative sentence; in writing it is marked in Spanish with an exclamation point both at the beginning and the end of the sentence:

¡Hace mucho frío!	*It is very cold!*
¡La cena está deliciosa!	*Supper is delicious!*

Exclamatory sentences and declarative sentences

With the appropriate punctuation, you can use declarative sentences to express strong feelings. In both English and Spanish, an exclamatory sentence is a forceful, declarative sentence that shows strong emotion. Remember the inverted exclamation point that precedes exclamatory sentences and the regular exclamation point that ends them.

¡ + declarative sentence + ! → exclamatory sentence

Exclamatory sentences have several possible word orders. You can use the *subject + verb + object* word order studied in Unit 1. The exclamation points add emphasis: an element of surprise, astonishment, admiration, or happiness. Note the difference in these examples:

El hombre ganó la lotería.	*The man won the lottery.*
¡El hombre ganó la lotería!	*The man won the lottery!*

There are other possible patterns for exclamatory sentences, depending on which word or words the speaker chooses to stress:

¡ + verb + subject + object + !

¡**Ganaron** + el partido + los chicos!
*The boys **won** the match!*

¡ + adverb + verb + subject + object + !

¡**Muy lindo** + canta + Marla + esa canción!
*Marla sings that song **beautifully**!*

Exclamatory sentences and negative declarative sentences

Negative declarative sentences, with added exclamation marks, can also be the starting point for building an exclamatory sentence:

¡ + **negative declarative sentence** + ! → **exclamatory sentence**

¡ + Lula **no** hizo la tarea + !
*Lula did **not** do her homework!*

EJERCICIO
4·1

En español. *¡No olvides los signos de admiración (¡!)!*

1. There is a beautiful moon! _____

2. We (*fem.*) are going to walk on the beach! _____

3. It is very hot outside! _____

4. The lemonade is cold! _____

5. Lucy is so tired! _____

6. Now we (*fem.*) are ready to rest! _____

7. I am not going to sleep! _____

8. I agree (**estar de acuerdo**)! _____

EJERCICIO
4·2

Te toca a ti. *¡Usa los signos de admiración (¡!)! Ahora usa las oraciones para crear exclamaciones afirmativas o negativas para decir cómo tú eres.*

1. Soy muy aburrido/a. _____

2. Bailo mucho en las fiestas. _____

3. Tengo muchos amigos. _____

4. Me gusta mi trabajo. _____

5. Tengo mucho dinero. _____

6. Ahorro dinero todos los meses. _____

7. Tengo mucha suerte en el amor. _____

8. Soy muy feliz. _____

Exclamation words and word order in exclamatory sentences

Exclamation words express the attitude and emotions of the speaker. A formal exclamatory sentence, used in writing, is one that begins with an exclamation word such as **¡Qué...!** (*What . . . !*), **¡Cómo...!** (*How . . . !*), as well as others. In Spanish, exclamation words, like question words, have a written accent mark:

¡Cómo!	*How!*
¡Cuán!	*How!*
¡Cuánto/a!	*How much!*
¡Cuántos/as!	*How many!*
¡Cuánto!	*How!*
¡Qué!	*What!*
¡Qué de!	*What!*
¡Quién! / ¡Quiénes!	*Who!*

These exclamation words underscore the quantity, quality, nature, or intensity of the noun, adjective, adverb, or verb that follows:

¡Qué mentiras dices!	***How many** lies you tell!*
¡Qué ruido hace!	***What** noise it/he/she makes!*
¡Qué caro es!	***How** expensive it is!*
¡Qué mal toca la niña la guitarra!	***How** badly the girl plays the guitar!*
¡Cómo llueve!	*It is raining **so** hard! / **How** hard it's raining!*

EJERCICIO
4·3

¡Así es la vida! *Escribe la puntuación y la ortografía apropiada para escribir oraciones exclamativas.*

1. cuanto cuestan estos zapatos

2. que largo es el vestido

3. como ha subido el precio de la vida

4 cuanto ganan

5. que amable es el camarero

6. cuantas entradas vendieron para el concierto

7. que bien hacen la paella en este restaurante

8. cuanta belleza hay en este lugar

Exclamation words in colloquial expressions

Some exclamations are used only in colloquial language, typical of informal conversation. The exclamations emphasize admiration, praise, or their opposite, ironically: contempt, disdain, scorn, dislike, etc. Note the following constructions and what they emphasize. These exclamations may have several meanings.

◆ **¡Qué + ... que... !**

> **¡Qué** auto **que** tienes!   *What a car you have!*

¡Qué auto que tienes! could praise the size, value, or qualities of the car; or the context may suggest the car is ugly, old, or small. A similar construction with similar meanings uses the interjection **vaya**:

◆ **¡Vaya + ... que... !**

> **¡Vaya** casa **que** tienes!   *What a great house you have!*
>   or *What a horrible house you have!*

◆ The adjectives **menudo**, **menuda**, **menudos**, **menudas** (*small*) and **valiente** (*brave*) communicate an ironic or opposite sense, different from the usual meaning:

◆ **¡Menudo + ... que... !**

> **¡Menuda** mentira **que** dices!   *Some big lie you tell!*
> **¡Valiente** trabajo **que** has hecho!   *Some work you have done!*
>   or *What a disaster you have made!*

EJERCICIO
4·4

Elige la reacción a cada una de las siguientes oraciones. ¿Cuál es la opción más apropiada?

1. _____ Francisco lava su ropa él mismo.   a. ¡Qué disciplinado que es!

2. _____ Su padre le regaló un auto.   b. ¡Qué listo que es!

3. _____ Juega a la baraja y siempre gana.   c. ¡Menuda suerte que tiene!

4. _____ Siempre pide un descuento en la tienda.   d. ¡Qué generoso que es!

5. _____ Va al gimnasio cuatro días a la semana.   e. ¡Qué limpio que es!

Interjections and exclamatory sentences

Interjections are words or phrases that add emotion to the delivery of a sentence. These utterances frequently appear in exclamatory sentences to express a reaction to what we perceive around us, what we remember, feel, or wish. Interjections are usually separated by a comma in writing:

> **¡Ah**, el concierto empieza a las ocho!   *Oh, the concert starts at eight!*
> **¡Ay**, tengo dolor de cabeza!   *Ouch, my head hurts (I have a headache)!*

Some interjections are euphemisms, inoffensive expressions that replace expressions that may offend the listener or that allude to something perceived as unpleasant. They are more common in speech:

> **¡Diantre**, el examen es difícil!   *Darn, the exam is hard!*

The English equivalents of interjections in a new language can be difficult to determine, because their meaning depends on the context: **¡ay!** may communicate pain, surprise, or delight.

Nouns, adverbs, and verbs are also used as interjections. Here is a list of frequently used interjections in Spanish. Note the exclamation points:

¡Ah!	*Oh!*	¡Eh!	*Hey!*
¡Aj!	*Yuck!*	¡Fo!	*Ugh!*
¡Anda!	*Oops!*	¡Hala!, ¡Hale!	*Go!, Do it!, Hurry!*
¡Arre!	*Giddyup!*	¡Hola!	*Hi!*
¡Aupa!	*Up!* (especially with children)	¡Huy!	*Ouch!*
		¡Oh!	*Oh!, Oh really!*
¡Ay de mí!	*Poor me!*	¡Ojalá!	*I wish!, Let's hope!*
¡Ay!	*Oh!, Ouch!*	¡Olé, olé!	*Bravo!*
¡Bah!	*No way!*	¡Puaj!	*Yuck!*
¡Bravo!	*Bravo!*	¡Pobre!, ¡Pobre de mi!	*Poor thing!, Poor me!*
¡Caramba!	*Good grief!*		
¡Caracoles!	*Good grief!*	¡Pst!	*Hey!*
¡Caray!	*Oops!*	¡Puf!	*Yuck!, Hmm!*
¡Chist!	*Hey!*	¡Quia!	*No way!*
¡Chitón!	*Hush!, Quiet!*	¡Uf!	*Phew!* (tiredness), *Ugh!* (dislike, repugnance)
¡Cielos!	*Good heavens!*		
¡Córcholis!	*Good grief!*		
¡Diantre!	*Heck!*	¡Vale!	*Bye!, OK!*
¡Ea!	*Go!*	¡Vaya!	*Great!*

En español. *Usa las interjecciones apropiadas de acuerdo al contexto.*

1. Hush, there is too much noise!

_____

2. Heavens, the lecture starts at eight o'clock!

_____

3. Hey, we are here!

_____

4. Poor me, I have no time!

_____

5. Let's hope, I need to win!

_____

6. Oh, the watch is beautiful!

_____

¡Usa la lógica! *Elige la reacción a cada una de las siguientes oraciones. ¿Cuál es la opción más lógica?*

1. _____ Marta siempre gana.

2. _____ Su esposo tuvo un accidente.

3. _____ La comida no sabe bien.

4. _____ Su padre le regaló doscientos euros.

5. _____ Mario sabe muchos chistes.

a. ¡Oh, fue terrible!

b. ¡Ah, qué suerte que tiene!

c. ¡Uf, tiene mucha suerte!

d. ¡Puaj, es un desastre!

e. ¡Qué cómico que es!

Imperatives

Most imperatives are commands that give an order or a strong suggestion directly to the second person, *you* (singular or plural).

Escuche las noticias.	***Listen*** *to the news.*
¡**Abre** la puerta!	***Open*** *the door!*
Regresen.	***Come back.***

To give a command in English, you use an infinitive without the particle *to*. Spanish uses stand-alone verb forms in the imperative mood.

verb in the imperative mood → imperative sentence

Depending on how strong the command is, imperatives may end with a period or an exclamation point. When the written Spanish imperative ends in an exclamation point, an inverted exclamation point is also placed at the beginning of the sentence.

Imperatives and the imperative mood

Let's see more examples of forms of the imperative mood, also known as *commands* or, in Spanish, **los mandatos.**

Vengan aquí inmediatamente.	***Come*** *here immediately.*
Estudia los diez primeros capítulos.	***Study*** *the first ten chapters.*

The subject of an imperative is implied. In Spanish, verb endings identify the individual or individuals to whom you are giving the command:

Encien**de** la tele.	*Turn on the television.* (to one person)
¡Termin**en** la tarea!	*Finish your homework!* (to several people)

In the first sentence above, *you* is the person **tú**. In the second example, the English equivalent of the people (more than one) receiving the command is also *you*. For the sake of emphasis or clarity, a proper or common noun (called a *vocative*) can be used to address the person for whom the imperative is intended:

(vocative) + imperative verb form + complement(s)

(Señorita,) + **abra** + la ventana.
(Miss,) open the window.

In Spanish, nouns referring to the people addressed can be placed at the beginning or the end of the utterance. Note the comma separating the vocative from the command:

Camarero, sirva el vino.   **Waiter**, *serve the wine.*
Contesta el teléfono, **Juan**.   *Answer the phone,* **Juan**.

The imperative mood

Forms of the imperative mood are, with one exception, the same as the Spanish present subjunctive forms. However, the *informal affirmative* command is the third-person singular of the present indicative. Let's quickly review the informal imperative forms:

-ar   Camina.   *Walk.*
-er   Bebe agua.   *Drink water.*
-ir   Vive la vida.   *Live your life.*

A review of the following situations will help determine which form, the *familiar* or *formal*, you should use:

◆ **Formal commands.** The use of formal commands indicates respect or unfamiliarity between the speakers. Most Spanish speakers use the **usted** form to communicate a formal command. The subject pronouns **usted** (*you*) or **ustedes** (*you, pl.*) may follow the verb as a sign of politeness. **Ud.** and **Uds.** are abbreviations of the subject pronouns.

Pase **Ud.**   *Come in,* **please**.
Hablen **ustedes** con el director.   **Please** *speak to the principal.*

◆ **Informal commands.** These commands indicate familiarity with the individual or individuals receiving the command:

tú (*you, sing., informal*)   Termina el examen.   *Finish the exam.*
vosotros/as (*you, pl., informal,*   Salid de la clase.   *Leave the classroom.*
    used in Spain only)
ustedes (*you, pl., informal*)   Cierren la puerta.   *Close the door.*

The subject pronoun may also be used with the **tú** and **vosotros** command forms for clarification or emphasis:

Compra **tú** los boletos.   *Buy the tickets* **yourself**.
Id **vosotros**.   **You** *go.*

EJERCICIO
5·1

¿Familiar o formal? *Escribe las oraciones en español. En el paréntesis aparece el sujeto implícito. Usa la puntuación apropiada.*

1. (tu hermana) Bring the bag. _____

2. (la Sra. Godínez) Read the letter. _____

3. (Dr. Ramos) Come in! _____

4. (tu hermanito) Please, answer the phone! _____

5. (tú) Decide! _____

6. (los Sres. Alvarado) Listen, please. _____

7. (dos chicos) Cross (**cruzar**) the street now! _____

8. (tu amiga Alicia) Go to the bus station. _____

The imperative mood in affirmative commands

Here is another point to consider when creating imperatives: is the command *affirmative* or *negative*?

- ◆ Affirmative formal commands. Forms of the affirmative formal commands are the same as the forms of the present subjunctive:

Firm**e** el documento.	*Sign the document.* (**usted**)
Borr**en** la pizarra.	*Erase the board.* (**ustedes**)

- ◆ Affirmative informal commands. Remember that the informal or familiar **tú** command, with some exceptions, is the same as the third-person singular of the *present indicative*:

Abre el regalo.	***Open** the gift.*
Cierra la ventana.	***Close** the window.*

Here are some of the frequently used irregular affirmative **tú** command forms:

decir	*to say, tell*	**di**
hacer	*to do, make*	**haz**
ir	*to go*	**ve**
poner	*to put, place*	**pon**
salir	*to leave, go out*	**sal**
ser	*to be*	**sé**
tener	*to have*	**ten**
venir	*to come*	**ven**

To form the affirmative plural form of **vosotros**, drop the **-r** of the infinitive and add **-d**:

Entra**d** al salón.	*Go into the living room.*
Hace**d** la tarea.	*Do the homework.*

EJERCICIO
5·2

Mandatos. *Cambia las oraciones siguientes. Usa la persona **tú** del singular. Algunas formas verbales son irregulares.*

1. Escriban la carta ahora mismo.

_____

2. Limpien el cuarto enseguida.

_____

3. Hagan la tarea de español.

_____

4. Pongan los papeles en la papelera.

_____

5. Digan la verdad.

_____

6. Salgan a la una de la tarde.

_____

7. Vengan a mi fiesta esta noche.

_____

8. Tengan paciencia.

_____

The imperative mood and negative commands

You already know how to create negative sentences in Spanish: The adverb **no** precedes the verb. However, for a negative command, you must be aware of which verb form to use, depending on whom you are addressing. The forms of all negative commands, both formal and informal, are the same as the present subjunctive forms.

No esperes a tu hermano.	*Do not wait for your brother.*
No suba al segundo piso.	*Do not go up to the second floor.*
No entréis al auto.	*Do not get into the car.*
No vayan Uds. a esa ciudad.	*Do not go to that city.*
No jueguen a la baraja.	*Do not play cards.*

EJERCICIO
5·3

En la oficina. *Cambia las oraciones siguientes. Usa la forma afirmativa o negativa **tú** del mandato de acuerdo a la información.*

1. Anita, (llamar) al gerente.

_____

2. Después, (invitar) a los empleados.

_____

3. No (hacer) más copias de estos documentos.

_____

4. (Llevar) los modelos al Sr. Martínez.

_____

5. Por favor, no (revisar) las listas de clientes.

_____

6. Y no (ayudar) al secretario.

_____

EJERCICIO

5·4

¿Cuáles son las oraciones imperativas? _Lee el diálogo. Subraya las oraciones imperativas._

1. —Buenas tardes. ¿En qué puedo servirle?
2. —Necesito una corbata para mi esposo. Saque esa corbata de la vitrina, por favor.
3. —¿Cuánto cuesta?
4. —La etiqueta dice $90.00 y un descuento del veinte por ciento.
5. —Cargue la corbata a mi tarjeta de crédito.
6. —Por favor, vaya a la otra caja (_cashier_). La computadora no acepta su tarjeta.
7. —¡Eso es un error! Llame inmediatamente al gerente.
8. —Lo siento. El gerente no está disponible.
9. —Guarde la corbata. No voy a comprar nada más en esta tienda.
10. —Lo siento.

Pleading

Imperative sentences are also used to plead or make an appeal or exhortation:

Den sangre.	_**Give** blood._
Protege el medio ambiente.	_**Protect** the environment._

The message in these sentences directs a person or sways or convinces someone to follow an idea or path. The speaker may be included as part of the implied subject in such an exhortation. Use the forms of the _first-person plural_ (**nosotros**) of the subjunctive for this type of imperative:

first person plural subjunctive + predicate → exhortation

Seamos pacientes.	_**Let's be** patient._
Ayudemos a estas señoras.	_**Let us help** these ladies._
Cenemos en la cocina.	_**Let's have dinner** in the kitchen._

Exhortación para mejorar el vocabulario. *Usa la forma* **nosotros.** *Usa la puntuación apropiada e incluye los signos de admiración (¡!).*

1. usar el diccionario _____

2. hacer preguntas a la maestra _____

3. viajar a México _____

4. ver telenovelas colombianas _____

5. repasar la gramática _____

6. escuchar las canciones españolas _____

Imperative sentences and word order

You know that an imperative sentence may consist of a single verb in the imperative mood. You have already been using sentences that include a direct and/or indirect object. The word order of sentences with noun or pronoun objects in Spanish also applies to imperatives: direct objects and indirect objects follow the verb, in that order.

> **verb + direct object noun + indirect object noun**
>
> Lleven + **el correo** + **a la secretaria.**
> *Take **the mail to the secretary.***
> ¡Escuchen **este programa**!   *Listen **to this program!***
> Devuelve **el dinero al dependiente.**   *Return **the money to the salesperson.***

Vas a dar una fiesta. *Da las instrucciones a tus amigos. Usa la forma afirmativa* **Uds.**

1. el salón / preparar _____

2. limpiar / las mesas _____

3. comprar / las bebidas _____

4. enviar / las invitaciones _____

5. envolver / los regalos _____

6. traer / las flores _____

En la cocina del restaurante. *¿Es correcto el orden de las palabras? Si no es correcto, cámbielo!*

1. Marta, ponga la carne en la nevera. _____

2. La cebolla corte. _____

3. La botella abra de aceite. _____

4. Felipe, lave los platos en la fregadora. _____

5. Las cervezas sirva a los invitados. _____

6. Prepare el café, Mario. _____

Word order in imperative sentences with object pronouns

In Unit 9 you will study other *pronouns*, words that replace nouns in a sentence. With affirmative commands, object pronouns are attached to the verb. Exclamation marks are used to indicate a sense of urgency.

affirmative command + object pronoun

¡Haz + **la**!
*Do **it**!*
¡Haz **la tarea**!   *Do **the homework**!*
¡Hazla!   ***Do it!***

Some sentences have more than one object pronoun. If there are two pronouns, the indirect object pronoun *precedes* the direct object pronoun: IO + DO.

A written accent mark appears on the stressed vowel of the imperative verb form when it is followed by one or two object pronouns. To place the accent, count back *three* vowels from the end of the imperative plus pronouns, and add the accent. (When an imperative verb form of more than one syllable has two object pronouns, count back *four* vowels, and add the accent mark.)

affirmative command + indirect object pronoun + direct object pronoun

Dá + **me** + **lo**
¡Dá**melo**!
*Give **it to me**!*
Dame el cuaderno, **¡dámelo!**   ***Give me** the notebook, **give it to me!***
Chicos, **llévenselo**.   *Boys, **take it with you**.*
Escribamos **la lista**.   *Let's write **the list**.*
Escribámosla.   ***Let's write it**.*
Lleva la taza **a Lisa**.   *Take the cup **to Lisa**.*
Llévale la taza.   ***Take her** the cup.*
Tráeme la tarea.   ***Bring me** the homework.*
Tráemela.   ***Bring it to me**.*

With negative commands, object pronouns are placed *immediately before the verb* in a Spanish sentence. Again, if there are two pronouns, the indirect object pronoun precedes the direct object pronoun.

negative word + object pronoun(s) + verb

¡**No** + **lo** + hagas!
¡**No lo** hagas!
Don't do it!
¡No leas **el periódico**!   *Do not read **the newspaper!***
No **lo** leas.   *Do not read **it**.*
No **me** des **las malas noticias**.   *Do not give **me the bad news**.*
No **me las** des.   *Do not give **it to me**.*

EJERCICIO 5·8

En español. *Sustituye el nombre subrayado con el pronombre de objeto directo correspondiente. Después, escribe la oración otra vez. Usa la forma* **tú**.

1. Call Diana! _____

2. Get (**recoger**) the tickets! _____

3. Buy the sodas for us! _____

4. Tell me the time! _____

5. Read me the program! _____

6. Wait for me! _____

EJERCICIO 5·9

Usa la lista de palabras para escribir una oración imperativa. Debes usar la forma **tú**. *¡Cuidado! Coloca los pronombres en el orden correcto. Usa los signos de admiración (¡!) y escribe acentos si son necesarios.*

MODELO   ¿Las llaves? / buscar / las / cajón / el / en

        ¿Las llaves? Búscalas en el cajón.

1. ¿La ventana? la / cerrar / mismo / ahora

_____

2. ¿Tus zapatos? los / al / no / tirar / suelo

_____

3. ¿El perro? lo / no / molestar

_____

4. ¿Tus amigos? los / su / llamar / a / casa

_____

5. ¿Las toallas? las / buscar / en el dormitorio

_____

6. ¿El auto? llevar / lo / al mecánico

_____

7. ¿Las manzanas? las / lavar / antes / comerlas / de

_____

8. ¿Las luces? no / las / apagar

_____

9. ¿Los vegetales? comprar / los / en / mercado / el

_____

10. ¿Los ejercicios? los / entregar / no

_____

Imperative sentences with reflexive object pronouns

Reflexive verbs are conjugated with reflexive pronouns. Imperative sentences with reflexive verbs have the same word order you have already studied for object pronouns: the pronoun is attached to the affirmative command, but it precedes the verb in negative commands. Add a written accent mark on the stressed syllable of the verb form.

¡Lá**va**te la cara!	*Wash **your** face!*
¡No **te** laves las manos!	*Do not wash **your** hands!*
¡Leván**tense**!	*Get up!*
¡No **se** levanten!	*Do not get up!*

EJERCICIO
5·10

Tú eres el/la líder. *Usa tu imaginación. Usa las formas afirmativas o negativas del imperativo para animar a un grupo de jóvenes. Usa el acento si es necesario.*

1. ¡_____ temprano! (despertarse)

2. ¡_____ antes de las ocho! (levantarse)

3. ¡_____ pronto! (prepararse)

4. ¡_____ la cara antes de salir! (lavarse)

5. ¡_____ los dientes! (cepillarse)

6. ¡No _____! (desanimarse)

7. ¡No _____ en el espejo! (mirarse)

8. ¡_____ la chaqueta! (ponerse)

9. ¡_____ ya! (sentarse)

10. ¡_____ tranquilos! (quedarse)

Building sentences with coordinating conjunctions

A coordinating conjunction connects two words, two phrases, or two clauses. By definition, a *clause* is a group of words containing a subject and a predicate that functions as *part of another sentence*. In this unit, we will build sentences that consist of more than one clause, joined by coordinating conjunctions.

The clause usually consists of a subject followed by a verb, but other elements may be included. If you can understand the idea presented, if the utterance communicates a complete thought and does not depend on any other elements to complete an idea or thought, it is an *independent* clause.

subject + predicate → sentence = independent clause

Each of the following examples of Spanish clauses includes a subject and a verb; each one makes complete sense when it stands alone. Remember that in Spanish the subject is usually understood by the ending of the verb:

Los candidatos no lleg**aron**.	*The candidates did not arrive.*
Viajar**emo**s a Buenos Aires.	*We will travel to Buenos Aires.*
¡Termin**en** ahora!	*Finish now!*

The most common coordinating conjunctions are:

y, e	*and*
ni	*nor*
ni... ni	*neither . . . nor*
pero	*but, yet*
sino	*but*
o, u	*or*

Remember that **y** (*and*) changes to **e** when followed by a word that starts with the vowel sounds **i-** and **hi-**:

Luisa **e** Irene son hermanas.	*Luisa **and** Irene are sisters.*
Sofía **e** Hilario son primos.	*Sofia **and** Hilario are cousins.*

Note that **u**, not **o** (*or*), is used when the word following starts with the vowel sounds **o-** and **ho-**:

¿Tienes siete **u** ocho hermanas?	*Do you have seven **or** eight sisters?*

Building sentences with coordinating conjunctions

Coordinating conjunctions can join two or more independent clauses. The result is a *compound sentence*, which means that the new sentence is the result of the combination of separate, independent elements.

independent clause + conjunction + independent clause

Luis juega al fútbol **+ y +** Jorge juega al tenis.
*Luis plays soccer **and** Jorge plays tennis.*

The typical word order for declarative, interrogative, or imperative sentences is used in the clauses that surround a coordinating conjunction:

El Dr. Mena es cardiólogo **y** la Dra. Manfredi es inmunóloga.	*Dr. Mena is a cardiologist **and** Dr. Manfredi is an immunologist.*
¿Quieres descansar **o** quieres ir de compras?	*Do you want to rest **or** do you want to go shopping?*
Devuelve los zapatos **y** regresa a casa inmediatamente.	*Return the shoes **and** come back home immediately.*

In previous units you built *sentences*: affirmative and negative sentences, direct questions, imperatives, and exclamatory sentences. They resemble the examples below:

Me levanto a las cinco todos los días.	*I get up at five o'clock every day.*
Los fines de semana no trabajo.	*On weekends I do not work.*
Salgo de compras.	*I go shopping.*
Regreso al mediodía.	*I come back at noon.*
Quiero un vestido nuevo.	*I want a new dress.*
No tengo mucho dinero.	*I do not have much money.*
¡Préstame el dinero!	*Lend me the money!*
No voy a la fiesta.	*I am not going to the party.*

Coordinating conjunctions can be used to join the simple sentences you just read. Independent clauses are linked with coordinating conjunctions to create longer sentences, each balanced in length:

Me levanto a las cinco todos los días, **pero** los fines de semana no trabajo.	*I get up at five o'clock every day, **but** I do not work on weekends.*
Salgo de compras **y** regreso al mediodía.	*I go out shopping **and** return at noon.*
Quiero un vestido nuevo, **pero** no tengo mucho dinero.	*I want a new dress, **but** I do not have a lot of money.*
¡Préstame el dinero **o** no voy a la fiesta!	*Lend me the money **or** I will not go to the party!*

A comma may be used in Spanish to mark the two clauses when combining sentences with these conjunctions. The comma can be placed *before* **y**, **e**, and **ni**, but only if you need to avoid confusion when linking the two clauses:

Mi jefe trabaja mucho**, y** el descanso le parece absurdo.	*My boss works hard, **and** he thinks resting is absurd.*

Combina las dos oraciones independientes. Elige la conjunción apropiada que aparece en cada paréntesis para crear una oración.

1. (y / ni) Fui a casa de Laura. Jugué con su perro.

   _____

2. (y / pero) Yo quería cenar con ella. Laura tenía una cita con el dentista.

   _____

3. (pero / o) Laura no faltará (*miss*) a la cita. No le gusta ir al dentista.

   _____

4. (ni / o) Laura no come de día. Duerme por la noche.

   _____

5. (sino / o) Va al dentista. Tomará calmantes por mucho tiempo.

   _____

6. (o / pero) Tengo mucha paciencia. Laura me enoja (*annoys*).

   _____

7. (pero / y) Es una linda persona. Es muy indecisa.

   _____

8. (y / o) Regresé a casa. Cené solo.

   _____

Omitting the subject and the verb in the second clause

In Spanish, as in English, when the subject of both the first and second clause is the same, it is frequently omitted:

Bertina cerró los ojos y no vio el accidente.	*Bertina closed her eyes and did not see the accident.*
El detective concluyó la investigación y se fue.	*The detective concluded the investigation and left.*

For different reasons, it is also possible to omit the verb of the second clause: for the sake of brevity, to balance the sentence, or as a simple matter of style:

Ni tiene trabajo ni dinero.	*He/she does not have a job or money.*
Se despide de mí y de sus amigos.	*He/she says good-bye to me and his/her friends.*
Preparo una paella de mariscos u otro plato.	*I prepare a seafood paella or another dish.*

Subraya los sujetos o los verbos que se pueden eliminar en cada oración. Después, escribe la oración otra vez.

MODELO   Fernando y Rosa compraron una casa y <u>ellos </u>vendieron su auto viejo.

Fernando y Rosa compraron una casa y vendieron su auto viejo.

1. Alicia y yo limpiamos la casa los sábados y los domingos nosotras cenamos con mis padres.

   _____

2. Yo no como carne ni como pollo.

   _____

3. Alicia prepara la ensalada de lechuga con aguacate y prepara la limonada.

   _____

4. Mis padres invitan a mis primos o invitan a sus amigos, los López.

   _____

5. A veces, nosotros tomamos una copa de vino o nosotros bebemos un vaso de cerveza.

   _____

6. Nos gusta un café con el postre o nos gusta un té de camomila.

   _____

7. Después, Alicia y su novio dan un paseo por la ciudad o ellos dan un paseo por la playa.

   _____

8. Los domingos no son días buenos ni son días malos.

   _____

9. Los domingos yo ceno con mis padres pero yo prefiero una cena con mis primos.

   _____

10. Mis primos van al cine conmigo o van al "Café Nostalgia".

    _____

Spanish coordinating conjunctions and their functions

At the beginning of this unit you reviewed common coordinating conjunctions. Get acquainted with their use and focus on the message each one communicates, and you will be able to use them correctly as you build sentences in Spanish.

- **Y, e** (*and*), and **ni** (*neither, nor*) join independent clauses:

  Marisa canta **y** yo bailo.   *Marisa sings **and** I dance.*

- **O** or **u** (*or*) link independent clauses that exclude each other:

  Loli camina **o** nada en la piscina.   *Loli takes a walk **or** swims in the pool.*

- **Pero** expresses opposition or contrast:

  Estoy cansada, **pero** terminaré la tarea.   *I am tired **but** I will finish the homework.*

- **Ni** (*neither, nor*) means **y no**. It joins two negative independent clauses. For emphasis, **ni** may precede each clause:

  No dormí **ni** estudié.   *I **did not** sleep or study. (I neither slept nor studied.)*

  Ni dormí **ni** estudié.   *I **did not** sleep or study. (I neither slept nor studied.)*

- **Sino** (*but, rather*) introduces an affirmative idea or concept in the second clause, which has been preceded by a negative idea in the first clause:

  No peleó Pedro **sino** Juan.   *Pedro **did not** fight, Juan **did**.*

EJERCICIO
6·3

Usa la lógica. *Con cada grupo de palabras vas a crear oraciones.*

1. y / la escritora / su novela / llegó / la oficina / a / se sentó / a / escribir

   _____

2. el / final / escribió / capítulo / pero / no / gustó / le

   _____

3. escribió / otro / muy / capítulo / aburrido / pero / resultó

   _____

4. o / el comienzo / cambiaba / o / el / sería / final / imposible

   _____

5. y / no / ideas / tenía / salió / de / oficina / la

   _____

6. no / ganas / escribir / tenía / de / ni / buscar / más / de / ideas

   _____

7. de / salió / la / oficina / y / fue / librería / a / la

   _____

8. se / en / sentó / una / café / silla / y / un / tomó

   _____

9. la / observó / gente / a / alrededor / su / a / el / inició / capítulo / e

_____

10. la / autora / inteligente / era / y / el / terminar / capítulo / logró

_____

Vas a crear oraciones nuevas. Usa la conjunción más apropiada para combinar las oraciones. ¡Ojo! En algunos casos, es posible usar más de una conjunción, pero el significado será diferente.

o / pero / sino / ni / y

1. Bailas muy bien. Tocas la guitarra mejor.

_____

2. No habla. No llora.

_____

3. Entras. Sales.

_____

4. No eres amable con tus colegas. Tampoco eres cortés con tus amigos.

_____

5. Es muy caro. Tengo dinero suficiente.

_____

6. No cerraron la tienda a las nueve. A las diez.

_____

7. Viajaremos por las montañas. Luego por la costa.

_____

8. Llévame al aeropuerto ahora. Pierdo mi vuelo a Arizona.

_____

9. Me gusta esta novela. Es muy larga.

_____

Punctuation of sentences with more than two independent clauses

In Spanish, a comma is usually not needed with the coordinating conjunctions **y**, **e**, and **ni**. However, when a sentence includes more than two independent clauses, the coordinating conjunction usually precedes the last clause, and a comma separates the previous clauses. Some styles *in English* also include a comma before the conjunction.

> **independent clause 1 + comma + independent clause 2 + conjunction + independent clause 3 → sentence**

Nos levantamos, fuimos al correo y regresamos.

*We got up, went to the post office, **and** came back.*

Corro, hago gimnasia olímpica y levanto pesas.

*I run, practice gymnastics, **and** do weight training.*

**EJERCICIO
6·5**

Completa cada oración. Usa la conjunción que aparece entre paréntesis, y cuando sea necesario, usa la coma.

1. Mi amiga y yo iremos al cine. Compraremos las entradas.

   (y) _____

2. No nos gustan las películas de horror. No preferimos las películas muy dramáticas.

   (ni) _____

3. No llueve mucho. Date prisa.

   (pero) _____

4. Tenemos poco dinero. Tenemos muchas deudas. Nuestro apartamento es muy caro.

   (y) _____

5. Ahorramos (*we save*) mucho. No somos tacaños (*stingy*).

   (pero) _____

6. O ganamos más dinero. Pedimos un aumento de sueldo. Buscamos otro trabajo.

   (o) _____

7. No somos ambiciosos. Cautelosos.

   (sino) _____

8. Somos jóvenes. Tenemos el futuro por delante.

   (y) _____

Building sentences with subordinating conjunctions

Another element to consider when building a complex sentence is the *subordinating conjunction*. A subordinating conjunction links a clause to a *main clause*. A main clause always includes a subject and a verb. The main clause makes complete sense when it stands alone. However, more elements may be needed to add information to such a sentence, with the help of a subordinating conjunction. Subordinating conjunctions introduce *dependent clauses* that cannot stand alone. A dependent clause, also called a *subordinate clause*, depends on the main clause to communicate its full meaning.

> **main clause + subordinating conjunction + dependent clause →**
> **sentence**

In the following example, the subordinating conjunction **aunque** (*although*) introduces a subordinate clause. Note that the idea presented in this clause is incomplete:

Aunque tengo miedo.	***Although** I am afraid.*

Adding the dependent clause, as follows, to an independent (main) clause results in a complete, complex sentence with a clearer meaning:

Aunque tengo miedo, **volaré a Cancún**.	*Although I am afraid, **I will fly to Cancún**.*

The subordinate clause and the main clause may be separated by a comma. The elements or building blocks of a sentence with a subordinate conjunction can be placed in either order:

> **main clause + subordinating conjunction + clause**
>
> Volaré a Cancún, + **aunque** + tengo miedo.

> **subordinating conjunction + clause + main clause**
>
> **Aunque** + tengo miedo + volaré a Cancún.

Spanish subordinating conjunctions and their functions

A conjunction is a word or a group of words that connect or join parts of a sentence, clauses, or full sentences. A *subordinating conjunction* is placed at the beginning of the clause it introduces. There are a number of subordinating conjunctions. They indicate the nature of the relationship between the main clause and the subordinate clause, such as time, cause, effect, or condition. Some of these clauses behave like adverbs; they are called *adverbial clauses.* Here are some of the most frequently used conjunctions and their relationship to the main clause:

- Time

    cuando *when*
    Juan me llama todos los días **cuando** llega a casa.

    *Juan calls me every day **when** he gets home.*

    desde que *once*
    Desde que empieza el verano, se van a la casa de la playa.

    ***Once** summer begins, they go to their beach house.*

    después (de) que *after, once*
    Después que entro, saludo a mis colegas.

    ***After** I get in, I greet my colleagues.*

    hasta que *until, by the time*
    Ana me espera todos los días **hasta que** termino mi trabajo.

    *Ana waits for me every day **until** I finish work.*

    siempre que *whenever*
    Ayudo a mis hermanos **siempre que** puedo.

    *I help my brothers **whenever** I can.*

- Cause and effect

    como *because, since*
    Como es muy violento, no veo este programa.

    ***Because** it is very violent, I do not watch this program.*

    de modo que *so*
    Lucas perdió el partido, **de modo que** pagaré la apuesta.

    *Lucas lost the match, **so** now I will pay the bet.*

    porque *because*
    Salgo ahora mismo **porque** llevo prisa.

    *I am leaving right now, **because** I am in a hurry.*

    puesto que *since*
    Puesto que no tienen dinero, no van de vacaciones.

    ***Since** they have no money, they are not going on vacation.*

    ya que *because, since*
    Ya que estás aquí, voy a ayudarte con la tarea.

    ***Since** you are here, I will help you with your homework.*

- Condition

    si *if*
    Si Uds. están en el museo, iré con mi novio.

    ***If** you are at the museum, I will go with my boyfriend.*

- A difficulty, a concession

    aunque *although, even though*
    Aunque tiene novia, Felipe no quiere casarse.

    ***Although** he has a girlfriend, Felipe does not want to get married.*

    por más que *even though*
    Por más que trabajo duro, no gano mucho dinero.

    ***Even though** I work hard, I do not earn a lot of money.*

Note that the examples above include a main clause in the indicative mood that states a fact, a certainty, or a good probability; the verb in the dependent clause is also in the indicative.

Another frequently used subordinate conjunction, **que** (*that*), introduces a clause that functions as a direct object of the main clause:

Tomasina dice **que** aprobó el examen de conducir.	*Tomasina says (**that**) she passed the driving test.*
Mi padre sabía **que** yo estaba en Venezuela.	*My father knew (**that**) I was in Venezuela.*

In English, for reasons of style, the conjunction *that* may be omitted. Its presence or absence does not affect the meaning of the sentence. Note that the conjunction **que** cannot be omitted in Spanish.

EJERCICIO 7·1

¿Cuál es la conjunción adecuada? *Elige la conjunción que ayuda a completar la oración de una manera lógica. Escribe la respuesta en el espacio en blanco.*

porque / desde que / después que / aunque / si / por más que / ya que / que

1. Antonia es muy tacaña (*stingy*), _____ a veces nos sorprende su generosidad.

2. No compró la chaqueta _____ no le ofrecieron un descuento.

3. _____ se probó varios vestidos, ¡no compró nada!

4. _____ Antonia no cambia su manera de ser, no iré de compras con ella.

5. _____ me gusta salir de casa, no tengo paciencia para ir de compras con Antonia.

6. Antonia ha sido tacaña siempre, _____ era una niña.

7. Estoy convencida de _____ será siempre igual.

8. _____ hablamos de Antonia, ahora sabes que soy chismosa.

EJERCICIO 7·2

Combina las dos cláusulas. De acuerdo al sentido de la oración, usa la conjunción apropiada de las dos que aparecen en cada paréntesis.

MODELO (cuando / ya que) ... no vienes conmigo, voy a salir al jardín.

Ya que no vienes conmigo, voy a salir al jardín.

1. (después que / aunque) Necesito trabajar en mi jardín... llueve mucho.

_____

2. (aunque / ya que) Tengo unos guantes... quiero proteger mis manos.

_____

3. (si / después que) ... me pongo los guantes, me pongo mi sombrero.

_____

4. (aunque / si) Tomaremos una limonada... tienes sed.

_____

5. (cuando / desde que) ... empecé a trabajar en el jardín, he rebajado doce libras de peso.

_____

6. (como / desde que) ... tengo mucha paciencia, trabajo lento, despacio.

_____

7. (puesto que / aunque) ... quieres limonada, voy a cortar los limones de mi jardín.

_____

8. (aunque / ya que) Necesitamos hielo ... quieres tomar la limonada fría.

_____

EJERCICIO
7·3

Completa cada una de las oraciones siguientes con una frase original y apropiada. Observa la conjunción delante del espacio en blanco para escribir tu respuesta.

MODELO Ellos viajarán al espacio porque (confiar) ____*confían en los científicos*____ .

1. Doce españoles viajarán al espacio porque (ser) _____ .

2. Una agencia prepara el viaje porque (querer) _____ .

3. Tenemos interés en este viaje ya que (pensar) _____ .

4. Como (tú) (tener dinero) _____ , no puedes ir al espacio.

5. Los viajeros preparan este viaje que (ofrecer) _____ .

6. Si tú (tener) _____ puedes comprar tu billete por $150.000.

7. Aunque (parecer) _____ , esta aventura atrae a mucha gente.

8. Es fácil creer esta noticia si (nosotros) (creer) _____ .

9. Aunque (los turistas) (estar listos) _____ , nos sabemos la fecha de salida.

10. Sueña con un viaje a las estrellas si (tú) (confiar) _____ .

Indicative mood in the dependent clause

The verb in the main clause establishes the subject's attitude or mood. In turn, that attitude or mood determines the mood of the verb in the dependent clause. A main clause with a verb that states a fact, a certainty, or a good probability requires the indicative mood in the dependent clause. Note that an adjective such as **seguro** (*sure*) or an adverb, **jamás** (*never, ever*) that leaves no doubt, may appear in the main clause, helping you determine the correct mood for the dependent clause.

In the following examples, the verb in the main clause indicates certainty or probability; thus, the verb in the dependent clause introduced by the conjunction **que** is in the *indicative*. The verb in the dependent clause can be in various tenses of the indicative mood, as required by the context.

Sé **que la Tierra no es el centro del universo.**	*I know **the Earth is not the center of the universe.***
Se dice **que descubrieron nuevos planetas.**	*They say **they have discovered new planets.***
Los astrónomos afirman **que se parecen a la Tierra.**	*The astronomers state **that they resemble the Earth.***
Los pesimistas creen **que jamás llegaremos a Marte.**	*Pessimists think **that we will never get to Mars.***

Note that the slightest hint of doubt or uncertainty in the main clause requires a *subjunctive* form in the dependent clause:

Dudamos **que el alcalde sea reelegido.**	*We doubt **that the mayor will be reelected.***

In Unit 16 you will study more about the subjunctive mood in dependent clauses.

EJERCICIO
7·4

El pronóstico optimista del tiempo. *Completa cada oración en español con la respuesta sugerida entre paréntesis.*

1. ¡Dios mío! Se anuncia... (*that there will be a snowstorm*).

   _____

2. Mi esposo dice... (*that it already snowed a lot during the night*).

   _____

3. Yo sé... (*that in winter this is possible*).

   _____

4. Creo... (*that we will be able to drive up the mountain*).

   _____

5. Pienso... (*that it will be a great day for skiing*).

   _____

6. Ah, otro boletín de "El tiempo" dice... (*that the weather conditions are ideal for winter sports*).

   _____

7. Sabía... (*that it was going to be a beautiful day*).

_____

8. Mi marido sabe... (*that I am an optimist*).

_____

9. Lo cierto es... (*that I love* [**me encantar**] *snow*).

_____

10. Me siento feliz... (*when I am in a cold place*).

_____

EJERCICIO
7·5

Tu futuro y las condiciones. *Usa los verbos entre paréntesis en la primera persona del singular (**yo**) del futuro de indicativo, y después del presente de indicativo para crear oraciones complejas. Sigue el modelo.*

MODELO   (ser) trilingüe si (estudiar) portugués y español
       Seré trilingüe si estudio portugués y español.

1. (ganar) mucho más dinero si (trabajar) más horas

_____

2. (terminar) mi máster si (tomar) dos cursos en línea este semestre

_____

3. (casarme) en agosto de este año si (convencer) a mi novia

_____

4. (viajar) a Buenos Aires si (ganar) el premio gordo

_____

5. (conseguir) mis metas (*goals*) si (tener) claros mis objetivos

_____

6. (tener) el apoyo de mi familia si (necesitar) ayuda en algún momento

_____

7. (comprar) un apartamento si (tener) un aumento de sueldo

_____

8. (visitar) a mis amigos si (poder) conseguir un billete a buen precio

_____

9. (ir) a Brasil si (aprender) suficiente portugués para hablar con la gente

_____

10. (aumentar) mi fortuna si (invertir) el dinero de manera sensata

_____

Using interrogatives to build subordinate clauses

In Units 2 and 3 you practiced building interrogative sentences, the word order of interrogatives, and how to answer questions. Now you can use some of that information to build subordinate sentences. Let's start with *yes/no* questions:

¿Está Lucía contigo?	*Is Lucia with you?*
Sí, está conmigo.	*Yes, she is with me.*
No, no está conmigo.	*No, she is not with me.*

In this unit, you studied **si** (*if, whether*) as a subordinating conjunction. A possible answer to a question can be built with **si**, the subordinating conjunction. Note that the adverb **sí** (*yes*) has an accent mark.

¿Tiene Lucía una cita hoy?	*Does Lucía have an appointment today?*
No sé **si** Lucía tiene una cita hoy.	*I don't know if (whether) Lucía has an appointment today.*
¿Hay peras y manzanas maduras (*ripe*)?	*Are there any ripe pears and apples?*
No sé **si** hay peras y manzanas maduras.	*I do not know whether there are ripe pears and apples.*

Using interrogative words to build subordinate clauses

Interrogative pronouns (**quién**, **cuál**, etc.), adverbs (**dónde**, **adónde**, **cuándo**), and other interrogative words can function as subordinating conjunctions. Here is a quick review of interrogative words:

¿Cómo?	*How?*
¿Cuál?, ¿Cuáles?	*Which?*
¿Cuándo?	*When?*
¿Cuánto?, ¿Cuánta?	*How much?*
¿Cuántos?, ¿Cuántas?	*How many?*
¿Dónde?	*Where?*
¿Adónde?	*Where (to)?*
¿Por qué?	*Why?*
¿Qué?	*What?*
¿Quién?, ¿Quiénes?	*Who?*
¿A quién?, ¿A quiénes?	*(To) Whom?*

These words are used to create direct questions with question marks. They are also used without question marks, but with an accent mark, in answers to introduce a *subordinating element*:

—¿**Quién** habla?   —***Who's speaking?***
—No sé **quién** habla.   —*I do not know **who** is speaking.*
—¿**A quién** le pertenece este abrigo?   —***Who(m)** does this coat belong to?*
—Pregunta **a quién** le pertenece este abrigo.   —*Ask **to whom** this coat belongs.*
—¿**A qué hora** sale el tren a Madrid?   —***At what time** does the train leave for Madrid?*
—Dime **a qué hora** sale el tren.   —*Tell me **at what time** the train leaves.*

Note that interrogative words in answers retain the interrogative accent mark. When interrogative words function as subordinating conjunctions, the elements of the sentence follow the same order as do clauses with other subordinating conjunctions.

main clause + interrogative word + subordinate clause

No sabemos + quiénes + compraron los regalos.
We do not know who bought the gifts.

Note the use of the indicative mood in the dependent clause introduced by an interrogative adverb. Verb tenses may vary as required by the context:

Yo no sabía **cómo** llegar a tu casa.   *I did not know **how** to get to your house.*
Me preguntó **cuántas** llamadas recibiste ayer.   *He asked me **how many** calls you received yesterday.*
Queremos saber **quiénes** vendrán a la cena.   *We want to know **who** will attend the dinner.*
Explícame **por qué** te enojabas con frecuencia.   *Explain to me **why** you used to get angry so often.*
Pronto sabrán **adónde** iremos.   *Soon you will know **where** we will go.*

EJERCICIO
7·6

Elige una palabra apropiada de la lista siguiente para completar la respuesta.

qué / dónde / quién / si / cómo / por qué / cuándo / quiénes

1. Me pregunto _____ ha llegado al estudio de televisión.

2. Voy a preguntar _____ se llama.

3. Ante todo, quiero que nos explique _____ ha llegado aquí.

4. Le pediré su autógrafo, _____ es una estrella del cine mexicano.

5. Voy a preguntarle _____ hace en esta ciudad.

6. Soy muy chismoso y me pregunto _____ se va a quedar esta noche.

7. Vamos a saber _____ se irá a Ciudad México, ¿tal vez mañana?

8. Ah, y tengo que saber _____ la acompañan.

En la estación de policía. *Usa las preguntas para crear cláusulas. Usa **si** cuando sea necesario. Observa el ejemplo:*

MODELO ¿Qué hora es?

Dime _____qué hora es_____ .

1. ¿Dónde están las joyas robadas?

   Nadie sabe _____ .

2. ¿A qué hora llegarán los agentes?

   Me pregunto _____ .

3. ¿Quién escribió la nota?

   No recordamos _____ .

4. ¿Adónde llevaron a la víctima?

   Dime _____ .

5. ¿Cuándo descubrieron el robo?

   Pregúntales _____ .

6. ¿Por qué abandonaron la casa de la víctima?

   Ignoro _____ .

7. ¿Cómo se llama la sospechosa?

   Nadie sabe con certeza _____ .

8. ¿A quiénes vamos a interrogar después?

   Decide tú _____ .

9. ¿Asignaron un especialista a este caso?

   Avíseme _____ .

10. ¿Desde cuándo no hay un boletín de noticias?

   Olvidé _____ .

Escribe una oración original con cada una de las siguientes conjunciones o interrogativas. Puedes escribir acerca de tus experiencias.

MODELOS   si

    Si tengo tiempo, preparo la cena en casa.

    Si no tengo tiempo, compro la cena en el supermercado.

    desde que

    Aprendí a cocinar desde que tenía doce años.

1. si

_____

2. cuando

_____

3. por qué

_____

4. aunque

_____

5. desde que

_____

6. hasta que

_____

7. quién

_____

8. porque

_____

9. por qué

_____

10. cuántas

_____

Relative pronouns

A *relative pronoun* refers to someone or something previously mentioned (*the antecedent*) in a sentence, or understood as such by those who are communicating. That someone or something can be a *noun* or a *pronoun*.

antecedent → relative pronoun

las calles + **que**
las calles **que**   *the streets **that***
el hombre **quien**   *the man **who***

In the following sentences, the antecedent precedes a relative pronoun **que** (*who, that*) or **quien** (*who*). Note also the use of **el/la que** (*he/she/the one who*).

Armando es **el empleado que** me ayuda.	*Armando is **the clerk who** helps me.*
Alquilé **una película que** es aburridísima.	*I rented **a movie that** is very boring.*
Este es **Martín, quien** quiere conocerte.	*This is **Martín, who** wants to meet you.*
¡El culpable es **el que** dice mentiras!	*The culprit is **he who** tells lies!*

Relative pronoun forms

The most frequently used relative pronouns are the following:

que	*that, who, which*
quien, quienes	*who, whom*

Que is the most frequently used relative pronoun. It can refer to people, animals, things, ideas, or events, in the singular and plural. English equivalents vary according to the context.

Marcos trae las flores **que** le gustan a María.	*Marcos is bringing the flowers **that** María likes.*
Leo la vida de Goya, **que** es mi pintor favorito.	*I am reading the life of Goya, **who** is my favorite painter.*
Prefiero esta camisa, **que** es más cómoda.	*I prefer this shirt, **which** is more comfortable.*
Esta idea, **que** es tuya, es excelente.	*This idea, **which** is yours, is excellent.*

Note that in Spanish, unlike English, the relative pronoun cannot be omitted:

Compré el abrigo **que** vimos ayer.	*I bought the coat (**that**) we saw yesterday.*

61

Que, quien, and quienes

The relative pronoun may be preceded by a preposition. After a preposition, **quien** and **quienes** are used when referring to people; the form **que** does not refer to people in such cases:

Los candidatos **en quienes** confío recibirán mi voto.	*The candidates **whom** I trust will get my vote.*
El dueño de la casa, **a quien** conozco, es mexicano.	*The owner of the house, **whom** I know, is Mexican.*
Vimos a Marcos, **con quien** nos encontramos ayer.	*We saw Marcos, **whom** we met yesterday.*

Remember that **quien** and **quienes** can also be interrogative pronouns in direct or indirect questions. In those cases, they require a written accent mark to indicate their function as interrogatives.

—¿**Quién** llama?	*—**Who** is calling?*
—¿No sabes **quién** te llama?	*—You do not know **who** is calling you?*

Quien/quienes may also function as indefinite pronouns, and as such they replace *he, she, those,* etc., as the subject. In these sentences, the true antecedent may be implied, especially in sentences such as the following:

Quienes rompen las reglas son castigados.	*__Those who__ break the rules are punished.*
Quien trabaja debe ser compensado.	*__He/she who/whoever__ works must be compensated.*

EJERCICIO
8·1

*Elige **que**, **quien** o **quienes**. En cada espacio en blanco, escribe la forma del pronombre que corresponde. En algunos casos, hay más de una respuesta correcta.*

1. Mariano, a _____ quiero mucho, es hipocondríaco.

2. No toma café, _____, de acuerdo a su opinión, provoca dolor de estómago.

3. Cuando llueve, _____ en la Florida es frecuente, Mariano sufre de sinusitis.

4. Va a la consulta del Dr. Valeriano, _____ es amigo de la familia.

5. Mariano sigue los consejos _____ sus amigos le dan.

6. Mariano es un hombre _____ teme a las enfermedades.

7. Sus hermanos, con _____ nos reunimos a menudo, no son como Mariano.

8. Las razones _____ provocan los temores de Mariano pueden ser imaginadas.

9. Tenemos un amigo _____ es sicólogo y va a ayudar a Mariano.

10. ¡Qué casualidad! Ahí viene el sicólogo de _____ te hablaba.

En español. *Escribe las frases siguientes en español. Usa los verbos en el pretérito. ¡Cuidado! Algunas de las frases en inglés no necesitan un pronombre relativo, pero en español sí.*

1. the invitation that I received

_____

2. the person who sent (**enviar**) the invitation

_____

3. the answer that I wrote

_____

4. the stamps (**estampillas**) that I bought

_____

5. the gifts that I chose (**escoger**)

_____

6. the person I met at the party

_____

7. the music they played

_____

8. the suit I wore (**llevar**)

_____

Te toca a ti. *Vas a construir un párrafo con las respuestas del Ejercicio 8-2. Tienes dos ejemplos:*

MODELOS   *La invitación que recibí me sorprendió.*

La persona que me invitó es mi jefe.

1. _____

2. _____

3. _____

4. _____

5. _____

6. _____

7. _____

8. _____

More relative pronouns: **el que, la que, los que, las que**

The relative pronouns **el/la/los/las que** are considered alternate forms of **quien** and the plural **quienes**. Remember that the order of the subject and predicate in a sentence may vary in Spanish.

Pasen al frente **los que** se matricularon.	***Those who*** *registered, step up to the front.*
Los que se matricularon pasen al frente.	*Step up to the front **those who** registered.*
Vamos a entrevistar a **las que** están presentes.	*We will interview **those who** are present.*

The **el que** pronouns frequently appear in proverbs or sayings as the subject of the sentence. Note that literal translation into English does not always convey the exact meaning:

El que no trabaja no come.	*No work, no money.*

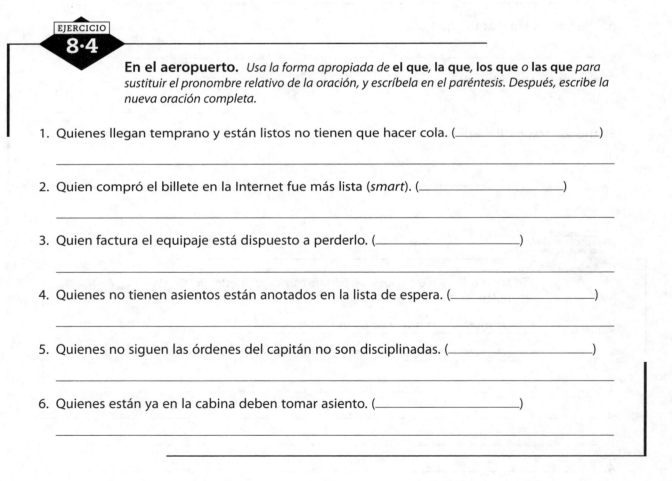

EJERCICIO 8·4

En el aeropuerto. *Usa la forma apropiada de* **el que, la que, los que** *o* **las que** *para sustituir el pronombre relativo de la oración, y escríbela en el paréntesis. Después, escribe la nueva oración completa.*

1. Quienes llegan temprano y están listos no tienen que hacer cola. (_____)

_____

2. Quien compró el billete en la Internet fue más lista (*smart*). (_____)

_____

3. Quien factura el equipaje está dispuesto a perderlo. (_____)

_____

4. Quienes no tienen asientos están anotados en la lista de espera. (_____)

_____

5. Quienes no siguen las órdenes del capitán no son disciplinadas. (_____)

_____

6. Quienes están ya en la cabina deben tomar asiento. (_____)

_____

Cuyo

Forms of the relative **cuyo** (*whose*) refer to both people and things.

        cuyo/a/os/as   *whose*

    In a sense, the relative pronoun **cuyo** functions as a possessive adjective; it does not agree with the antecedent but with the person or thing *possessed*, which follows **cuyo** (or any of its forms) in the sentence. **Cuyo** is used mostly in written Spanish.

> **antecedent + cuyo/a/os/as + person or thing possessed**
>
> Conocí a Laura, + **cuyas** + **hermanas** viven aquí.
> *I met Laura, **whose sisters** live here.*
>
> Las jóvenes **cuyos padres** admiras son cubanas.   *The young girls **whose parents** you admire are Cuban.*
>
> El profesor, **cuyas ideas** no comparto, es estricto.   *The professor, **whose ideas** I do not share, is strict.*

EJERCICIO 8·5

¿Sabías esto? *Escribe las oraciones en español. Usa la forma apropiada:* **cuyo, cuya, cuyos** *o* **cuyas.**

1. The man whose brother arrived is my boss.

    _____

2. Luli, whose husband is not here, wants to buy a luxury car.

    _____

3. That lady, whose handbag is horrible, thinks she is elegant.

    _____

4. This girl, whose boyfriend is very handsome, is so boring!

    _____

5. Do you like *The Shadow of the Wind*, whose author is Spanish?

    _____

6. Miranda, whose parents do not live here, is too young to drive alone.

    _____

Relative clauses

In Unit 7 you learned how to build subordinate clauses with subordinating conjunctions. Now you will study *relative clauses* that require *relative pronouns* to build sentences with two clauses: a main clause and a *relative clause*. To build a sentence with a relative clause you need the following elements:

main clause containing the antecedent + relative pronoun in a dependent clause

Hablé con **el empleado** + **que** tiene las entradas.
*I spoke to **the employee who** has the tickets.*

Remember that a dependent clause requires a main clause in order to communicate its entire meaning. Relative pronouns serve as links to create longer, more complex sentences with both a main clause and a relative clause. As you build sentences and put them in specific contexts, you will also be creating paragraphs.

The verb in a relative clause can be in the *indicative* or *subjunctive mood*, depending on whether the main clause suggests certainty or uncertainty. In Unit 16 you will review the subjunctive mood and its uses. Read the following sentences. They do not suggest uncertainty; therefore all the verbs are in the *indicative mood*:

Estoy en el museo Reina Sofía.	*I am at the Reina Sofía Museum.*
Ves el cuadro *Guernica*.	*You see the painting Guernica.*
Tienen varios cuadros de Salvador Dalí.	*They have some paintings by Salvador Dalí.*
Son muy interesantes.	*They are very interesting.*
Vale la pena visitar el museo.	*It is worth visiting the museum.*
Es uno de muchos en Madrid.	*It is one among many in Madrid.*
Compré dos libros sobre la pintura moderna.	*I bought two books about modern painting.*
Es mi favorita.	*It is my favorite.*
Vine con Julio Saravia.	*I came with Julio Saravia.*
Es un experto en arte contemporáneo.	*He is an expert in contemporary art.*

The following examples show how a *relative pronoun* may link each pair of sentences. In each case, the first sentence has become the main clause; the second sentence in each pair is now a dependent clause, introduced by a relative pronoun. Note that some slight changes have been made in the original sentences, for style.

Estoy en el museo Reina Sofía, **en el cual** está el cuadro *Guernica*.	*I am at the Reina Sofía Museum, **where (in which)** the painting Guernica can be found.*
Tienen varios cuadros de Salvador Dalí, **cuyas obras** son muy interesantes.	*They have several paintings by Salvador Dalí, **whose** works are very interesting.*
Vale la pena visitar el museo, **que** es uno de muchos en Madrid.	*It is worth visiting the museum, **which** is one of many in Madrid.*
Compré dos libros sobre la pintura moderna, **la cual** es mi favorita.	*I bought two books about modern painting, **which** is my favorite.*
Vine con Julio Saravia, **quien** es un experto en arte contemporáneo.	*I came with Julio Saravia, **who** is an expert in contemporary art.*

In the first example above, the preposition **en** precedes the relative pronoun. A comma may be used before the relative pronoun **el cual** and its forms.

Relative clauses and punctuation

Commas separating the relative clause from the rest of the sentence help clarify the information contained in the clause. If the information is essential for the meaning of the sentence, *no* commas are used. In Spanish and English, clauses introduced with **que** or *that* are considered essential:

Veo las estrellas **que aparecen** por el telescopio.	*I see the stars **that appear** in the telescope.*

In the following example, the information in the dependent clause is not considered essential. In this case, it is separated by two commas:

Investigaciones de muchos astrónomos, **a quienes admiro**, revelan los misterios del espacio.	*Research by many astronomers, **whom I admire**, reveals the mysteries of outer space.*

Lo que and lo cual in relative clauses

These relative pronouns are used to refer to an idea, a concept, or a clause. **Lo que** translates into *what* or *that which*. **Lo que** and **lo cual** translate into *which*, referring to a fact if the antecedent is a *clause* or an *idea*.

Me dice **lo que** quiere.	*He/she tells me **what** he/she wants.*
Votaron por el otro candidato, **lo cual** enojó a mi abuelo.	*They voted for the other candidate, **which** annoyed my grandfather.*

A relative clause with **lo que** or **lo cual** can also act as the subject of the verb in the main clause. The relative clause usually follows the main clause in Spanish, but the reverse order is also acceptable. In that case, a comma separates the two clauses, because the usual order has been inverted.

Es rarísimo **lo que** me dices.	***What** you are telling is bizarre.*
Lo que sucedió, permanecerá en mi recuerdo.	***What** happened will remain in my memory.*

EJERCICIO
8·6

En el concierto. *De acuerdo al sentido de la oración, usa el pronombre relativo apropiado del paréntesis para unir las dos cláusulas.*

1. (el cual / lo cual) No tenemos entradas para el concierto. Me enfurece.

_____

2. (las cuales / quien) Quiero sentarme con Carla y Lupe. Son fanáticas del rap.

_____

3. (cuyo / cuya) Hay que hacer cola con Juan. Su paciencia es corta.

_____

4. (el que / lo cual) Podemos darle una propina a Mario. Me parece lógico.

_____

5. (que / el cual) Mario hace la cola. Es muy larga.

_____

6. (quienes / que) Así, nos vamos al café con Marcos. Tiene el auto aquí mismo.

_____

7. (de que / a quien) Mario vio a Rolando Villazón. Escuchó en el concierto ayer.

_____

8. (en que / en las que) Detesto esta situación. Me encuentro aquí ahora.

_____

EJERCICIO
8·7

Noticias. _Completa cada oración en español con la respuesta sugerida en los paréntesis. Usa comas (,) cuando sean necesarias._

1. La prensa publica la reacción del Presidente (_which is not clear to me_).

_____

2. Según el Presidente (_who was elected by popular vote_) no hay crisis económica.

_____

3. El Presidente mencionó entre otras cosas una crisis económica (_which is real_).

_____

4. El pueblo (_that is very well informed_) necesita confiar en su gobierno.

_____

5. La crisis internacional (_which affects many nations_) es una prioridad.

_____

6. Un líder necesita comunicar claramente (_which is very important_).

_____

7. El discurso del Presidente (_whose words I am reading now_) no aclara la situación.

_____

8. El partido de la oposición (_that hopes to win the next election_) no ha comentado.

_____

Relative clauses with pronouns after a preposition

You are already aware that some relative pronouns follow certain _prepositions_. A relative clause can also be introduced by a preposition followed by the relative pronouns **que** (_that, which_), **quien/ quienes** (_whom_), or a form of the pronoun **el cual** (_which_).

Que and **quien/quienes** may be used after some prepositions (**a**, **de**, **en**, and **con**), but in those cases **que** does not refer to people. The forms **el cual**, **los cuales**, **la cual**, **las cuales** may be used after *all* prepositions, regardless of the position of the antecedent. Word order is more strict in such clauses: the main clause, containing the main verb, is always followed by the other elements:

main clause with antecedent + preposition + relative pronoun + clause

Salieron a **la ventana,** + **desde** + **la cual** + nos saludaron.
*They went out to **the window, from which** they greeted us.*

Fueron a la ciudad de Valencia, **desde la cual** enviaron una carta.	*They went to the city of Valencia, **from which** they sent a letter.*
Visitaron a mi hermana, **con quien** estudiaron en Barcelona.	*They visited my sister, **with whom** they studied in Barcelona.*
Regresaron al hotel, **del cual** salieron para el aeropuerto.	*They went back to the hotel, **from which** they left for the airport.*

Note that the relative clause introduced by a preposition follows the main clause in both English and Spanish. Also note that the verb in the relative clause can be in various tenses of the indicative mood.

EJERCICIO
8·8

¿Cuál es la respuesta apropiada? Subráyala.

1. Juan compró un televisor (que / quien) tiene una pantalla gigante.

2. Llegó a la tienda en (quien / la que) encontró la enorme pantalla.

3. Se sentó y apretó el botón del mando del televisor con (que / la que) encendió el aparato.

4. Vio un partido de fútbol en (lo que / el que) se enfrentaban España y Alemania.

5. Su equipo favorito, (el cual / lo cual) es España, ganó uno a cero.

6. Juan decidió llevarse la pantalla gigante (que / quien) le había gustado.

7. Su esposa no estaba en casa, (que / lo cual) era bueno para Juan.

8. Juan pensó cómo explicar a Marta la pantalla delante de (la que / que) la esperaba.

EJERCICIO
8·9

Escribe una oración original con cada uno de los siguientes pronombres relativos.

1. que

_____

2. quienes

_____

3. los que

_____

4. cuyo

_____

5. los cuales

_____

6. desde la que

_____

7. quien

_____

8. cuyas

_____

9. la que

_____

10. lo que

_____

Using pronouns

Pronouns are sets of words that *substitute* for nouns or noun phrases. A pronoun replaces an element that is either named or understood in a sentence or a larger context. Everyone involved must know which elements (or *referents*) the pronouns refer to. Notice how the referent of the pronoun **ellos** (*they*) needs to be clarified in the following dialogue:

—**Ellos** hablan dos idiomas.	—**They** speak two languages.
—¿Luis y Fernando?	—Luis and Fernando?
—No, mis hermanos. Ellos hablan francés.	—No, my brothers do. **They** speak French.

Now, let's break a short paragraph into five sentences. Note that the proper noun **Marta** and the common noun **alumnos** (*students*) must be repeated in each sentence:

Marta era la maestra de español.	*Marta was the Spanish teacher.*
Marta trabajaba en la escuela secundaria.	*Marta used to work at the secondary school.*
Los chicos adoraban a **Marta**.	*The kids adored Marta.*
Todos agradecieron a **Marta** su dedicación.	*Everyone thanked Marta for her dedication.*
Sus alumnos y **mis alumnos** fueron a su casa.	*Her students and my students went to her house.*

In the sentences that follow, let's look at which pronouns replace the proper noun **Marta** and where they are placed. The first sentence establishes who **Marta** is. In grammatical terms, **Marta** is the *subject* and also the *referent* or noun the paragraph refers to.

Marta era la maestra de español.	*Marta was the Spanish teacher.*

In the second sentence, **Ella** is a pronoun that takes the place of the subject noun:

Ella trabajaba en la escuela secundaria.	*She used to work at the secondary school.*

In the third sentence, the pronoun **la** replaces the proper noun **Marta**. Now either **Marta** or **la** is the *direct object* of the verb.

Los chicos **la** adoraban.	*The kids loved her.*

In the fourth sentence the *indirect object pronoun* **le** represents **Marta**, the person *to whom* or *for whom* the action of the verb is done. Notice the *indirect object* **le** and the *direct object* **la** in the previous sentence. Both correspond to the English pronoun *her*, which follows the verb in the English sentences.

Todos **le** agradecían su dedicación.	*Everyone thanked **her** for her dedication.*

In the fifth and last sentence **alumnos** is replaced by **los míos**, to avoid repetition.

Sus alumnos y **los míos** fueron a su casa.	***Her students** and **mine** went to her house.*

These are examples of pronouns, small but powerful words loaded with meaning. Now read the sentences combined in a short paragraph:

> **Marta** era la maestra de español. **Ella** trabajaba en la escuela secundaria. Los chicos **la** adoraban. Todos **le** agradecían su dedicación. **Sus alumnos** y **los míos** fueron a su casa.

Pronouns are *substitutions* that make sentences run smoother, make them less clunky, and help avoid tedious repetition.

Pronouns that replace the subject

The pronouns that replace subject nouns are called *subject pronouns*, because they do the action of the verb. The usual word order of a sentence or clause with subject pronouns is the same as that of a sentence with the *subject-noun* word order:

subject pronoun + predicate

Ellos + protegen el medio ambiente.
They protect the environment.

In previous units you learned that the subject in Spanish sentences can also follow the verb in interrogatives and in exclamatory and declarative sentences. The same is true for subject pronouns:

—¿Conoce él a la novia de Juan?	—*Does **he** know Juan's girlfriend?*
—¡Sí, sí, él la conoce!	—*Yes, **he** knows **her**!*

Let's review the Spanish subject pronoun forms, their gender, their number, and their uses.

SINGULAR SUBJECT PRONOUNS		PLURAL SUBJECT PRONOUNS	
yo	*I*	nosotros, -as	*we*
tú	*you (familiar)*	vosotros, -as	*you (familiar)*
usted (Ud.)	*you (polite)*	ustedes (Uds.)	*you*
él	*he*	ellos	*they*
ella	*she*	ellas	*they*

Keep in mind the following tips when using subject pronouns in Spanish to build your sentences:

- As a general rule *subject pronouns* are not often used in Spanish because the verb endings identify the subject.
- Use *subject pronouns* only when you need to *clarify* or *emphasize* the subject in a sentence.
   Clarify if you need to differentiate between **él** or **ella,** or **ellos** and **ellas**:

Eso, **ellos** son los culpables.	*That's it, **they** are the guilty ones.*

Emphasize if you need or want to stress the difference between two subjects, even when the verb is clearly understood. The second subject may be implied:

Yo no quiero trabajar hoy. *I do not want to work today.*

Show politeness by adding **usted** (**Ud.**) and **ustedes** (**Uds.**):

¿Son **ustedes** los padres de Lolita? *Are you Lolita's parents?*
Pase **usted**, por favor. *Come in, please.*

◆ **Tú** is used to address friends and family.
◆ **Vosotros/as** is used in most of Spain, but *not* in the rest of the Spanish-speaking world; it is a familiar form for addressing friends and family.
◆ **Usted** and **ustedes** are polite forms throughout most of the Hispanic world; **Ud.** and **Uds.** are abbreviations.
◆ **Ustedes** is the plural of the informal **tú**, except in Spain (**vosotros**).

EJERCICIO
9·1

En español. *Usa los pronombres solamente si son necesarios en español.*

1. Marcos, he is Marta's brother. _____

2. He works with Marta. _____

3. He is the chef, not Marta. _____

4. I know Marta well. _____

5. I want to go to the movies tonight; not Marta. _____

6. Do you want to go to the movies? _____

EJERCICIO
9·2

¿Tú o usted? *¿Qué forma del pronombre necesitas para dirigirte (address) a estas personas? Escribe la forma apropiada del pronombre en el espacio en blanco.*

1. la Dra. Balerdi _____

2. Don Augusto, el gerente de la compañía _____

3. tu primo _____

4. el alcalde (*mayor*) de tu ciudad _____

5. el director de la escuela _____

6. tus padres _____

7. los abuelos de tus amigos _____

8. un viejo amigo _____

En español. *Ahora sí necesitas los pronombres de sujeto para dar énfasis a tu mensaje. ¡Cuidado! Los verbos aparecen en el pasado y en el presente.*

1. They (*masc.*) wanted to eat.

   _____

2. You sing (*sing., familiar*) but she plays the guitar.

   _____

3. They (*fem.*) can finish their homework!

   _____

4. You (*pl., polite*) started at ten but we finished early.

   _____

5. Now, you (*sing., familiar*) rest while I wash the clothes.

   _____

Pronouns that replace object pronouns and word order

Direct and *indirect object pronouns* replace the direct and indirect object nouns in a sentence. The following charts and examples will give you a quick review of direct and indirect object pronouns:

DIRECT OBJECTS

SINGULAR		PLURAL	
me	*me*	nos	*us*
te	*you*	os	*you*
lo/la	*him, her, you, it*	los/las	*them, you*

INDIRECT OBJECTS

SINGULAR		PLURAL	
me	*me*	nos	*us*
te	*you*	os	*you*
le	*him, her, you, it*	les	*them, you*

Let's look at some examples:

—¿Luisa conoce a **Jacobo**?	—*Does Luisa know **Jacobo**?*
—Sí, **lo** conoce.	—*Yes, she knows **him**.*
—Y **le** regaló una corbata.	—*And she gave **him** a tie.*
—**Me lo** dijo mi hermana.	—*My sister told **me** (**it**).*

These pronouns normally precede the conjugated verb in *affirmative* and *negative* sentences that have a single verb. Consider the position of one object pronoun:

Laura + **la** + compró.   *Laura bought **it**.*
Mayra + no + **la** + quiere.   *Mayra does not want **it**.*
Laura + **me** + dio + la billetera.   *Laura gave **me** the wallet.*

Note the word order in sentences with two object pronouns:

indirect object pronoun + direct object pronoun + verb

Laura + **me** + **la** + compró.
*Laura bought **it for me**.*

An important detail to remember: the third-person singular and plural *indirect* object pronouns **le** and **les** change to the form **se** when followed by a direct object pronoun that begins with the letter **l**: **la**, **lo**, **las**, or **los**.

Laura **se la** compró.   *Laura bought **it for him/her/them**.*
Marcos **se las** regaló.   *Marcos gave **them to him/her/them**.*

EJERCICIO
9·4

En el juzgado (*court*). *Sustituye los objetos directos e indirectos con los pronombres correspondientes. Después, escribe la oración otra vez con los pronombres en el orden apropiado.*

MODELO   El hombre saludó a su amigo.

Pronombre ___lo___

El hombre lo saludó.

1. La policía encontró al criminal.

Pronombre _____

_____

2. Llevaron a la víctima al hospital.

Pronombre _____

_____

3. La víctima no reveló su nombre.

Pronombre _____

_____

4. El médico diagnosticó un trauma leve a la víctima.

Pronombre _____

_____

5. La enfermera llevó un calmante a la víctima.

Pronombre _____

_____

6. El noticiero local comunicó <u>el incidente</u> <u>a la comunidad</u>.

Pronombre _____

_____

7. Al día siguiente la policía investigó <u>los detalles del asalto</u>.

Pronombre _____

_____

8. El criminal recibirá <u>su sentencia</u>.

Pronombre _____

_____

The redundant use of indirect object pronouns in Spanish

In Spanish, it is not unusual for *both* the indirect noun *and* the indirect pronoun to appear in the same sentence. We see a similar structure with the use of the stressed pronouns (**mí, ti, usted, él, ella, nosotros/as, vosotros/as, ustedes, ellos, ellas, sí**, placed after **a**) that repeat the indirect object pronoun. At first, this may seem unnecessary. That is why we refer to these pronouns as *redundant*. One explanation: since the third-person indirect object pronouns **le** (*to him, to her, to you*) and **les** (*to them, to you*) are ambiguous, the redundancy clarifies who the receiver is.

a + indirect object noun or stressed pronoun → redundant indirect object

Ana **le** dio mi recado **a su hermana**.	*Ana gave my message **to her sister**.*
Ana **le** dio mi recado **a ella**.	*Ana gave **her** my message.*
Le regalé una camisa roja **a Ana**.	*I gave **Ana** a red shirt.*
Y **le** compré un libro **a su hermano**.	*And I bought a book **for her brother**.*

Another reason to add the redundant, stressed indirect object pronoun (after **a**) is the need, at times, to put emphasis on the indirect object:

Laura **me** llamó **a mí**.	*Laura called **me**.*
Raúl **nos** invitó **a nosotros**.	*Raúl invited **us**.*

EJERCICIO
9·5

En español: un mensaje claro. *Usa **a** + el objeto indirecto o **a** + el pronombre acentuado para aclarar el mensaje al final de la oración.*

1. I gave a note <u>to her</u>.

_____

2. We asked (**pedir**) <u>her brother</u> a favor.

_____

3. They brought a new computer to us.

_____

4. Luis y Ana asked their boss for a raise.

_____

5. Marcela sent flowers to them.

_____

6. You prepared the reception for us.

_____

7. Cindy told a few jokes (**chistes**) to my brother.

_____

8. Robert announced his retirement (**jubilación**) to his friends.

_____

EJERCICIO
9·6

En orden. *Coloca las palabras en el orden apropiado en español. Observa las reglas de ortografía. ¡Ojo! Necesitas usar a veces sustantivos indirectos redundantes.*

1. devolvieron / los clientes / los zapatos / le

_____ al empleado.

2. el empleado / otro modelo / mostró / les

_____ a los clientes.

3. compraron / ese par de zapatos / le

_____

4. la tienda / les / un descuento / dio

_____ a los clientes.

5. los clientes / gastaron / más dinero

_____

6. una comisión / el jefe / dio / una comisión / le

_____ al empleado.

7. los clientes / la amabilidad / agradecieron / les

_____ a los empleados de la tienda.

Gustar, indirect object pronouns, and word order

In Spanish, **gustar** is a frequently used verb to communicate *to like*. In English, the word order in a sentence with *to like* is the usual *subject + verb + object*: *We like cool weather.* The subject is the person or persons who *like* something or someone. In the previous example, the subject is *we*. In Spanish (see the example below), the subject is the thing or person that is *pleasing to someone*, in this case *music*.

If you focus on the notion of *to someone*, the preposition *to* tells you how to build your sentence in Spanish: it always requires an *indirect object*. Word order in sentences or clauses with **gustar** is the following:

> **indirect object pronoun + a form of gustar + subject**
>
> **Nos** + **gusta** + la música.
> *We like music.*

In this structure, the form of **gustar**, the verb determined by a following subject, is always *third-person* singular or plural.

Me gustan las esculturas de Botero.	*I like Botero's sculptures.*
No me gusta la última película de Almodóvar.	*I do not like Almovodar's last movie.*

Infinitives that refer to actions can also be the subject of a sentence with **gustar**. Note (in the last example below) that the English element *it* does not translate into Spanish:

¿**Te gusta** correr o nadar?	*Do you like running or swimming?*
No **le gusta** ni trabajar ni estudiar.	*He/she does not like to work or study.*
—¿**Les gusta** bailar?	—*Do you (pl.) like dancing?*
—Sí, **nos gusta**.	—*Yes, we like it.*

For emphasis or clarification, the preposition **a**, followed by a noun or a *stressed or prepositional pronoun*, may precede the indirect object:

> **a + noun or stressed pronoun + indirect object pronoun + a form of gustar + subject**
>
> **A** + **nosotros** + **nos** + **gusta** + la música.
> *We do like music.*

EJERCICIO
9·7

Sondeo de opinión. *Para cada respuesta, vas a escribir una pregunta con el sustantivo sugerido. Usa la forma apropiada del objeto indirecto y el verbo* **gustar** *con las formas* **usted** *o* **ustedes***.*

MODELO   la comida japonesa

      ¿Les gusta la comida japonesa?

      Sí, nos gusta la comida japonesa.

1. el té

_____

No me gusta, prefiero el café.

2. la comida mexicana

_____

Sí, efectivamente, nos gusta la comida mexicana.

3. correr

_____

¡Claro!, me gusta correr por la playa.

4. nadar

_____

¡Ah, no! No nos gusta mucho nadar en la piscina. Preferimos la playa.

5. los programas cómicos o dramáticos

_____

A mí, particularmente me gustan más los programas cómicos.

6. esta encuesta

_____

Sí, nos ha gustado esta encuesta (*survey*). ¡Gracias!

Other verbs with indirect object pronouns

Here are some frequently used verbs that behave in the same manner as **gustar**. They will be useful for building sentences:

agradar	*to please*
bastar	*to suffice, to be enough*
caer bien (mal)	*to like (to dislike)*
doler	*to hurt*
encantar	*to love someone or something*
faltar	*to be lacking in, to be in need of*
fascinar	*to be fascinating to*
hacer(le) falta (a alguien)	*to need*
importar	*to be important to*
interesar	*to be interesting to*
molestar	*to be bothersome to*
parecer	*to seem to*
sobrar	*to be in surplus/excess*
tocar(le) (a alguien)	*to be someone's turn*

Mi vida. *Usa la primera persona del singular en el presente del verbo entre paréntesis para completar las oraciones.*

MODELO   (tocar) la cancha de tenis a las tres

                Me toca la cancha de tenis a las tres.

1. (fascinar) las novelas de misterio

_____

2. no (interesar) las biografías, son aburridas

_____

3. (doler) la cabeza y tomo una aspirina

_____

4. (hacer falta) dinero y voy al banco

_____

5. (bastar) con poco, soy modesto/a

_____

6. (caer mal) Carolina; es antipática

_____

7. (caer bien) Nina porque es agradable

_____

8. (faltar) diez dólares

_____

9. (tocar) descansar porque he terminado el ejercicio

_____

10. (encantar) estudiar español

_____

Reflexive object pronouns and word order

The function of reflexive object pronouns is not the same as that of other object pronouns: reflexive object pronouns always stay with their subject. In English, the reflexive object pronoun is compounded with *-self*. Note that the subject and object of the verb always refer to the same person, animal, or entity.

Let's compare this sentence in Spanish and in English:

Lucía **se** lava **los pies**.   *Lucia washes **her feet**.*

In Spanish, the reflexive pronoun **se** precedes the verb. It indicates that the *subject* receives the action of the verb. It is not translated in the English equivalent. (The reflexive pronoun *myself* is not needed in English because the possessive adjective *her* is used with *feet*.) In Spanish, because of the reflexive form, we understand that Lucía is washing her own feet. Note also that a form of the definite article (**el/la; los/las**) usually appears in the Spanish sentence with a part of the body. The word order is:

subject + reflexive pronoun + verb

Ana + **se** + peina.
*Ana is combing **her** hair.*

In the next example, the verb is *not* reflexive. The *indirect object pronoun* **le** indicates who receives the action of the verb, in this case, a person other than the subject.

Lucía **le** lava los pies **a su niña**.   *Lucía washes **her daughter's feet**.*

Reflexive pronouns in Spanish are closely related to *direct and indirect object pronouns* in that they follow the same word order and use many of the same forms.

SINGULAR		PLURAL	
me	*myself*	nos	*ourselves*
te	*yourself*	os	*yourselves*
se	*himself, herself, yourself*	se	*themselves, yourselves*

In Spanish, many verbs are classified as *reflexive*. Many of those describe routines we follow every day, in grooming, for example. However, almost all Spanish verbs can be turned into reflexives, which often changes the meaning of the verb. In this construction, the *reflexive pronoun* is always placed before the verb, whether in affirmative, negative, or interrogative sentences.

Carlos **no se despierta** temprano.   *Carlos **does not wake up** early.*
¿Por qué **te peinas los cabellos** otra vez? *Why **are you combing your hair** again?*
Se ponen las botas.   *They **put on their boots.***

EJERCICIO
9·9

La rutina y los verbos reflexivos. *Coloca el pronombre reflexivo que corresponde en cada oración.*

me / te / se / nos / os / se

1. Juan _____ acuesta a las ocho cada día.

2. Nosotros _____ ponemos el pijama para dormir.

3. Luisa y Ana _____ duermen mirando la tele.

4. Ustedes siempre _____ enojan con los niños.

5. Yo _____ voy a dormir.

6. Tú _____ miras siempre en el espejo.

7. Vosotros _____ preparáis para descansar.

8. Yo siempre _____ lavo los dientes después de comer.

EJERCICIO
9·10

El orden de los pronombres. *Sustituye los sustantivos* subrayados *con los pronombres de objeto directo y objeto indirecto para escribir de nuevo el párrafo con los pronombres correspondientes y en el orden apropiado.*

Eduardo Benítez dirige una agencia de publicidad. Eduardo dirige (1) <u>esa empresa</u> con éxito. El año pasado dobló las ganancias. Y logró (*achieve*) (2) <u>las ganancias</u> con su esfuerzo. Los inversionistas (*investors*) agradecen (3) <u>a Eduardo</u> su perseverancia. Eduardo asegura (4) <u>a los inversionistas</u> que al año próximo doblará las ganancias: más dinero. Y van a ganar (5) <u>más dinero</u> porque hay una gran demanda en el mercado internacional. Eduardo conoce muy bien (6) <u>ese mercado</u>.

_____

_____

_____

_____

_____

_____

_____

Word order of direct, indirect, and reflexive pronouns with more than one verb

Now let's concentrate on sentences with more than one verb. This construction usually consists of a conjugated verb followed by an *infinitive* (-**ar**, -**er**, -**ir** ending) or a *present participle*, -**ndo** (the English -*ing* form).

◆ Pronouns may be placed *before the conjugated verb*:

direct object + conjugated verb + infinitive
Te + **quiere** + **ver**.
He/she wants to see you.

indirect object + conjugated verb + present participle
Paco **les** + **está** + **hablando**.
Paco is speaking to them.

Melisa **lo** quiere ver.	*Melisa wants to see **him/it**.*
Melisa no **te** quiere ver.	*Melisa does not want to see **you**.*
¿**Te** quiere ver Melisa?	*Does Melisa want to see **you**?*

◆ Spanish object pronouns may also be attached to *infinitives* and *present participles*:

conjugated verb + infinitive (pronoun)
Quiere + **verte**.
*He wants **to see you**.*
Queremos **visitarte** en Guadalajara.　　*We want **to visit you** in Guadalajara.*

conjugated verb + present participle (pronoun)
Viene + **riéndose**.
*He comes along **laughing**.*
Estaba **cantándote** una canción.　　*He was **singing you** a song.*
Estaba **cantándotela**.　　*He was **singing it to you**.*

Note the written accent mark on the next-to-last syllable of the present participle, when one or more syllables have been added by attaching pronouns.

EJERCICIO
9·11

Otra posibilidad. *Observa la posición de los pronombres subrayados. Escribe la oración otra vez y une (attach) los pronombres a la forma del verbo que corresponde.*

1. Es una pintura famosa. <u>La</u> estoy admirando. _____

2. Buscan unas notas. <u>Las</u> van a encontrar. _____

3. Necesitas un préstamo. (*loan*) <u>Lo</u> vas a pedir. _____

4. No tiene ayuda. No <u>la</u> va a tener. _____

5. ¿Quieren ellos dejar el auto? ¿<u>Lo</u> quieren dejar? _____

6. Vamos a terminar este ejercicio. <u>Lo</u> vamos a terminar. _____

Using adjectives

When we write sentences to communicate thoughts, ideas, beliefs, feelings, or opinions, we often include *adjectives*. They specify and clarify nouns; for example, they state how many (*some, many*) we want to emphasize. Adjectives also describe the origin or material of an object or the color, size, age, or shape of nouns (persons, places, or things).

Adjectives modify all nouns: nouns used as subjects, as direct or indirect objects, as prepositional phrases, and so on.

adjective → describes or limits a noun

Consider the following sentences, the relationship of the adjectives to the nouns, and the position of nouns and adjectives:

Diez científicos **españoles** investigan regiones **montañosas**.	*Ten Spanish scientists are doing research in **mountain** regions.*
Estudian cambios **climáticos** en **varias** áreas.	*They are studying **climatic** changes in **several** areas.*
Es **necesario** comprender los cambios del medio **ambiente**.	*It is **necessary** to understand changes in the environment.*
Estudian las **antiguas** épocas **climáticas**.	*They study **remote climatic** eras.*
Este estudio incluye la adaptación a escenarios **futuros**.	*This study includes adaptation to future scenarios.*
Los científicos quieren comunicar **sus** ideas a la población.	*The scientists want to communicate **their** ideas to the public.*

The words in boldface above are all adjectives. They fall into several categories. In the first sentence, two adjectives refer to the same plural masculine noun, **científicos: diez** is a *limiting adjective of quantity* that determines the *number* of the noun **científicos**, while **españoles** denotes the origin of the noun.

The adjective **climáticos** describes **cambios**; **varias** determines the number of **áreas**. The adjective **necesario** is part of the impersonal expression with **es,** or another form of **ser,** that indicates the necessity of what is to follow. **Ambiente** is part of the fixed expression **medio ambiente** (in English, a single word, *environment*). **Antiguas** denotes the age of **épocas**. And the demonstrative adjective **este** determines the noun e**studio**; that is, *this study*, not another. Finally, **sus**, a possessive adjective, shows that the ideas belong to the scientists working on this project.

The words discussed in the previous paragraph are all adjectives: words that *describe*, *modify*, or *limit* the name of a person, being, or thing appearing in a sentence.

Let's go back to the first sentence in the previous examples. If we eliminate the adjectives in the first sentence, the message is not complete; it is rather vague:

Científicos investigan regiones.   *Scientists are doing research in regions.*

Completed by its adjectives, the sentence is clearer and more informative.

Note that adjectives agree in *number* and *gender* with the nouns they modify. However, the adjective **diez**, like most other Spanish numerals, does not change with number or gender of the noun. Impersonal expressions with adjectives always use the masculine singular form of the adjective: **es necesario**, **es bueno**, etc.

Adjectives and gender and number

Let's review the gender formation of adjectives. Adjectives ending in **-o** change the ending to **-a** in the feminine. Adjectives of nationality often *add* an **-a** in the feminine when the masculine ends in a consonant (**español/española, irlandés/irlandesa**).

El chico es **pequeño** pero la nena no es **pequeña**.	*The boy is **little**, but the girl is not **little**.*
El periódico **francés** y la revista **francesa** son de Alba.	*The **French** newspaper and the **French** magazine are Alba's.*

Most adjectives ending in a consonant have the same singular form for both genders:

El reguetón es **popular**; y también es **popular** la salsa.	*Reguetón is **popular**; and salsa is **popular** too.*
El trabajo parece **difícil**, pero esta actividad es muy **fácil**.	*The job seems **difficult**, but this activity is very **easy**.*

The *plural* of adjectives ending in a vowel is formed by adding **-s**:

Las **rosas rojas** alegran la sala.	*The **red roses** cheer up the room.*
Compré los **zapatos caros**.	*I bought the **expensive shoes**.*

The plural of adjectives ending in a consonant is formed by adding **-es**:

Los estudiantes **alemanes** viajarán al Perú.   *The **German** students will travel to Peru.*

Adjectives ending in **-z**, such as **feliz**, change the **-z** to **-c** before adding the **-es** plural ending. You may wish to review the spelling rules in Unit 18.

Me acuerdo de esos días **felices**.   *I remember those **happy** days.*

EJERCICIO
10·1

En el zoológico. *Subraya los adjetivos que describen los sustantivos en el párrafo siguiente.*

El zoológico de San Diego, California, está entre los más famosos del mundo. El área de los trópicos incluye bellas cascadas de agua y zonas elevadas, imitando las montañas africanas donde viven los gorilas. La sección de los gorilas, gigantes vegetarianos que viven en una sociedad muy compleja, tiene gorilas jóvenes y ágiles que se deslizan (*tumble down*) rápidamente para ir a observar a la gente curiosa. Cerca, están otros simios, monos inteligentes y simpáticos que divierten a los visitantes. Hay rocas enormes, palmas tropicales. ¡Es como si estuvieras en África!

Tu capacidad creativa. *Coloca un adjetivo en el espacio en blanco para construir oraciones más completas. Usa la forma apropiada de los adjetivos de la lista de sugerencias.*

rápido / fiel / incapacitado / cariñoso / humano / simpático / inteligente / agresivo / hablador / tropical / anfibio

1. Los perros _____ pueden ayudar a las personas _____.

2. Las cotorras (*parrots*) _____ me parecen cómicas.

3. Los peces _____ tienen una gran variedad de colores bonitos.

4. ¿Tienes un tigre en tu casa? Los tigres son _____

   pero _____.

5. Dos características de la mascota ideal: _____ y _____.

6. Los gorilas tienen características casi _____.

7. Las gacelas son _____.

8. La rana (*frog*) es un animal _____.

¿Cómo eres? *Construye oraciones para hacer una descripción de tus cualidades físicas e intelectuales.*

Tu descripción física

1. Soy _____, _____, _____

   y _____.

2. Mis ojos _____, un poco _____.

3. Mi nariz _____ pero _____.

4. La forma de mi cara es _____ y _____.

5. Mi pelo no es _____ sino _____.

6. Me gusta(n) mi(s) _____ porque _____.

Ahora, tu personalidad y características intelectuales

7. Soy una persona _____ porque puedo _____.

8. Creo que soy _____ y además _____.

9. Mis amigos me aprecian porque _____.

10. En el futuro, puedo cambiar y ser más / menos _____.

Adjectives and word order

The nature of an adjective determines its place in a sentence. Most combinations with *descriptive* adjectives follow this order in Spanish:

> noun + adjective → descriptive adjective combination
>
> una rosa **amarilla**
> *a **yellow** rose*

Limiting adjectives are demonstratives, possessives, and adjectives of number and quantity. Limiting adjectives precede the noun in Spanish:

> adjective + noun → limiting adjective combination
>
> **mis cuatro** perros
> ***my four** dogs*

Adjectives that follow nouns

In English, with some exceptions, descriptive adjectives usually appear immediately before the noun they modify. In Spanish, descriptive adjectives are usually placed *after* the noun:

Los libros **interesantes** deleitan a los lectores.	***Interesting** books delight their readers.*
Una montaña **alta** separa las provincias.	*A **tall** mountain separates the provinces.*

Descriptive adjectives may appear in a sequence, separated by commas:

Alto, **delgado**, **musculoso** y a**tractivo**.	***Tall**, **slender**, **muscular**, and **attractive**.*
Tienes una colega **leal**, **lista**, **persistente**.	*You have a **loyal**, **sharp**, **persevering** colleague.*

Adjectives that precede nouns

Descriptive adjectives can be placed *before* the noun when the adjective underscores or contains an innate or inherent quality of the noun it modifies. In the first example below, the writer focuses on **duras**, placing the adjective immediately before the noun. In the second sentence, **valientes** serves a similar purpose:

Las **duras** experiencias fortalecen el carácter.	***Tough** experiences build character.*
Los patriotas son recordados por sus **valientes** hazañas.	*Patriots are remembered for their **courageous** deeds.*

Demonstrative adjectives, possessive adjectives, and adjectives of number and quantity *precede* the nouns they modify:

Este chico es un amigo de **mi** hermano Luis.	***This** young man is a friend of **my** brother Luis.*
Tus amigos y **mis** hermanos se reúnen mañana.	***Your** friends and **my** brothers are meeting tomorrow.*
Quieren ver **tres** películas argentinas en la tele.	*They want to see **three** Argentinean movies on TV.*
Muchas veces salen a cenar juntos.	***Many** times they go out to dinner together.*
Algunos amigos de Luis son italianos.	***Some** of Luis's friends are Italian.*

Note that the following adjectives of quantity are frequently used in the plural form:

algunos/as	*some*
muchos/as	*many*
ningunos/as	*none, not any*
pocos/as	*few*
unos/as	*some*
varios/as	*several*

EJERCICIO
10·4

¿Qué adjetivo asocias con cada sustantivo? *Escribe la letra de la respuesta que consideres más apropiada. Después, escribe la forma apropiada del adjetivo. Observa si el sustantivo es masculino o femenino, singular o plural.*

1. _____ largo _____

2. _____ bello _____

3. _____ dulce _____

4. _____ fuerte _____

5. _____ destructivo _____

6. _____ suave _____

a. flores

b. dolor

c. piel

d. bebida

e. huracán

f. pelo

EJERCICIO
10·5

Ahora regresa al ejercicio anterior. Usa los sustantivos y los adjetivos para crear oraciones completas. Usa los verbos en el presente.

MODELO   interesante pasajes

Me gustan los pasajes interesantes de la novela El juego del ángel.

1. _____

2. _____

3. _____

4. _____

5. _____

6. _____

Position and meaning of adjectives

In Spanish, some adjectives change their meaning according to their position *before* or *after* a noun:

ADJECTIVE	BEFORE A NOUN	AFTER A NOUN
antiguo/a	*former*	*old*
cierto/a	*certain*	*sure*
gran(de)	*great*	*big*
mismo/a	*same*	*himself/herself*
pobre	*unlucky*	*poor*
viejo	*old time*	*old*

La madre de mi amiga es una **señora vieja**.	*My friend's mother is an **old woman**.*
Me encanta charlar con mis **viejos amigos**.	*I love to chat with my **old friends**.*
¿Quieres ver la **misma película**, otra vez?	*Do you want to see the **same movie** again?*
¡Bueno, lo hicieron **ellas mismas**!	*Well, **they themselves** did it!*

Shortened adjective forms

Some adjectives drop the **-o** (or the **-e**) ending when they precede a masculine noun (**buen amigo**, **gran hombre**):

alguno, algún	*some*
bueno, buen	*good*
grande, gran	*big, great*
malo, mal	*bad*
ninguno, ningún	*no, not any*
primero, primer	*first*
tercero, tercer	*third*
Algún día entenderás a tus padres.	***Someday** you will understand your parents.*
Carlos se porta como un **buen estudiante**.	*Carlos behaves like a **good student**.*
No me gusta el **primer día** de clases.	*I do not like the **first day** of school.*
Ese plato me dejó **mal sabor** en la boca.	*This dish left me with a **bad taste** in my mouth.*

Here are more uses of the shortened adjectives:

◆ **Cien** is used when it precedes all nouns, except the numbers 1 to 99:

Cien años es un siglo.	***One hundred** years is a century.*

◆ **Grande** is also shortened when it precedes a feminine singular noun:

Gloria Fuertes era una **gran poeta**.	*Gloria Fuertes was a **great poet**.*

◆ **San**, the shortened form of the title **Santo**, is used before the names of all male saints, *except* those whose names start with the letters **Do-** or **To-**:

Santo Tomás y **Santo Domingo** son venerados.	***Saint Thomas** and **Saint Dominick** are revered.*

EJERCICIO 10·6

En Quito. *Escribe la forma apropiada del adjetivo que aparece entre paréntesis.*

1. Mi _____ amigo Franklin vive en Quito con su esposa Susi. (bueno, buen)

2. Creo que _____ día lo voy a visitar en su casa. (alguno, algún)

3. Tenemos una _____ amistad. (grande, gran)

4. Tuve un _____ sueño anoche: Franklin se había caído de la moto. (malo, mal)

5. Nunca conocí a _____ hombre más fanático de las motocicletas. (ninguno, ningún)

6. Hace dos años, Franklin tuvo su _____ accidente en la moto. (primer, primero)

7. Y este año tuvo su _____ problema con la moto: ¡se la robaron! (tercero, tercer)

8. ¡Pobre Franklin! El seguro le pagará solamente _____ dólares por la moto. (ciento, cien)

En español. *Lee el párrafo completo antes de empezar a escribir las oraciones en español.*

1. Yesterday my brother went to visit his old friend, Mario.

2. Mario told me himself that he admires my father.

3. He believes our father is a great influence in his own life.

4. Mario's father is very old and he is ill.

5. Mario's father used to live in an old house in Guatemala.

6. One day, he decided to move to New Mexico.

7. Mario's family was not poor.

8. An old friend (*fem.*) of mine met Mario and his father, Don Julián.

9. Poor Don Julián, he is too ill now to go back to Guatemala.

1. _____

2. _____

3. _____

4. _____

5. _____

6. _____

7. _____

8. _____

9. _____

Words that function as adjectives

Past participles may function as adjectives in both English and Spanish. In Spanish, they must agree with the noun they modify in gender and number. Remember that Spanish past participles are formed by dropping the **-ar**, **-er**, and **-ir** infinitive endings of a verb and adding **-ado** or **-ido**.

Alina encontró las joyas **robadas** en su habitación.	*Alina found the **stolen** jewels in her room.*
¿No estuviste en Chile la semana **pasada**?	*Didn't you go to Chile **last** week?*
Suenas como un disco **rayado**.	*You sound like a **broken** record.*
¿No has encontrado los libros **perdidos**?	*Haven't you found the **lost** books?*

Remember that some common verbs have irregular past participle forms:

abrir	*to open*	abierto	*opened*
escribir	*to write*	escrito	*written*
hacer	*to do*	hecho	*done*
imprimir	*to print*	impreso	*printed*
morir	*to die*	muerto	*dead*
romper	*to break*	roto	*broken*
volver	*to turn*	vuelto	*returned; turned over*

Prefixes such as **en-**, **re-**, **des-**, and others can be added to the infinitive of some of these verbs, changing their meaning. Their irregular past participles are like those of the original verbs:

envolver	*to wrap*	envuelto	*wrapped*
desenvolver	*to unwrap*	desenvuelto	*unwrapped*
revolver	*to stir*	revuelto	*stirred*
deshacer	*to undo*	deshecho	*undone*
rehacer	*to redo*	rehecho	*redone*
reescribir	*to rewrite*	reescrito	*rewritten*

Son promesas **rotas**.	*They are **broken** promises.*
Lleva los paquetes **envuelto**s al correo.	*Take the **wrapped** packages to the post office.*
¿Donde está la versión **impresa**?	*Where is the **printed** version?*

EJERCICIO
10·8

Ayer fue un día terrible. *Usa la forma apropiada del participio pasado para incluir más información en el espacio en blanco.*

MODELO   Llegué a casa y encontré los papeles ___*revueltos y deshechos*___ .

desenvuelto / muerto / revuelto / roto / impreso / reescrito / desecho / abierto

1. Entré en mi dormitorio y vi las ventanas _____ .

2. Fui al patio y encontré dos lagartijas (*lizards*) _____ .

3. En la cocina, había varios platos _____ .

4. Los paquetes _____ de los regalos del cumpleaños de Alicia estaban en el comedor.

5. Una extraña hoja con mi nombre _____ estaba en la mesa.

6. ¡El documento _____ en mi computadora estaba alterado!

7. ¡Toda mi casa _____ me daba miedo!

8. Comprendí las promesas _____ de mi sobrino: no me había ayudado a cuidar la casa en mi ausencia.

Using adverbs

In previous chapters, you studied categories of words. You know that these elements, when used properly and placed in the correct word order, are necessary to build sentences and communicate ideas clearly. In this chapter, we turn to adverbs, reviewing their functions and use in sentence structures.

Unlike adjectives, nouns, verbs, or pronouns, adverbs are *invariable*; they do not change in gender or number. Adverbs add information to the meaning of a verb, an adjective, or another adverb. In most cases, adverbs reveal circumstances under which something happens or someone acts.

adverb → modifies a verb, an adjective, or another adverb

Note that adverbs in the sentences that follow can be easily spotted if we ask specific questions. You may wish to review Unit 3 on interrogatives.

In the first four example sentences below, the circumstances reveal the answers to *where*, *when*, *how*, and *how much*. The last two sentences include adverbs that communicate an *affirmation*, *denial*, and *doubt*, respectively. These are answers to *yes/no* questions. You may wish to review Unit 1 on how to use adverbs to make negative statements.

Hay un paquete para ti **aquí**.	*There is a package **here** for you.*
Llegó **ayer**.	*It arrived **yesterday**.*
Veo que el paquete llegó **bien**.	*I see the package arrived **well** (without problems).*
Pero este paquete pesa **mucho**.	*But this package weighs **a lot**.*
Inicialmente rechacé la entrega.	***At first**, I refused the delivery.*
Sí, pensaba que era del vecino.	***Yes**, I thought it was our neighbor's.*
No te había visto todo el día.	*I had **not** seen you all day.*
Tampoco sabía que estabas **aquí**.	***Besides**, I did not know you were **here**.*

In Spanish, the words **donde** (*where*), **cuando** (*when*), **como** (*how*), and **cuanto** (*how much*) are adverbs. They can also function as relative pronouns or conjunctions to introduce subordinate clauses. With written accent marks, they are used in interrogative and exclamatory sentences.

La ciudad **donde** vivían nuestros padres es Buenos Aires.	*The city **where** our parents used to live is Buenos Aires.*
Cuando vivieron en esa ciudad, eran muy jóvenes.	***When** they lived in that city, they were very young.*
¿**Cómo** llegaron a Canadá?	***How** did they get to Canada?*
¿**Cuánto** gastaron en ese viaje?	***How much** did they spend on that trip?*

More about adverbs

Adverbs appear in different forms. They may consist of one word, an adjective that ends in **-mente**, or a phrase, called an *adverbial phrase* or *adverbial expression* (**una locución adverbial**).

Adverbs

The following is a short list of adverbs and the circumstances they express or clarify.

Adverbs of place

aquí	*here*
delante (de)	*ahead, in front (of)*
lejos	*far*
allá, allí	*there*
dentro	*inside*
—¿Trabajas **aquí**?	—*Do you work **here**?*
—No, mi oficina está **allí**.	—*No, my office is **over there**.*

Adverbs of time

ayer	*yesterday*
hoy	*today*
jamás	*never*
luego	*later, afterwards, then*
mientras	*while*
nunca	*never*
siempre	*always*
Mientras Ud. espera, Marian va a cambiar los zapatos.	***While** you wait, Marian will exchange the shoes.*
No nos visitas **nunca**.	*You **never** visit us.*

Adverbs of manner

bien	*well*
despacio	*slowly*
mal	*badly, poorly*
rápido	*quickly*
Camina **despacio**, por favor.	*Walk **slowly**, please.*
¿Por qué el niño se porta **mal**?	*Why is the boy behaving **poorly**?*

Adverbs of quantity

bastante	*enough*
mucho	*much, a lot*
muy	*very*
poco	*a little*
Trabajo **mucho**.	*I work **a lot**.*
Eso sí, gano **bastante**.	*But yes, I earn **a lot**.*

Adverbs that express addition of ideas

además	*besides*
incluso	*even*
también	*also*
tampoco	*either, neither*
Voy a quejarme **también**.	*I am going to complain **too**.*
Incluso voy a ver al gerente.	*I am **even** going to see the manager.*
No estudio. **Tampoco** trabajo.	*I do not study. I do not work, **either**.*

Repasa los adverbios que aparecieron en las listas anteriores. ¿Cuál de los adverbios puedes usar en cada oración? Es posible que puedas usar más de uno.

1. Catalina se graduó _____, consiguió un trabajo excelente.

2. Su casa está _____, a unos cuarenta kilómetros de Medellín.

3. _____ estudiaba, Catalina estudiaba _____.

4. Pero _____ dejó de asistir a clase.

5. _____, todos los días, llegaba a tiempo a clase.

6. La constancia ha sido _____ una característica de Catalina.

7. _____, en la empresa donde trabaja ahora Cata, la aprecian.

8. Por cierto, Cata habla _____ bien francés e inglés.

Adverbs that end in -mente

Many adverbs are formed by adding the ending **-mente** to the *feminine singular* form of the adjective. Note that adjectives such as **fácil** and **difícil** keep the written accent mark after adding the ending **-mente**:

El ejecutivo va **discretamente** vestido.	*The executive appears to dress **discreetly**.*
Subieron la cuesta **lentamente**.	*They climbed the slope **slowly**.*
Seguimos las instrucciones **fácilmente**.	*We followed the instructions **easily**.*
Actualmente, las novelas históricas son populares.	*Nowadays, historical novels are popular.*

Note that **actualmente** (*currently, nowadays*) is not an exact cognate. It refers to the *present*, from the point of view of the narrator. Two or more adverbs may appear in a series, but only the *last* one ends in **-mente**. If such a series is marked with commas, the adverbs may all end in **-mente**. Stylistically, this adds to the effect created by the sentence:

Leíamos las noticias **rápida** y **silenciosamente**.	*We read the news **quickly** and **quietly**.*
Lentamente, pacientemente respondí a todas las preguntas.	*Slowly and patiently, I answered all the questions.*

*¿Cuál es el adverbio que corresponde a la descripción de cada oración? Usa el adverbio que termina en **-mente**.*

1. Nuestro gobernador es una persona discreta. Habla _____.

2. Además es muy paciente. Trabaja _____.

3. Es puntual. Llega a las entrevistas _____.

4. Sobre sus contrarios, hace comentarios con delicadeza. Hace comentarios _____.

5. Colabora con los representantes de la oposición con frecuencia. Trabaja con ellos _____.

6. Trata a sus empleados con respeto. Se comporta _____.

7. En las sesiones de su gabinete, trabaja rápido. Hace los quehaceres _____.

8. En resumen, es una persona tranquila. Nuestro gobernador vive _____.

EJERCICIO
11·3

¿Qué adverbio asocias con cada verbo? *Escribe la letra de la respuesta que consideres más apropiada. Después, en cada línea, escribe el verbo seguido del adverbio terminado en -***mente***.*

1. _____ valientemente _____

2. _____ cuidadosamente _____

3. _____ profundamente _____

4. _____ elegantemente _____

5. _____ frecuentemente _____

6. _____ silenciosamente _____

7. _____ agradablemente _____

8. _____ cortésmente _____

a. hacer ejercicios
b. oler (**hue-**)
c. conducir
d. tratar

e. vestirse
f. meditar
g. luchar
h. respirar

EJERCICIO
11·4

Tus costumbres (*habits*). *Ahora regresa al Ejercicio 11-3. Usa los verbos en el presente y los adverbios para crear oraciones completas. Si quieres, puedes añadir otros adverbios para comunicarte con claridad.*

MODELO   luchar valientemente

Siempre lucho valientemente por mis derechos.

1. _____

_____

2. _____

_____

3. _____

_____

4. _____

_____

5. _____

_____

6. _____

_____

7. _____

_____

8. _____

_____

Adverbial phrases

Both English and Spanish have an endless number of adverbial expressions (**locuciones adver-biales**). They can be built in several ways, combining a *preposition* with other words. The first group below consists of a preposition followed by a noun; it may also include an adjective:

preposition + (adjective) + noun (adjective) → adverbial phrase

a buen precio	*at a good price*
al cabo de	*after*
a mano	*at hand; handmade*
a manos llenas	*abundantly, lavishly*
con alegría	*happily*
con elegancia	*elegantly*
con gusto	*with pleasure*
con los brazos abiertos	*with open arms*
con una voz tajante	*categorically, unequivocally*
de boca	*facedown*
de buena (mala) gana	*happily/unwillingly*
de día	*during the day, in daylight*
de noche	*at night*
en ninguna parte	*nowhere*
en seguida	*immediately*
en voz baja (alta)	*softly/loudly*
por todas partes	*everywhere*
sin duda	*undoubtedly, without a doubt*
Gastan el dinero **a manos llenas**.	*They spent their money **lavishly**.*
Salen a bailar **de noche**.	*They go out dancing **at night**.*

Se cayó **de boca**.	He fell **facedown**.
Trabajamos **de buena gana**.	We work **happily**.
La modelo camina **con elegancia**.	The model walks **elegantly**.
La respuesta, **sin duda**, fue elocuente.	The answer was, **undoubtedly**, eloquent.
Por todas partes puedes ver manifestaciones de protesta.	You can see protest demonstrations **everywhere**.

Comentarios y elogios (*praise*). *Estudia la lista de las locuciones adverbiales y úsalas para completar las ideas de una manera lógica.*

MODELO   Eres rico porque gastas el dinero ___*a manos llenas*___.

1. Debes ser muy tímido porque hablas _____.

2. Veo que eres cariñoso (*affectionate*) porque me recibiste _____.

3. Eres sensato (*sensible*) porque compras todo _____.

4. Ahorras dinero porque encuentras rebajas _____.

5. Yo gasto mucho; no encuentro rebajas _____.

6. Tus hijos son felices y hacen los quehaceres (*chores*) de la casa _____.

7. En cambio los hijos de tus vecinos son gritones. Siempre hablan _____.

8. No me extraña. La madre de esos niños nunca habla _____.

A number of adverbial phrases are formed with a preposition followed by an adjective; others are formed with a preposition plus an infinitive.

preposition + adjective → adverbial phrase

en general	*in general, generally*
en particular	*especially, particularly*
por supuesto	*of course*
por consiguiente	*consequently*
Por supuesto, entendemos su preocupación.	**Of course**, we understand your concern.
Les preocupa la falta de asistencia médica **en particular**.	**In particular**, they are concerned about the lack of medical services.

preposition + infinitive → adverbial phrase

al amanecer	*at dawn, at daybreak*
al anochecer	*at nightfall*
al atardecer	*at sunset*
sin cesar	*incessantly*
sin parar	*without stopping*
sin hablar	*without a word*
Los pescadores salen al mar **al amanecer**.	*Fishermen go out to sea **at daybreak**.*

Los candidatos hacen campaña **sin parar**.   *The candidates are campaigning **without stopping (ceaselessly)**.*

Sin hablar, me hace entender lo que quiere.   ***Without a word**, he lets me know what he wants.*

Note in the preceding examples that the preposition **a** + the article **el** results in the contraction **al**.

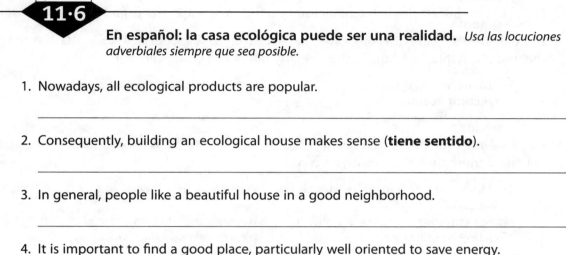

En español: la casa ecológica puede ser una realidad. *Usa las locuciones adverbiales siempre que sea posible.*

1. Nowadays, all ecological products are popular.

_____

2. Consequently, building an ecological house makes sense (**tiene sentido**).

_____

3. In general, people like a beautiful house in a good neighborhood.

_____

4. It is important to find a good place, particularly well oriented to save energy.

_____

5. The wind can help consume less electricity, especially in summertime.

_____

6. Ecologists gladly receive news about new green technology.

_____

7. Without a doubt, there is more demand for ecological homes.

_____

8. It is extremely important to consider all possibilities, particularly plants inside the house to reduce pollution.

_____

Adverbs and word order

You have probably noticed that adverbs do not appear to fit a particular word order. In determining word order in the sentence, you will need to consider the length of the adverb, whether the verb it modifies is in a simple or compound tense, and the intended emphasis placed on the adverb.

- Adverbs appear at the beginning of the sentence in both English and Spanish as *transitional words* (**enlaces** or **conectores**). A comma usually follows an adverb used this way. When the emphasis is on the action of the verb, the adverb may appear at the end of the sentence:

El nadador llegó **ayer**. **Hoy**, ganó la medalla de oro.	*The swimmer arrived **yesterday**. **Today**, he won a gold medal.*
Se entrenará **bien**. **Además**, levantará pesas.	*He will train **well**. He will **also** lift weights.*

Note that in the last English sentence above, the adverb appears *before* the verb.

- In English sentences with compound tenses, adverbs may separate the auxiliary verb and the past participle. In Spanish, they usually follow the entire verb form:

Pedro me **ha escrito** cartas **frecuentemente**.	*Pedro **has frequently written** me letters.*
Lisa me **ha llamado ya**.	*Lisa **has already called** me.*

- Review Unit 1 for use of adverbs in negative statements. Remember that Spanish verbs may have more than one negative adverb:

No sabemos francés, pero hablamos italiano.	*We do **not** know French, but we speak Italian.*
Nunca salimos a pescar en el invierno.	*We **never** go fishing in the winter.*
No haremos **jamás** este trabajo.	*We will **never** do this work.*

Adverbs that add meaning to a message

Adverbs and adverbial phrases often add shades of meaning to the words they modify by highlighting, amplifying, or softening the tone of the message. Adverbs emphasize the idea conveyed by the verb in the following examples:

Realmente, no creemos en su inocencia.	*We **really don't believe** in his innocence.*
Los deportistas **están literalmente extenuados**.	*The athletes **are literally exhausted**.*
Llenan simplemente la planilla y la entregan.	***Just fill out** the form and turn it in.*

The strong message communicated by the following adverbs emphasizes the idea presented by the sentence:

La situación en el Golfo es **extremadamente** peligrosa.	*The situation in the Gulf is **extremely** dangerous.*
El informe del periódico es **absolutamente** cierto.	*The newspaper report is **absolutely** true.*

Note the softer tone created by the adverbs in these examples:

Apenas llueve.	*It's **barely** raining.*
Estamos **medio** decididos a viajar.	*We **are sort of ready** to travel.*

Te toca a ti. *Vas a sustituir los adverbios o locuciones adverbiales por otras que comunican una idea similar. El mensaje no debe cambiar de significado.*

MODELO   La noticia es <u>totalmente</u> falsa. El director ha hablado <u>con sinceridad</u>.

La noticia es *absolutamente* falsa. El director ha hablado *con honestidad*.

or La noticia es *completamente* falsa. El director ha hablado *con franqueza*.

Katrina buscaba al pez en la pecera. (1) <u>De repente,</u> _____ lo vio en el fondo,

inmóvil, (2) ¡<u>totalmente</u> _____ inmóvil! Katrina estaba (3) <u>verdaderamente</u>

_____ preocupada. (4) <u>Inmediatamente,</u> _____ fue a su

cuarto y llamó al veterinario. (5) <u>Después de</u> _____ unos minutos, regresó a la

pecera y el pez estaba flotando pero respiraba (6) <u>con dificultad</u> _____ . Fue a

su cuarto y (7) <u>rápidamente</u> _____ buscó en la Internet información para ayu-

dar al pez. Después de un rato, regresó a la pecera. El pez (8) <u>obviamente</u> _____

 no estaba allí. Empezó a buscar a sus familiares (9) <u>por todas partes</u> _____ .

(10) <u>Por fin</u> _____ fue al garaje. Encontró a su hermano sacando la basura.

(11) ¡<u>Encima de</u> _____ un cesto de la basura estaba el pez! Katrina sacó al pez

de la basura, corrió a la pecera y colocó al pez (12) <u>en el agua</u> _____ . (13) <u>En</u>

<u>unos segundos,</u> _____ el pez comenzó a nadar. Es un misterio y, (14)

<u>afortunadamente,</u> _____ Katrina está feliz.

Using infinitives

The *infinitive*, the name that identifies a verb, is the most basic form of a verb. The infinitive does not indicate a person, or by itself, a notion of time. In English, the infinitive is the *root* of the verb and usually refers to the form *to + first person of the verb*. In Spanish, verb infinitives are grouped in three conjugations that have the same infinitive endings: **-ar**, **-er**, and **-ir**.

root of the verb + -ar, -er, or -ir → infinitive

The infinitive is basically a verb, but it performs many functions of a noun. When translated alone, the Spanish infinitive **salir** is the English equivalent of *to leave*. However, in other contexts, the English equivalent may be different. In the first example below, the Spanish infinitive **merendar** (*to snack*) is the *subject* of the sentence and plays the role of a noun. In the second, it also functions as a noun but as the *object* of the sentence:

Merendar es saludable.	*Having a snack is healthy.*
¿Quieres **merendar**?	*Do you want **to have a snack**?*

Infinitives as nouns

Infinitives acting as nouns belong to the category of *verbals*: words that have the characteristics of a verb (an action) but function in a sentence as a noun.

El errar es humano.	*To err is human.*
Mis padres decidieron **ir**.	*My parents decided **to go**.*
Me relaja **tocar el piano**.	*Playing the piano relaxes me.*
¡Me encanta **correr**!	*I love **to run**!*
el ser celoso/a	*being jealous*

Keep in mind the following points:

◆ Infinitives used as nouns are always masculine and generally appear in the singular form; some are also used in the plural:

los deberes	*homework; duties*
los quehaceres	*duties, work, responsibilities*

Infinitives as nouns may be used with or without a *masculine* article. They may also be modified by *adjectives*, *possessive adjectives*, *demonstrative adjectives*, or *adverbs*:

El comer en exceso es **peligroso**.	*Eating too much is **dangerous**.*

Los deberes de un ciudadano son **exigentes**.	*The duties of a citizen are **demanding**.*
Conducir velozmente puede ser **fatal**.	***Driving too fast** can be **fatal**.*
Su melodioso cantar deleita a los pacientes.	***His/her delightful singing** pleases the patients.*
Errar es **humano**.	***To err** is **human**.*

- The English present participle (the *-ing* ending), which appears in some of the previous example translations, is frequently used to translate the Spanish infinitive (**-ar**, **-er**, or **-ir**). In English, both the infinitive and the present participle can function as nouns (according to certain rules); in Spanish, the present participle is *never* used as a noun.
- In Spanish, infinitives that refer to actions can be the *subject* of a sentence. Spanish infinitives can also be the *object* of a verb or a predicate nominative, as in the following examples:

¿Te gusta **correr**?	*Do you like **to run**?*
¿Prefiere **trabajar** y no **estudiar**?	*He/she prefers **to work** and not **to study**?*
Es un placer **conocerlo/la**.	*It is a pleasure **to meet you**.*

- Split infinitives are possible in Spanish. In English, an infinitive can be split for clarification, although such constructions are often restricted to proverbs and sayings:

... **para verdaderamente saber** la verdad	*. . . **to truly know** the truth*

- The infinitive of **haber** (the auxiliary verb in compound tenses) may be combined with a past participle and used as a noun, with or without an article or an adjective. This construction may function as the subject or as the direct object of the main verb or in a subordinate clause. Note the English equivalent, which uses the present participle (or *gerund*, *-ing* form) of *to have*, followed by a past participle or a conjugated form:

El haber aprendido chino me ayudará a conseguir esa plaza.	***Having learned Chinese** will help me to get the position.*
No creo **haber conocido** a ese chico.	*I do not think **I have met** that young man.*

EJERCICIO
12·1

Los beneficios de los deportes. *Escribe en español. Usa los infinitivos (**-ar**, **-er**, o **-ir**).*

1. Walking is healthy.

_____

2. Swimming opens (= improves) your (**el**) appetite.

_____

3. Running burns a lot of calories.

_____

4. Playing golf is very relaxing.

_____

5. Rowing can be hard.

_____

6. Climbing a mountain is not my favorite activity.

_____

7. Dancing is almost a sport.

_____

8. But sleeping is my favorite activity.

_____

EJERCICIO

12·2

Construye las oraciones con lógica. *Usa los infinitivos como sujetos de la oración. Coloca el sujeto al principio de la oración.*

1. no mejora (*improve*) / en exceso / comer y beber / la salud

_____

2. un concierto / a / de música / inspira / a / concierto / personas / muchas / asistir / clásica

_____

3. mensajes / amigos / con / nuestros / email / por / compartir / comunica / nos

_____

4. fortuna / una / invertir / en / la / bolsa / fortuna / aumentar / dinero / puede

_____

5. satisface / contribuir / electoral / una / los / campaña / a / ciudadanos / los / a

_____

6. mérito / tiene / a / desamparados / los / ayudar

_____

EJERCICIO

12·3

*Elige una de las opciones para completar tu párrafo. Usa el artículo **el** + infinitivo.*

dormir / comer y charlar / trabajar / ahorrar / perder / leer

1. Me encanta _____ el periódico los domingos por la mañana. No tiene sentido 2. _____ toda la mañana. Además, 3. _____ en exceso me cansa mucho. 4. Me enoja (*annoys*) _____ cuando juego al tenis. 5. _____ para el futuro, es prudente. 6. Eso sí, _____ con mis amigos me relaja.

Prepositions placed before infinitives

In Spanish, the only form of a verb used after a *preposition* is the infinitive. In English, the present participle (-*ing* form) is used after prepositions. A number of prepositions and prepositional phrases may precede the infinitive in Spanish:

a	*to, at*
al (a + el)	*upon, on*
a condición de	*provided that*
antes de	*before*
después de	*after*
en lugar de	*instead of*
en vez de	*instead of*
para	*in order to*
por miedo de	*for fear that*
por	*because of*
sin	*without*

Note that in this construction, the main verb and the following infinitive have the same subject. When the subjects of the two clauses are different, you will need to use the conjunction **que** + a *subjunctive* verb form. You may review that structure in Unit 16.

main verb + preposition + infinitive

Se levantó + **después de** + tomar el café.	*He got up **after** having coffee.*
Lávate las manos **antes de** comer.	*Wash your hands **before** you eat.*
Descansa **después de** cenar.	*Rest **after** you eat your dinner.*
Estudia **en vez de** dormir.	*Study **instead of** sleeping.*
Me dejó su auto **a condición de** cuidar al perro.	*He lent me his car **provided that** I take care of the dog.*
Salió temprano **por miedo a** perder el avión.	*She left early **for fear (that)** she might miss her flight.*

The following examples are infinitive clauses that cannot stand alone but complete the meaning of the main clause, preceding or following it. An infinitive clause ends with a comma when it precedes the main clause.

Para conducir, necesitas un carnet vigente.	***In order to drive**, you need a valid license.*
Sin saber la verdad, acusó a un inocente.	***Without knowing the truth**, she accused an innocent person.*

The contraction al + the infinitive

The contraction **al** is made up of the preposition **a** plus the masculine definite article **el**: **a** + **el** = **al**. The construction **al** + *infinitive* indicates an action or state that is happening at a certain time, present, past, or future. The English equivalent is:

al + infinitive → upon or when + the -ing form of a verb

Vi a Ramona **al llegar** al supermercado.	*I saw Ramona **when I got** to (**upon arriving** at) the supermarket.*
Al salir de casa, te llamo.	***When I leave** (**upon leaving**) the house, I will call you.*
Al entrar, saluda; **al salir**, despídete.	***On entering**, say hello; **upon leaving**, say good-bye.*
Encontramos un perrito **al pasear** por el parque.	*We found a puppy **when (we were) strolling** in the park.*

The most frequently used English equivalent for **al** + *infinitive* in everyday language is *when*. Note that the comma is necessary when the infinitive clause with **al** precedes the main clause in Spanish.

EJERCICIO
12·4

La rutina de mi hermana. *Vas a construir oraciones con una cláusula + una preposición + un infinitivo. Conjuga el verbo principal en el pretérito y usa la puntuación apropiada.*

1. al / despertarse / mi hermana / llamar por teléfono / a su amiga Loli

_____

2. en vez de / preparar / el desayuno / perder / mucho tiempo

_____

3. antes de / salir / a su trabajo / no apagar / la cafetera

_____

4. en lugar de / ayudar / en la casa / complicar / mi situación

_____

5. sin / despedirse / de mí / salir / de casa

_____

6. después de / llegar / a la oficina / llamar / a mi madre

_____

EJERCICIO
12·5

Los políticos y sus campañas. *Ahora vas a construir tus propias oraciones con tu opinión acerca de los políticos. Usa la preposición + infinitivo para comunicar tus ideas. Puedes usar uno de estos verbos:*

prometer / mentir / persuadir / construir / engañar / ayudar / recibir

MODELO   después de ganar

Después de ganar las elecciones, se olvidan de sus promesas.

or *Se olvidan de sus promesas después de ganar las elecciones.*

1. al empezar

_____

2. en vez de

_____

3. después de

_____

4. por miedo de

_____

5. a pesar de

_____

6. sin

_____

7. para

_____

8. en vez de

_____

Infinitives after verbs

In Spanish and English, there are many verbs that may be directly followed by an infinitive. They can be grouped into verbs of *perception*, *emotion*, *want*, *possibility*, and *movement*, and verbs that emphasize the effect of an action.

Infinitives after verbs of *want*, *likes and dislikes*, *opinion*, *obligation*, and *appearance*

Infinitives are used after the following verbs:

Verbs of want, likes and dislikes

desear	*to desire*
detestar	*to dislike, to detest*
encantar	*to adore, to love*
exigir	*to demand*
gustar	*to like*
querer	*to want*
Susi **prefiere esperar** el autobús.	*Susi **prefers to wait** for the bus.*
Nos **encanta cocinar**.	*We **love to cook**.*
Tú **exiges terminar** con el abuso.	*You **demand to end** (**an end to**) the abuse.*
Ellos **quieren ir** a Puerto Rico.	*They **want to go** to Puerto Rico.*
Me **gustaría perder** un poquito de peso.	*I **would like to lose** a little weight.*
¿**Te gustaría hacerte** médico?	***Would you like to become** a doctor?*

In the previous examples, the subject of the verb in the infinitive clause is the *same* as the subject—the conjugated verb—of the main clause.

EJERCICIO
12·6

Te toca a ti. *Contesta las siguientes preguntas desde tu propia perspectiva. Después del verbo principal (main verb), usa el infinitivo para completar la oración.*

MODELO   ¿Qué te gusta hacer en tu tiempo libre?

Me gusta descansar y conversar con mis amigos por teléfono o chatear por Internet.

1. ¿Qué deseas lograr (*accomplish*) en los próximos dos meses?

   _____

2. ¿Qué quieres estudiar en el futuro?

   _____

3. En tu opinión, ¿qué prefieren hacer los jóvenes?

   _____

4. ¿Qué exigen los hijos de sus padres hoy en día?

   _____

5. ¿Qué te encanta hacer en tu tiempo libre?

   _____

6. ¿Qué detestas, por encima de (*above*) todo?

   _____

EJERCICIO
12·7

Ahora, lee las respuestas y escribe las preguntas a esas respuestas. Usa la forma de respeto (UD) del verbo principal + infinitivo.

MODELO   Deseamos viajar a China estas vacaciones.

   qué   _¿Qué desean hacer estas vacaciones?_

1. Prefiero tomar un taxi yo sola al salir del trabajo.

   qué _____

2. Necesito llegar al aeropuerto a las diez en punto.

   a qué hora _____

3. Quiero hacer escala (*stopover*) en Japón antes de llegar a China.

   dónde _____

4. Necesito facturar estas maletas y también estos paquetes.

   qué _____

5. Bueno, me gustaría ir a Corea y Tailandia.

   adónde _____

6. En mi próximo viaje, preferiría viajar con mis amigos al Himalaya.

   con quién _____

Infinitive after verbs of perception

A simple infinitive clause can be used after a verb of *perception*:

ver	*to see*
escuchar	*to listen*
mirar	*to watch, to see*
oír	*to hear*
sentir	*to feel*

Note the word order in the following Spanish and English infinitive clauses. There are two possible word orders for the Spanish infinitive clause, but only one in English.

Veo **el tren salir**.	*I see **the train leave/leaving**.*
Veo **salir el tren**.	*I see **the train leave/leaving**.*
Oigo **a los pájaros cantar**.	*I hear **birds sing/singing**.*
Oigo **cantar a los pájaros**.	*I hear **birds sing/singing**.*

Also note above that the English equivalent can be in the present tense or the present participle (-*ing* form).

Infinitive after verbs of movement

Infinitives are used after conjugated verbs of movement. The preposition **a**, **de**, or **por** usually follows the verb of movement:

ir a	*to go*
comenzar a	*to start, to begin*
empezar	*to begin, to start*
ponerse a	*to begin*
volver a	*to do (an activity) again*
volver de	*to return from*
venir de	*to come from*
subir a	*to go up*
bajar a	*to go down*
salir de, a, por, etc.	*to go out, exit*
Voy a comprar una botella de vino.	*I am going to buy a bottle of wine.*
Venimos a cenar contigo.	*We are coming to dine with you.*
Salgo a buscar los vasos en la terraza.	*I am going to get / look for the drinking glasses on the terrace.*
Bajaré a abrir la puerta a los invitados.	*I will go down to open the door for the guests.*

En español. *Usa el infinitivo.*

1. I saw the plane landing (**aterrizar**).

_____

2. We heard the agent greeting the passengers.

_____

3. Mary started to get ready to receive her family.

_____

4. She went to ask for a wheelchair.

_____

5. Luis started (**empezar**) to look for the suitcases.

_____

6. The children started (**ponerse**) crying when they woke up.

_____

7. Then Luis heard his cell phone ringing.

_____

8. He heard a familiar voice speaking.

_____

9. Then he saw his sister coming.

_____

10. Finally, they all went looking for their car.

_____

Other verbs followed by the infinitive

An infinitive is used after verbs that express authority or influence:

hacer, hacer(se)	*to make (someone do something)*
dejar	*to allow*
mandar	*to order*
impedir	*to stop, not to allow*
permitir	*to allow*
prohibir	*to forbid*
Fernanda **se hizo construir** una piscina.	*Fernanda **had** a pool **built**.*
Ahora **hace nadar** a sus hijos.	*Now she is **making / having** her children **swim**.*
Mañana, **hará organizar** los armarios.	*Tomorrow she will **make / have someone organize** her closets.*

Note below the use of the infinitive after **dejar** (*to allow*), **permitir** (*to let, to allow*), **atreverse a** (*to dare*), and **intentar** (*to try*):

¡**No dejes caer** la torta!	*Do not drop the cake!*
¡Ay, no! **Dejaste quemar** la carne.	*Oh, no!* ***You let*** *the meat* ***burn.***
No te atrevas a servirla a los invitados.	***Do not dare (to)*** *serve it to the guests.*

Infinitives also follow verbs of influence: a verb of *allowing, influencing, prohibiting,* or *obliging*—and similar verbs, such as those involving *requests*—can be followed by an infinitive that represents the action of someone other than the subject of the main verb. An *indirect object* is used to indicate who was asked to perform (or not perform) the action. The indirect object can be *a noun* or *an indirect object pronoun*. These sentences are similar in structure to their English equivalents:

María **me** dejó entrar.	*María allowed **me** to enter.*
Les mandamos escribir la carta.	*We required **them** to write the letter.*
Te prohíbo salir antes de las diez.	*I forbid **you** to leave before ten.*
Lidia **me** hace trabajar en casa.	*Lidia makes **me** work at home.*

EJERCICIO
12·9

Un misterio. *Lee las preguntas y después escribe las respuestas usando los verbos entre paréntesis y el verbo subrayado en la pregunta.*

MODELO ¿Escuchaste la noticia?

(permitir) No, el ruido _no me permitió escuchar la noticia_.

1. ¿Escapó el criminal?

   (dejar) No, la policía _____.

2. ¿El teniente hizo una investigación?

   (mandar) No, el capitán _____.

3. ¿Visitaste a la víctima en el hospital?

   (permitir) No, su familia no _____.

4. ¿Llegaron los periodistas al salón?

   (prohibir) No, los sicólogos _____.

5. ¿Revelaron el nombre de la víctima?

   (dejar) No, las autoridades _____.

6. ¿Llegaron ustedes a recepción en el hospital?

   (impedir) No, un guardia _____.

Infinitives after impersonal expressions

Infinitives are used after *impersonal expressions*. Impersonal sentences do not have a specific subject or person in the main clause. Most impersonal expressions consist of a form of **ser** in the third-person singular, followed by an adjective:

Es aconsejable	*It is advisable to*
Es bueno	*It is good to*
Es importante	*It is important to*
Es imposible	*It is impossible to*
Es indispensable	*It is indispensable to*
Es justo	*It is fair to*
Es malo	*It is bad to*
Es mejor	*It is better to*
Es necesario	*It is necessary to*
Es posible	*It is possible to*
Es preciso	*It is necessary to*
Es preferible	*It is better to*

Impersonal constructions are used to make suggestions and to give general instructions or commands. Note that some of the examples include other elements after the infinitive. English has similar constructions:

Es importante beber mucha agua.	***It is important to drink*** *a lot of water.*
Es bueno practicar deportes.	***It is good to participate in*** *sports.*
Es necesario animar a los jóvenes.	***It is necessary to encourage*** *young people.*
Es mejor no fumar ya en público.	***It is better to no longer*** *smoke in public.*

The word order in this type of construction is flexible. In spoken English, an infinitive with *to* may start a sentence; in written English, starting a sentence with *to* + *infinitive* is usually avoided:

Bailar salsa es divertido.	***To dance (Dancing)*** *salsa is fun.*
No cuidarse la salud es atroz.	***Not to take care*** *of one's health is atrocious.*

Other impersonal expressions are:

Más vale	*It is better to*
Conviene	*It is advisable to*
En el futuro, **más vale evitar** problemas.	*In the future,* ***it is better to avoid*** *problems.*
Conviene estar listo para salir.	***It is advisable to be ready*** *to leave.*

If impersonal expressions that communicate *uncertainty, doubt, conjecture, wishes, desires, requests, orders,* or other emotions are followed by a *different* subject, you will need to use the *subjunctive* in the subordinate clause:

impersonal expression + que + a subjunctive form

Es dudoso que el precio **baje.**	***It is doubtful that*** *the price* ***will go down.***

See Unit 16 to review the use of impersonal expressions followed by the subjunctive.

Te toca a ti. *Escribe una lista de sugerencias para progresar en la vida. Repasa las expresiones impersonales que has aprendido. Construye tus oraciones combinando una expresión impersonal + el infinitivo + tu sugerencia.*

MODELO   es aconsejable / invertir

Es aconsejable + invertir + en la bolsa de valores con prudencia.

Es aconsejable invertir en la bolsa de valores con prudencia.

1. es bueno / hacer una lista

_____

2. es beneficioso / tener fe

_____

3. es necesario / visualizar

_____

4. mas vale / enfrentar

_____

5. conviene / mantener

_____

6. es mejor / ser

_____

7. es malo / posponer

_____

8. es preferible / imaginar

_____

Infinitive to express the near future

Although it performs many functions as a noun, the infinitive still communicates the idea of an action. The future tense in Spanish is frequently replaced with a form of **ir** followed by the preposition **a** + the infinitive. In this construction, the time the infinitive communicates is *after* (= the future).

ir a + infinitive → action or event in the near future

Vamos a descansar en unos minutos.	*We **will rest** in a few minutes.*
Voy a terminar mis quehaceres.	*I **am going to finish** my chores.*

Note that the English equivalents include either a future tense or a form of *to be* and the gerund or present participle, *going.*

En el futuro. *Lee las oraciones para saber qué hicieron algunas personas. Después, escribe lo que van a hacer en el futuro. Usa la forma apropiada del verbo* **ir** + **a** + *el infinitivo.*

MODELO   Carlos fue de vacaciones a Europa hace dos años.

probablemente / este verano

     Probablemente, Carlos va a ir a Japón este verano.

1. Luisa y Jaco salieron de compras a Nueva York el invierno pasado.

   seguramente / el año que viene

   _____

2. Miranda y Alejandro no quisieron acompañar a sus padres la semana pasada.

   tal vez / la próxima vez

   _____

3. Mis sobrinos compitieron en el torneo de golf la primavera pasada.

   afortunadamente / este año

   _____

4. Cati y Luisa se entrenaron para participar en los Juegos Panamericanos en 1999.

   con toda certeza, no / en el futuro

   _____

5. Mis hermanos asistieron a la Fiesta de San Fermín hace dos años.

   desgraciadamente no / nunca más

   _____

6. Tú y yo no nos comunicamos por email desde hace dos años.

   desde ahora / con más frecuencia

   _____

Idioms and special phrases

In Spanish, an idiom is a **modismo**. Native speakers understand idiomatic phrases in their own language; however, often they may not be clear to language learners, since idioms and idiomatic phrases do not translate word-for-word from one language to another. Idiomatic expressions and phrases often combine words, creating different meanings from their dictionary definitions.

¿**Te das cuenta** de lo que pasa?	***Do you realize** what is going on?*
¡El libro no **está disponible**!	*The book **is** not **available**!*

Darse cuenta de (*to realize*) is an idiomatic expression. At first glance, you might think it means *to give* a *sum or* an *account*. Note that *going on* is an idiomatic expression in English. Sometimes an idiom is used in a context that appears to have little to do with the situation at hand. Note the following exchange between an employee and a manager:

—¿Vamos a firmar el nuevo contrato?	*Are we going to sign the new contract?*
—No estamos seguros.	*We are not sure.*
—Entonces, ¿no recibiremos un bono?	*So, we will not get a bonus?*
—No está **el horno para galletitas**.	*This is not **the right time**.*

If you translate the last Spanish sentence literally it says *the oven is not* (*ready*) *for* (*baking*) *cookies*. What would *an oven ready to bake cookies* have to do with a discussion about contracts and bonuses? **No está el horno para galletitas** is a special phrase that fits the dialogue, hinting clearly that most probably there will not be a bonus. Idiomatic phrases in Spanish, learned carefully and practiced consistently, will help you communicate effectively and avoid awkward situations or misunderstandings. Think of this type of phrase as:

a combination of words that creates a different meaning from common definitions → idiomatic phrase

Some idioms may be complete sentences, proverbs, or sayings. Note the idiomatic English equivalents:

A la tercera va la vencida.	*Three strikes, you're out.*
A buena hambre, no hay pan duro.	*Beggars can't be choosers.*
El casado, casa quiere.	*Married people need a home of their own.*
A palabras necias, oídos sordos.	*Take no notice of (turn a deaf ear to) thoughtless words people say.*

Other idioms are adverbial phrases. You may wish to go back to Unit 11 to review adverbial phrases. Remember that most of these phrases, functioning as adverbs, are formed with a preposition plus a noun, an adjective, or an infinitive. They are idiomatic since they do not translate literally into other languages. Note the following prepositional phrases and their English equivalents:

a cuentagotas	*in dribs and drabs*
a toda vela	*full speed ahead*
de mala gana	*unwillingly, reluctantly*
en esas condiciones	*in such condition(s)*
en mi opinión	*in my book*
en resumen	*in a nutshell*
Vamos **a toda vela**.	*We are moving **full speed ahead**.*
Nos dan las noticias **a cuentagotas**.	*They give us the news **in dribs and drabs**.*
No volverán a esta casa nunca **en esas condiciones**.	*They will never return to this house **in (under) those conditions**.*
Los chicos limpian su dormitorio **de mala gana**.	*The kids clean their room **reluctantly**.*

Many idioms, such as **soportar** (*to stand, to take*), are specific, idiomatic uses of verbs:

No soporta una broma.	*He **can't take** a joke.*

The context for these messages is often informal. A paragraph such as the following may appear in a conversation, a short e-mail, or a message you may find on your answering machine:

Hice unos recados. Fui al supermercado que **da al este**, **di con** los ingredientes que buscaba. Luego llamé a Carla pero **no dio la cara**.	*I ran a few errands. I went to the supermarket **facing east**, **I found** the ingredients I was looking for. Then I called Carla, **but she did not (refused to) answer me**.*

In a somewhat different tone, the following paragraph might appear in a Spanish newspaper. Note the highlighted idiomatic phrases:

La comisión creada por el Presidente, **llevará a cabo** la investigación del secuestro, sin **perder de vista** las necesidades de los ciudadanos. El Presidente ha manifestado que para los secuestrados, su situación **es un asunto de vida o muerte**. También, ha comunicado la necesidad de **mantener la calma** y **estar alertas** ante cualquier situación sospechosa.	*The commission created by the President **will carry out** the investigation of the kidnapping, **without losing sight** of the needs of the citizens. The President has declared that, for the kidnap victims, their situation **is a matter of life and death**. He also emphasized the need **to keep calm** and **be on the alert** for any suspicious situations.*

Idiomatic expressions are used:

◆ To express the accurate equivalent of a word or phrase that does not have a literal translation:

No soporto sus comentarios.	*I **cannot stand** his/her/their comments.*

◆ To clarify the meaning of what is being communicated:

Estás débil y tienes que **guardar cama** por unos días.	*You are weak and you have to **stay in bed** for a few days.*

◆ To further explain or emphasize ideas:

No durmieron anoche; **pasaron la noche en blanco.** | *They did not sleep at all;* ***they did not sleep a wink.***

Common phrases with verbs

Many common idiomatic phrases consist of a verb + another verb, a noun, or a preposition, followed by other elements. Here are some frequently used verbal expressions:

atar cabos	*to put two and two together*
dejar caer	*to drop*
dejar pasar la ocasión	*to miss the opportunity, to miss the boat*
deshacerse en lágrimas	*to burst into tears*
estar en ayuno, quedarse en ayuno	*to fast (not eat); to be unable to understand something*
guardar cama	*to stay in bed*
llevar a cabo	*to carry out, to realize*
llover a cántaros	*to rain cats and dogs*
meterse a alguien en el bolsillo	*to have someone eating out of one's hand, to buy someone off*
meterse en un lío	*to be in a pickle, to be between a rock and a hard place*
pasar la noche en blanco	*to not sleep a wink*
sacar una foto	*to take a picture / photo*
salir adelante	*to make headway / progress*
salirse con la suya	*to get one's way*
ser hombre muerto	*to be a marked man*
ser un asunto de vida o muerte	*to be a matter of life and death*
tirar la casa por la ventana	*to spend money excessively / left and right*
valer la pena	*to be worth it*
venderse como pan caliente	*to sell like hotcakes*
volverse + *adjective*	*to become*
Atando cabos, descubrieron las pistas.	***They put two and two together*** *and found the clues.*
Laura **dejó caer** el jarrón chino.	*Laura* ***dropped / let fall*** *the Chinese vase.*
Al ver la cara de su hija, la madre de Laura **se deshizo en lágrimas.**	*Upon seeing her daughter's face, Laura's mother* ***burst into tears.***
Juan tiene fiebre y debe **guardar cama.**	*Juan has a fever and must* ***stay in bed.***
Anoche estaba nervioso y **se pasó la noche en blanco.**	*Last night he was nervous and* ***could not sleep a wink.***
Se preocupa porque su esposa **tira la casa por la ventana.**	*He is concerned because his wife* ***spends money excessively.***
Pero **no vale la pena** preocuparse tanto.	*But* ***it is not worth*** *worrying so much.*

EJERCICIO
13·1

Vamos a narrar un cuento, pero con otras palabras. *Elige la frase que comunica en otras palabras el mensaje. Después escribe la nueva oración en el tiempo apropiado del pasado.*

1. _____ El detective hizo un excelente trabajo. _____

2. _____ No durmió en toda la noche. _____

3. _____ Afuera, caía mucha agua. _____

4. _____ Entendió todo lo que había pasado. _____

5. _____ No quería perder una oportunidad. _____

6. _____ Hizo una foto del sospechoso (*suspect*). _____

7. _____ Para el detective, el caso era muy importante. _____

8. _____ El sospechoso estaba enfermo. _____

9. _____ Pero el sospechoso no podía ganar. _____

10. _____ El detective iba a ganar (*win*). _____

11. _____ El trabajo no fue en vano (*in vain*). _____

a. atar cabos

b. llover a cántaros

c. sacar una foto

d. salirse con la suya

e. pasar la noche en blanco

f. dejar pasar la ocasión

g. valer la pena

h. ser un asunto de vida o muerte

i. guardar cama

j. ser hombre muerto

k. llevar a cabo

Idiomatic use of verbs in certain expressions

Some verbs appear in idiomatic expressions more often than others. The following list shows verbs frequently used in such expressions. Notice how words are combined in these expressions with **dar**:

verb + preposition

dar + con
No dimos con el edificio. *We could not find the building.*

verb + preposition + infinitive

dar + a + conocer
Dieron a conocer la noticia. *They revealed the news.*

verb + noun

hacer + preguntas
Les **hicieron preguntas**. *They asked them questions.*

verb + article + noun

perder + la + calma
No pierdan la calma. *Stay calm. (Don't lose your cool.)*

Verbs and idiomatic expressions

A few common Spanish verbs are particularly used in idiomatic expressions.

Verbal expressions with dar

If you open a Spanish-Spanish dictionary, the first definition of **dar** you will see is **donar** (*to give, to donate*) or **entregar** (*to turn in*). Keep looking under the same entry, **dar**, and a rather long list of verbal phrases appear. This is not the case for all verbs, but some (such as **dar**, **tener**, and **hacer**) are the bases of a rich list of idiomatic expressions. Here are some of the idiomatic verbal expressions that include **dar**. Note how they vary in meaning:

dar a conocer	*to reveal*
dar ánimo	*to encourage*
dar con	*to find*
dar cuerda	*to wind (a clock)*
dar gritos	*to scream*
dar la cara	*to face (up to) someone or something*
dar la hora	*to strike the hour*
dar la mano	*to shake hands*
dar las gracias	*to thank*
dar por hecho	*to take for granted*
dar un abrazo	*to embrace, to give a hug*
dar un paseo	*to take a walk; to go for a ride*
dar una bofetada	*to slap on the face*
dar una mano	*to give / lend a hand*
dar una vuelta	*to take a walk*
darse cuenta de	*to realize*
darse prisa	*to hurry*
La víctima **dio gritos**.	*The victim **screamed**.*
En ese momento, el reloj **dio las tres**.	*At that moment, the clock **struck three**.*
Un testigo **dio por hecho** que estaba loco.	*A witness **took for granted** that he was insane.*
Mi hermano **dio testimonio** bajo juramento.	*My brother **testified** under oath.*
Los miembros del jurado **se dieron cuenta** de su inocencia.	*The members of the jury **realized** that he was innocent.*
Los periodistas **se dieron prisa** para dar la noticia.	*The reporters **hurried** to report the news.*

Other verbal expressions with **dar** + *a noun of feeling* convey emotions or reactions to something or someone:

dar alegría a	*to make someone happy*
dar asco a	*to make someone feel sick*
dar ganas de (llorar) a	*to make someone feel like (crying)*
dar miedo a	*to scare, to frighten someone*
dar náuseas a	*to make someone nauseous / nauseated*
dar pánico a	*to make someone panic*
dar pena a	*to make someone feel sorry*
dar risa a	*to make someone laugh*
dar sueño a	*to make someone sleepy*
dar tristeza a	*to make someone sad*
El aburrimiento **da sueño**, y lo ridículo **da risa**.	*Boredom **makes one sleepy**, and silly things **make one laugh**.*
A Lina **le dan miedo** los ratones.	*Mice **frighten** Lina.*
A mí los ratones **me dan náuseas**.	*Mice **make me nauseous**.*
Las campañas llenas de mentiras **nos dan asco**.	*Campaigns full of lies **make us feel sick**.*

En la comunidad. *¿Cuál es la frase sinónima más apropiada? Escribe la oración otra vez. Usa una de las frases que aparecen en la primera lista de las expresiones con el verbo **dar**.*

1. Carlos conduce rápido. _____

2. Felipe ayuda a Mario. _____

3. Ahora, Ana entiende mi problema. _____

4. Luisa agradece mis consejos. _____

5. Cuando entramos, Ana nos saluda. _____

6. Benita revela los secretos de todos. _____

7. Berta y Alina animan a sus amigos. _____

8. A todos nos encanta pasear. _____

Te toca a ti. *Indica tu reacción a los siguientes estímulos. En tu respuesta usa la forma apropiada del verbo **dar**.*

MODELO   la crítica destructiva

   La crítica destructiva no me da risa, me da asco.

dar alegría / dar asco / dar ganas de llorar / dar miedo / dar náuseas / dar pánico / dar pena / dar risa / dar sueño / dar tristeza

1. los comentarios tontos

_____

2. los chistes de mal gusto

_____

3. las biografías de figuras militares

_____

4. los vuelos en avionetas (*small planes*)

_____

5. las películas de horror

_____

6. los animales abandonados

_____

Verbal expressions with hacer

hacer caso	*to heed, to pay attention*
hacer cola	*to stand in line*
hacer de + *noun*	*to work as*
hacer el papel de	*to play the role of*
hacer la vida imposible	*to make someone's life impossible*
hacer preguntas	*to ask, pose questions*
hacer un favor	*to do someone a favor*
hacer un recado	*to run an errand*
hacer(se) daño	*to harm; to hurt oneself*
hacerse + *noun*	*to become*
hacerse pedazos	*to break into pieces*
Juan **hace de** payaso en la fiesta de los niños.	*Juan **plays the role of** a clown at the children's party.*
Siempre **hace favores** a sus amigos.	*He always **does** his friends **favors**.*
Ayer, me **hizo un recado**.	*Yesterday he **ran an errand for me**.*
Marcos me **hace la vida imposible** con sus preguntas.	*Marcos **makes my life impossible** with his questions.*
Marcos quiere **hacerse abogado** pero no está seguro.	*Marcos wants **to become a lawyer** but he is not sure.*
Esta mañana dejé caer el jarrón y **se hizo pedazos**.	*This morning I dropped the vase and **it broke into pieces**.*

A number of expressions that refer to weather conditions use the verbs **haber** (**hay**) and **hacer** (**hace**). Remember to use the third-person singular of the verb tense to describe or talk about the weather:

hacer buen / hacer mal tiempo	*to be good / bad weather*
hacer calor / frío	*to be hot / cold*
hacer fresco	*to be cool*
hacer sol	*to be sunny*
hacer viento	*to be windy*
Pasó la tormenta tropical y **hace calor**.	*The tropical storm passed and **it is hot**.*
Hizo mal tiempo toda la semana pasada.	*All last week **the weather was bad**.*

haber luna	*the moon is out / is shining*
haber niebla	*to be foggy*
haber nubes	*to be cloudy*
haber sol	*to be sunny*
Esta noche **no hay luna** porque **hay muchas nubes**.	*Tonight **there is no moon** because **it is very cloudy**.*
Habrá sol esta tarde. Lleva los lentes de sol.	***It will be sunny** this afternoon. Take your sunglasses.*

EJERCICIO
13·4

Usa la lógica. *Contribuye a aclarar las siguientes preguntas. Usa una expresión verbal para contestar cada pregunta y escribe el verbo en el presente de indicativo.*

hacer favores / hacer el papel de / hacer caso / hacer daño / hacer preguntas / hacer la vida imposible

1. ¿Carlos es actor?

Claro, _____ un loco.

2. ¿Cómo sabes que es curioso?

   Porque siempre _____.

3. ¿Es amable?

   Sí, a menudo _____ a sus amigos.

4. Entonces, ¿es muy buena persona?

   Por supuesto, jamás _____ a nadie.

5. ¿Es un buen paciente?

   Efectivamente, _____ de los consejos de su médico.

6. Y, ¿también es paciente?

   Sin duda, pues soporta a su suegra, quien le _____.

Verbal expressions with **perder**

echar a perder	*to spoil, to ruin*
perder cuidado	*not to worry*
perder el autobús, el tren, etc.	*to miss the bus, the train, etc.*
perder la calma	*to lose patience*
perder la razón	*to lose one's mind*
perder de vista	*to lose sight of*
perder el turno	*to miss one's turn*

Verbal expressions with **poner**

poner(se) de acuerdo	*to agree, to come to an agreement*
poner en duda	*to doubt, to cast a doubt*
poner los puntos sobre las íes	*to cross your t's and dot your i's*
ponerle los pelos de punta	*to make your hair stand on end*

EJERCICIO
13·5

Una persona muy especial. *Usa la frase apropiada de la columna **B** para añadir énfasis a las oraciones de la columna **A**. Después, escribe las oraciones completas. ¡Cuidado! Algunas oraciones pueden ser negativas.*

MODELO   es muy tranquilo y tiene paciencia   (no) perder la calma

   Es muy tranquilo y tiene paciencia, no pierde la calma.

A

1. _____ habla con mucha claridad

2. _____ no gasta mucho dinero

B

a. (no) salirse con la suya

b. (no) perder el tren

3. _____ es convincente
4. _____ no es puntual, no llega a tiempo
5. _____ cuida sus intereses
6. _____ no discute ni pelea con sus hermanos
7. _____ acepta las explicaciones de sus amigos

c. (no) poner los puntos sobre las íes
d. (no) poner nada en duda
e. (no) ponerse de acuerdo
f. (no) perder nada de vista
g. (no) tirar la casa por la ventana

1. _____
2. _____
3. _____
4. _____
5. _____
6. _____
7. _____

Verbal expressions with tener

The English verb *to be* translates many of the verbal expressions with **tener**:

tener ansias	*to be anxious*
tener calor	*to be hot, warm*
tener celos	*to be jealous*
tener cuidado	*to be careful*
tener envidia	*to be envious*
tener éxito	*to be successful*
tener frío	*to be cold*
tener hambre	*to be hungry*
tener la culpa	*to be guilty*
tener mala suerte	*to be unlucky*
tener miedo	*to be afraid*
tener nervios	*to be nervous*
tener paciencia	*to be patient*
tener prisa	*to be in a hurry*
tener razón	*to be right*
tener sueño	*to be sleepy*
tener suerte	*to be lucky*

Other verbal expressions with **tener**:

tener escalofríos	*to have the chills*
tener dolor de cabeza	*to have a headache*
tener ganas de	*to feel like*
tener lugar	*to take place*
tener que ver (con)	*to have to do with*

*Estudia la lista de las frases con el verbo **tener**. Después, escribe la frase que completa la oración de una manera lógica. Debes usar la forma apropiada del verbo de acuerdo al sujeto.*

1. Duerme cuando _____.

2. Corro cuando _____.

3. Están felices si _____.

4. Se puso la chaqueta porque _____.

5. Tomó dos aspirinas porque _____.

6. No se van a la cama aunque _____ de dormir.

7. No nos gusta esperar, no _____.

8. Nunca gano un premio; _____.

9. Margo está equivocada porque _____.

10. Debes pedir perdón porque _____.

Refranes

A saying, **un refrán** in Spanish, states a commonsense observation and applies to certain situations. Like most idiomatic expressions, these phrases are not always easily translated. For example, an adolescent insists on keeping the wrong company. His/her parents are concerned about the consequences of associating with individuals with a bad reputation, and the worried parents give their child a warning:

> Dime con quién andas, y te diré quién eres.   *You are judged by the company you keep.*

The message can be interpreted as: *Tell me who your friends are, and I will tell you who you are.* Another example conveys a similar message about keeping bad company. Literally, it says: *God creates them, and they find a way to get together:*

> Dios los cría y ellos se juntan.   *Birds of a feather flock together.*

There are many such sayings, proverbs, and sentences in other languages. They vary depending on the region or country where they are popular; some are centuries old. As a cultural note, it is said that there are more than 100,000 **refranes** in Spanish.

The following is a list of commonly used sayings or **refranes** organized by themes or situations where they are used. Some belong to more than one category. Note the equivalents in idiomatic English; only rarely does the English vocabulary "match" the vocabulary in the Spanish saying.

Facing adversity

A mal tiempo, buena cara.   *When life gives you lemons, make lemonade.*
Borrón y cuenta nueva.   *Let bygones be bygones.*

Cuando una puerta se cierra, cien se abren.	*When one door closes, another always opens.*
El amor todo lo puede.	*Love will conquer all.*
El tiempo lo cura todo.	*Time heals all wounds.*
La risa es el mejor remedio.	*Laughter is the best medicine.*
Más vale tarde que nunca.	*Better late than never.*
No hay mal que por bien no venga ni cuerpo que lo resista.	*Nothing lasts forever.*
Nunca es tarde si la dicha es buena.	*Better late than never.*
Ojos que no ven, corazón que no siente.	*Long absent, soon forgotten. / Out of sight, out of mind.*
Peor es nada.	*Half a loaf is better than none.*
Persevera y triunfarás.	*If at first you don't succeed, try, try again.*
Quien espera, desespera.	*Hope deferred makes the heart sick.*
Siempre llueve sobre mojado.	*When it rains, it pours.*

Character and deception

Cría fama y acuéstate a dormir.	*You can rest on your laurels. / Give a dog a bad name and hang it.*
De noche, todos los gatos son pardos.	*All cats are gray in the dark.*
Hierba mala nunca muere.	*The devil looks after himself.*
No es oro todo lo que reluce.	*All that glitters is not gold.*
Poderoso caballero es Don Dinero.	*Money talks.*
Quien mal anda, mal acaba.	*If you live like that, you're bound to come to a bad end.*
Quien roba una vez roba diez.	*Once a thief, always a thief.*
Tanto tienes, tanto vales; nada tienes, nada vales.	*You are what you own.*

Friendship

Amigo en la adversidad es un amigo de verdad.	*A friend in need is a friend indeed.*
Dime con quién andas, y te diré quién eres.	*You are judged by the company you keep.*

Life situations

A la ocasión la pintan calva.	*Strike while the iron is hot.*
Tanto monta, monta tanto.	*It makes no difference.*

Mistakes/consequences

Al que no quiera caldo, dos tazas.	*It never rains, but it pours.*
El hombre propone y Dios dispone.	*Man proposes and God disposes.*
El que la hace, la paga.	*You've made your bed, now you must lie in it.*
El que no trabaje, que no coma.	*No bees, no honey; no work, no money.*
Lo pasado, pasado está.	*Let bygones be bygones.*

Popular wisdom

El mundo es un pañuelo.	*It's a small world.*
El saber no ocupa lugar.	*One can never know too much.*
Hecha la ley, hecha la trampa.	*Every law has its loophole.*
Ladrón que roba a ladrón tiene cien años de perdón.	*It's no crime to steal from a thief.*

Más sabe el diablo por viejo que por diablo.	*There's no substitute for experience.*
No solo de pan vive el hombre.	*Man cannot live by bread alone.*
Sobre gustos, no hay nada escrito.	*Different strokes for different folks.*

EJERCICIO
13·7

Situaciones y refranes. *Revisa la lista de refranes; después, escribe un refrán que se pueda usar en cada una de las situaciones siguientes.*

1. Un estudiante se queja porque tiene que estudiar mucho.

_____

2. Vas a una entrevista pero no te ofrecen el trabajo.

_____

3. Un buen amigo está enfermo pero no lo sabes.

_____

4. Compraste un billete de lotería pero sólo ganaste $5.

_____

5. Un amigo te debe $500 desde hace tres años y ¡por fin te devuelve tu dinero!

_____

6. Descubres con alegría que un amigo ha pagado una deuda que tenía.

_____

7. Un colega y tú han tenido problemas pero decides olvidar el pasado.

_____

8. Un senador va a la cárcel porque ha usado fondos públicos para ayudar a un criminal.

_____

Colloquial phrases

Most idiomatic expressions are used in colloquial exchanges: dialogues, informal conversations, or situations. However, colloquial phrases may be used in more formal writing to state an idea clearly, and to the point, that can be understood by everyone involved. For example, a political leader may use a phrase to state his/her position in difficult times: **En tiempo de tribulaciones no hacer mudanzas.** This expression says it is not wise to make hasty decisions during hard times. Other expressions are purely colloquial in nature:

Estás hasta en la sopa.	*There is no getting away from you.*
Te llegó la hora.	*Your time is up.*

Some phrases fall out of fashion and become outdated. It is not easy to keep up with usage. Note the possible English translations for the following example. The second one is more current:

Cada oveja con su pareja.   *Every Jack has his Jill. / Everyone has his soul mate.*

Some phrases are hard to understand if they are part of the jargon or slang of a particular group or consist of a combination of nonstandard vocabulary elements. Remember that the Spanish-speaking world is very large. As a learner, it's best to avoid certain expressions, especially if they convey offensive connotations that might be interpreted as demeaning. A given word or a phrase may be inappropriate in some areas while being completely acceptable in others.

One could create infinitely long lists of colloquial phrases. The following are commonly used. They are listed by groups for easier learning:

Animals

estar loco como una cabra	*to be mad as a hatter*
hacer patas de mosca	*to write like chicken scratching*
no oírse ni una mosca	*to hear a pin drop*
ponérsele a alguien la carne / la piel de gallina	*to get goose bumps*
ser un lince	*to be very very smart*
ser un/a gallina	*to be chicken, a coward*
ser un/a zorra	*to be (like) a fox*
No escribes claro, **haces patas de mosca**.	*You do not write clearly, **it's like chicken scratching**.*
Cuando el juez iba a leer el veredicto no **se oía una mosca**.	*When the judge was going to read the verdict, **you could hear a pin drop**.*
Cantó tan bien que **se me puso la carne de gallina**.	*She sang so well that **it gave me goose bumps**.*

Color

blanco como un papel	*as white as a sheet, as white as a ghost*
como de lo blanco a lo negro	*as different as day and night*
por si las moscas	*just in case*
un chiste verde	*a dirty joke*
un mosca muerta	*a hypocrite*
un viejo verde	*a dirty old man*
Tiene malos atributos: **es un viejo verde y un mosca muerta.**	*He has bad traits: **he is a dirty old man and a hypocrite**.*
Por si las moscas, no lo voy a invitar a la cena.	***Just in case**, I am not inviting him to dinner.*
Oyó la noticia y **se quedó blanco como un papel**.	*She heard the news and **she turned white as a ghost**.*

Food

con su pan se lo coma	*it's his/her own tough luck*
estar hasta en la sopa	*there is no getting away from*
estar más fresco/a que una lechuga	*to be cool as a cucumber*
importar un pepino	*not to care*

importarle a alguien un rábano / un pepino	*he/she could not care less*
ser pan comido	*to be easy as pie / a piece of cake*
Se han equivocado y **con su pan se lo coman.**	*They made a mistake and **it is their own tough luck.***
Vas a tomar el examen y te ves **más fresco que una lechuga.**	*You are going to take the exam, and you look **as cool as a cucumber.***
Me importa un pepino lo que digan de mí.	***I could not care less** about what they say about me.*
¡Ah!, este ejercicio es fácil: **es pan comido.**	*This exercise is easy: **a piece of cake.***

Numbers

bajo siete llaves	*under lock and key*
como que dos y dos son cuatro	*as certain as eggs is eggs*
seguir en sus trece	*to stick to one's guns*
igual Pascual	*even Steven*
Guardo mis secretos **bajo siete llaves.**	*I keep my secrets **under lock and key.***
Mi hermano es muy terco; **sigue en sus trece.**	*My brother is very stubborn; **he is sticking to his guns.***

Parts of the body

desternillarse de la risa	*to be in stitches*
estar para chuparse los dedos	*to be finger-licking good*
la niña de sus ojos	*the apple of his/her eye*
meter la pata	*to put one's foot in one's mouth*
patas arriba	*upside down*
poner los ojos en blanco	*to roll one's eyes*
Este plato está para **chuparse los dedos.**	*This dish is **finger-licking good.***
Su hija es **la niña de sus ojos.**	*His daughter is **the apple of his eye.***
Eres muy desordenado y tienes todo **patas arriba.**	*You are disorganized, and everything is **upside down.***

Various topics

chitón	*mum's the word*
de eso nada	*my eye*
en resumidas cuentas	*in a nutshell*
eso es otro capítulo	*that is another story*
estar en un lío	*to be in a jam*
ir como alma que lleva el diablo	*to run like hell*
llegarle la hora a alguien	*your number is up*
no pintar nada	*to be out of place*
no venir al caso	*to be beside / to miss the point*
ser un ladrillo	*to be extremely boring*
tener la sartén por el mango	*to have the upper hand, to run the show*
Ahora, no hablemos: **chitón.**	*Now, let' not talk: **mum's the word.***
No hablemos de mis problemas. **Eso es otro capítulo.**	*Let's not talk about my problems. **That is another story.***
Tu crítica y tus comentarios **no vienen al caso.**	*Your criticism and your comments **are beside the point.***
Este libro es **un ladrillo.**	*This book is **extremely boring.***

EJERCICIO
13·8

Estudia la lista de frases coloquiales; después, usa una de las frases para completar las oraciones con un sentido lógico. Debes conjugar los verbos en el tiempo y la persona apropiada.

1. Puedes confiar en mí, guardo mis secretos _____.

2. Dices cosas que no tienen sentido, ¡estás _____!

3. ¿Tienes miedo? Estás _____.

4. ¡Es verdad! ¡_____!

5. Es muy cómico, voy a _____.

6. No hagas lo que no debes hacer porque _____.

7. No hagas comentarios inapropiados, que _____.

8. Pues ahora es tu turno, _____.

EJERCICIO
13·9

Te toca a ti. *Para cada situación, escribe un refrán o una frase coloquial que sea apropiada.*

1. Haces un trabajo difícil y te sientes orgulloso/a.

_____

2. Quieres ser amigo/a de un/a chico/a pero sabes que tiene mala reputación.

_____

3. Has encontrado a la pareja perfecta para ti.

_____

4. Haces un comentario inapropiado, fuera de lugar.

_____

5. Has esperado mucho tiempo, pero has recibido la respuesta que esperabas.

_____

6. Sales de casa de prisa, no haces la cama, no lavas los platos.

_____

7. Preparas una cena y tus amigos dicen que todo está delicioso.

_____

8. Conociste al hermano de un amigo pero su conversación es aburridísima.

_____

Comparisons, contrasts, and antonyms

Comparisons and contrasts are part of everyday communication. We use adjectives and adverbs to compare items at the grocery store or to rate the performance of sports teams and at other competitions. In previous units you studied *adjectives* and *adverbs*. In this unit you will apply your knowledge to compare and/or contrast ideas with adjectives and adverbs that express degrees of quality, quantity, or relationship:

Las peras están **más baratas** que las manzanas.	*Pears are **cheaper** than apples.*
La **mejor** película no ganó el Oscar.	*The **best** movie did not win the Oscar.*

Comparisons and contrasts

The *comparison* establishes similarities: you may compare an object, an idea, or a person to another, to describe what they have in common.

comparison → similarities

Esta casa es **cómoda y grande**.	*This house is **comfortable and big**.*
Esta otra casa **también** es **placentera y espaciosa**.	*This other house is **also pleasant and spacious**.*

You may need to compare two or more people, ideas, items, etc., to establish similarities and dissimilarities. This may take the form of a school assignment, a report evaluating a product, your opinions about ideas stated in a letter, etc.

Esta consola de DVD es **mejor** que aquella.	*This DVD player is **better** than that one.*
Al compararlo, el precio de este aparato es **más bajo**.	*By comparison, the price of this appliance is **lower**.*
Las sandalias son **más cómodas** que los zapatos.	*Sandals are **more comfortable** than shoes.*

Establishing comparisons may require qualifying or descriptive adjectives, since they show levels or degrees of quantity, quality, or relationship:

¿Nadar es **tan emocionante como** escalar una montaña?	*Is swimming **as exciting as** climbing a mountain?*

A *contrast* usually highlights the differences between two people, objects, or ideas:

contrast → differences

Lucía ha cumplido cuarenta años y tiene canas.	*Lucía is forty years old and has white hair.*
En cambio, Alba tiene cincuenta y dos y se ve muy joven.	*By contrast, Alba is fifty-two and looks very young.*

De compras. *¿Semejanzas o diferencias? Indica **S** si es una semejanza, **D** si es una diferencia.*

1. _____ Este producto es caro. Este otro es barato.

2. _____ Las botas son cómodas. Y los zapatos también.

3. _____ Dos maneras de ahorrar son las rebajas y usar los cupones de descuento.

4. _____ Mi salario es muy bajo. Tú ganas más dinero.

5. _____ El porcentaje de las ganancias subió. Las ventas, también.

Adjectives and comparisons

Adjectives can express degrees of modification that indicate different levels of quality, quantity, or relationship. You may know them as *positive*, *comparative*, and *superlative adjectives*. Note that the positive degree does not show a degree of quality, but the comparative and the superlative do.

El diseño de la ropa italiana es **popular**.	*Italian clothing design is **popular**.*
La calidad de estas telas parece **excelente**.	*The quality of these materials seems **excellent**.*

Remember that adjectives must agree with nouns in gender and number.

Comparative adjective forms and word order

The comparative and superlative forms require a standard word order both in English and Spanish. Comparative adjectives highlight the *same* degree, a *lesser* degree, or a *greater* degree of intensity in the quality of an adjective. Consider the following examples of word order in Spanish sentences and the type of comparisons they establish:

tan + adjective + como = *as + adjective + as* → **comparison with equal degree of intensity**

Los diseñadores italianos son **tan creativos como** los diseñadores franceses.	*Italian designers are **as creative as** French designers.*
La salsa es **tan popular como** el merengue.	*Salsa is **as popular as** the merengue.*

más + adjective + que = *(more) + adjective (-er, -ier) + than* → **comparison with a greater degree of intensity**

La seda es **más cara que** el algodón.	*Silk is **more expensive than** cotton.*
La seda es **más suave que** la lana.	*Silk is **softer than** wool.*

Los niños se ven **más cansados que** sus
padres.

*The children seem **more tired than** their
parents.*

The English *-er* and *-ier* comparative endings are added to most English adjectives, usually
those with two syllables; otherwise the word *more* establishes the comparison:

menos + adjective + **que** = *(less)* + adjective *(-er, -ier)* + *than* → **comparison**
with a lesser degree of intensity

Las comidas mexicanas no son **menos**
populares **que** las españolas.

*Mexican dishes are not **less** popular **than**
Spanish dishes.*

EJERCICIO
14·2

La pasión por la tecnología. *Expresa tu opinión. Usa los comparativos **tan... como,
más... que** o **menos... que** y la forma apropiada del adjetivo entre paréntesis.*

MODELO   las películas extranjeras tienen escenas (violento) / americano

   *Las películas extranjeras tienen escenas menos violentas que las
   americanas.*

1. los autos japoneses son (elegante) / alemanes

_____

2. las pantallas de alta definición ofrecen imágenes (claro) / las pantallas de plasma

_____

3. una cámara digital toma fotos (preciso) / teléfono celular

_____

4. una casa ecológica puede ser (eficiente) / casa tradicional

_____

5. los videojuegos crean una dependencia (peligroso [*harmful*]) / cigarrillo

_____

6. un ordenador portátil (*laptop*) es (pesado) / bolsa de mano

_____

7. los equipos de sonido deben ser (potente) / computadora

_____

8. los mensajes electrónicos producen efectos (favorable) / carta por correo aéreo

_____

Superlative adjective forms and word order

The superlative adjective forms show degrees of quality within a group or class. Note that in both English and Spanish the definite article precedes the noun. Remember that in Spanish the article, noun, and adjective must agree in gender and number. Consider the following two degrees of superlative adjectives:

el/la/los/las + noun + **más** + adjective + **de** = *the* + adjective (*-est, -iest*) + noun + *of* → highest degree of intensity in a group

Era **el** jugador **más alto de** las Olimpiadas de 2008.	*He was **the tallest** player **of** the 2008 Olympic team.*
Son las playas **más románticas del** Caribe.	*They are the **most romantic** beaches **in the** Caribbean.*

el/la/los/las + **menos** + adjective + **de** = *the* + *least* + adjective + *of* → least degree of intensity in a group

Mis hermanos son **los menos divertidos de** los primos.	*My brothers are **the least amusing of** the cousins.*
Estos son **los** exámenes **menos difíciles**.	*These are **the least difficult** exams.*
Tomaste **la** decisión **menos favorable**.	*You made **the least favorable** decision.*

el/la/los/las + **más** + adjective = adjective (*-est, -iest*) → superlative

Definitivamente, Juan es **el más inteligente**.	*Juan is definitely **the smartest**.*
Y su novia es **la más dulce y bonita**.	*And his girlfriend is **the sweetest and prettiest**.*

In English, the *-est* or *-iest* endings appear in most superlative forms. The word *most* is also used to convey the superlative degree.

EJERCICIO
14·3

Los superlativos. *Usa la forma apropiada del presente del verbo* **ser** *y el adjetivo superlativo para escribir oraciones.*

MODELO   las ballenas / mamífero / grande / del planeta

Las ballenas son los mamíferos más grandes del planeta.

1. China / país / poblado / del mundo

   _____

2. Nueva York / ciudad / atractiva / de los EE.UU

   _____

3. los perros / animal / fiel / al hombre

   _____

4. los zafiros / piedra / caro / de la colección

   _____

5. el fútbol / deporte / popular / entre los jóvenes ecuatorianos

   _____

6. San Agustín / población / antigua / de la Florida

_____

7. las carreras de caballos / evento / popular / de la temporada

_____

8. el flamenco / música / española / conocida / del mundo

_____

Compara y contrasta. *Lee la información y escribe la conclusión. Usa la forma del verbo **ser** en el presente.*

MODELO   Juan tiene cuarenta y dos años / Pedro tiene sesenta / Raúl tiene veinticinco (joven)
          Pedro es el menos joven y Raúl es el más joven de los tres.

1. el paquete azul pesa 170 libras / el rojo 184 / el verde 155 (pesado)

_____

2. Alicia mide seis pies / Berta cinco pies y seis pulgadas / Rosalba cinco pies y tres pulgadas (alto) de

_____

3. el bolso de cuero vale $350 / el de tela $45 / el de piel de cocodrilo $550 (caro)

_____

4. Santo Domingo fue fundada en 1496 / San Agustín en 1563 / Nueva York en 1519 (antiguo)

_____

5. la carta tiene dos páginas / el artículo cinco / el correo electrónico tres (largo)

_____

6. mi bañador es talla seis / el de Lidia cuatro / el de Marta doce (grande)

_____

The absolute superlative

In an absolute superlative, *no comparison* is involved.

muy + adjective = *very* + adjective → absolute superlative

Sus abuelos son **muy viejos**.   *Her grandparents are **very old**.*
Y su familia es **muy respetada** en la   *And her family is **very respected** in this*
comunidad.   *community.*

In Spanish, the superlative (**-ísimo/a/os/as**) endings may be added to adjectives, after the final **-o** or **-a** is dropped. Note the accent mark on the **-ísimo** endings:

Pescaron un tiburón **grandísimo**.   *They caught a **very large** shark.*
Fue una aventura **interesantísima**.   *It was a **very interesting** adventure.*

Note the following spelling changes that apply when the adjectives have the following endings:

-co → -quísimo   poco (*little*) → poquísimo/a/os/as
-go → -guísimo   largo (*long*) → larguísimo/a/os/as
-oz → -císimo   veloz (*quick*) → velocísimo/a/os/as

EJERCICIO
14·5

Comentarios. *Usa las dos formas de los superlativos para escribir tus oraciones.*

MODELO   Roma es una cuidad con mucho tráfico. (congestionado)

     Roma es una ciudad muy congestionada. Es congestionadísima.

1. La novela *La casa verde* tiene más de 400 páginas. (largo)

_____

2. El tren de alta velocidad viaja a más de 300 km por hora. (veloz)

_____

3. El tango gana en popularidad de toda la América hispana. (popular)

_____

4. Margarita levanta pesas de 150 libras. (fuerte)

_____

5. Las pinturas del museo del Prado tienen un valor incalculable. (valioso)

_____

6. Los romanos crearon obras arquitectónicas. (importante)

_____

7. Los bienes raíces en Nueva York valen mucho. (costoso)

_____

8. Los tesoros en el fondo del mar Caribe son numerosos. (rico)

_____

En español. *Usa las dos formas del superlativo.*

MODELO   Marcos's brother is very well known.

        El hermano de Marcos es muy conocido / conocidísimo.

1. Marcos's family is very rich.

_____

2. They are very generous with their community.

_____

3. They used to have a very large mansion.

_____

4. Marcos's father sold the mansion for a very high amount.

_____

5. The family gave a very generous amount to charity (**obras de caridad**).

_____

6. Marcos donated a very valuable collection of coins.

_____

Irregular comparative and superlative forms

The comparative and superlative forms of the following adjectives are irregular:

bueno/ a/os/as	*good*	mejor(es)	*better*	el/la/los/ las mejor(es)	*the best*
malo/a/os/as	*bad*	peor(es)	*worse*	el/la/los/ las peor(es)	*the worst*
grande(s)	*big*	mayor(es)	*older*	el/la/los/ las mayor(es)	*the oldest*
		más grande	*larger*	el/la/los/ las más grande(s)	*the largest*
		menos grande	*less large*	el/la/los/ las menos grande(e)	*the least large*
pequeño/ a/os/as	*small*	menor(es)	*younger*	el/la/los/ las menor(es)	*the youngest*
		más pequeño/ a/os/as	*smaller*	el/la/los/las más pequeño/a/os/as	*the smallest*
		menos pequeño/ a/os/as	*less small*	el/la/los/las menos pequeño/a/os/as	*the least small*

Note that the irregular comparative forms precede the noun in the following phrases:

la mejor obra de Cervantes   *Cervantes's **best work***
la mayor contribución de los argentinos   *the **greatest contribution** of the Argentineans*
un asunto de **menor importancia**   *a matter of **lesser importance***

However, note that when **mayor** and **menor** refer to the age of an individual, they *follow* the noun:

la hermana menor de Julio   *Julio's **younger sister***
el hermano mayor de María   *María's **older brother***

EJERCICIO
14·7

En español: en las competencias. *Cuidado con las formas irregulares.*

1. The American athletes are younger than the Mexican athletes.

   _____

2. Julián's brother is the youngest winner.

   _____

3. The American team's best gymnast did not win a medal.

   _____

4. This is a larger group of fans (**fanáticos**).

   _____

5. The crowd said this tennis match was worse than yesterday's.

   _____

6. Canada's largest stadium will be ready for the competitions.

   _____

Adverbs and comparisons

Adverbs also have degrees of comparison. There are three comparative forms. In the examples that follow, you will find an adjective that functions as an adverb, or an adverb formed with the **-mente** (*-ly*) suffix:

◆ Positive: **lento, lentamente**:

     El equipo trabaja **lento**.   *The team works **slowly**.*

◆ Comparative: **más**, **menos rápido**, **rápidamente** + **que** = *more, less quickly + than*:

     Los botes navegan **más rápido que** en el otro río.   *Boats sail **more quickly than** in the other river.*
     Hablé **menos rápidamente que** otras veces.   *I spoke **less quickly than** on other occasions.*

- Superlative: **más, menos apasionadamente**:

Raúl defiende sus ideas **más apasionadamente**.	*Raúl defends his ideas **more passionately**.*
Marta las defiende **menos apasionadamente**.	*Marta defends them **less passionately**.*

- Absolute superlative: **lo** + **menos lentamente** + **posible**; **lo** + **más lentamente** + **posible**.

  The *adverbial superlative* formed with the neuter article **lo** is usually followed by a phrase expressing possibility:

Nos iremos **lo más rápidamente posible**.	*We will leave **the fastest we can / as fast as possible**.*

**EJERCICIO
14·8**

Te toca a ti. *Para tu respuesta, usa* **lo más** *o* **lo menos** + *el adverbio con la terminación* **-mente**. *Observa el modelo.*

MODELO   ¿Cómo te vistes? (elegante) poder

Lo más elegantemente que puedo.

or _Lo menos elegantemente que puedo._

1. ¿Cómo conduces? (cuidadoso) poder

_____

2. ¿Cómo trabajas? (rápido) saber

_____

3. ¿Cómo cocinas tú? (sano) poder

_____

4. ¿Cuándo duermes? (frecuente) ser posible

_____

5. ¿Cómo escribes? (claro) saber

_____

6. ¿Cómo comes? (lento) poder

_____

7. ¿Cómo saludas? (cortés) saber

_____

8. ¿Cómo nadas? (rápido) saber

_____

Antonyms and contrasts

You may also compare concepts and ideas using nouns, verbs, and expressions that denote *opposite* meanings. *Antonyms* are words of opposite meaning. They can be used to contrast ideas, people, and things. Transition words and phrases can also convey contrasts.

El mandatario dice **una mentira** y oculta **la verdad**.

*The statesman tells **a lie** and hides **the truth**.*

Al amanecer despierta y **al anochecer**, ya duerme.

*At **daybreak**, he wakes up and at **sundown**, he is already sleeping.*

La novela narra una anécdota ficticia. **En cambio**, la biografía incluye datos fidedignos.

*The novel narrates a fictitious anecdote. **On the other hand**, the biography includes reliable data.*

Adjectives, antonyms, and contrasts

Adjective opposites can be used to contrast ideas.

Opposite adjectives

Adjectives may be grouped according to positive and negative qualities. The following is a list of frequently used adjectival antonyms. They may describe physical appearance, size, personality, and other qualities.

aburrido/a / divertido/a	*boring / exciting, amusing*
activo/a / pasivo/a	*active / passive*
alegre / triste	*happy / miserable, sad*
ambicioso/a / generoso/a	*greedy / generous*
arrogante / humilde	*arrogant / humble*
arrugado/a / estirado/a	*wrinkled / smooth*
bajo/a / alto/a	*short / tall*
bello/a / feo/a	*beautiful / ugly*
cariñoso/a / frío/a	*affectionate / cold*
caro/a / barato/a	*expensive / inexpensive*
cobarde / valiente	*cowardly / brave*
cruel / compasivo/a	*cruel / compassionate*
delgado/a / grueso/a, gordo/a	*slim, thin / fat*
delicado/a / resistente, fuerte	*delicate / strong*
diminuto/a / enorme	*minuscule / enormous*
egoísta / solidario/a	*selfish, self-centered / altruistic*
fácil / difícil	*easy / hard, difficult*
famoso/a / desconocido/a	*famous / unknown*
generoso/a / tacaño/a	*generous / tightfisted, stingy*
grande / pequeño/a	*big, large / small*
guapo/a / feo/a	*handsome, good-looking / ugly, unattractive*
hábil / incompetente	*skillful / incompetent*
hablador(a) / callado/a	*talkative / quiet*
idealista / realista	*idealist / realist*
inteligente / ignorante	*intelligent / stupid*
lento/a / rápido/a	*slow / fast*
listo/a / tonto/a	*smart / foolish*
mentiroso/a / sincero/a	*lying, cheating / sincere*
nuevo/a / viejo/a	*new / old*
optimista / pesimista	*optimist / pessimist*

orgulloso/a / modesto/a	*proud, arrogant / modest*
oscuro/a / claro/a	*dark / clear, light*
perezoso/a / industrioso/a	*lazy / energetic, hardworking, productive*
pobre / rico/a	*poor / rich*
popular / impopular	*popular / unpopular*
puntual / informal	*punctual / unreliable*
rebelde / sumiso/a	*rebellious / submissive*
serio/a / frívolo/a	*serious / frivolous*
simpático/a / huraño/a, antipático/a	*friendly / unfriendly*
simple / complicado/a	*simple / complicated*
solitario/a / sociable, gregario/a	*solitary, lonely / gregarious, sociable*
suave / áspero/a, duro/a	*soft / hard, harsh, rough*
superficial / profundo/a	*superficial / deep*
tímido/a / atrevido/a	*shy, timid / daring, bold*
trabajador(a) / holgazán(a), perezoso/a	*hardworking / lazy*
Las personas **trabajadoras** contribuirán, pero las **perezosas**, no.	***Hardworking** individuals will contribute, but the **lazy** ones will not.*
Los colores **claros** son **agradables**; los colores **oscuros** son **desagradables**.	***Light** colors are **pleasant**; **dark** colors are **unpleasant**.*
La seda es **suave**; la lana es **áspera**.	*Silk is **delicate**; wool is **rough**.*

EJERCICIO
14·9

Los opuestos. *Escribe un antónimo para completar cada oración.*

1. Este no es un asunto simple sino (*but*) _____.

2. El cliente quiere un traje claro, no _____.

3. Pero el empleado trabaja lento, no _____.

4. No es realmente cariñoso, más bien _____.

5. Es un poco tonto, no es realmente _____.

6. No es grueso, no; él es un hombre _____.

7. La tela del traje no es suave, es muy _____.

8. El cliente quiere una colonia suave, no _____.

Prefixes, antonyms, and contrasts

The opposite form of an adjective can often be formed with a prefix. Many English and Spanish adjectives are cognates (words of similar origin and spelling), but they may use a different prefix to convey the opposite:

considerado/a / desconsiderado/a	*considerate / inconsiderate*

des-

afortunado/a / desafortunado/a	*fortunate / unfortunate*
agradable / desagradable	*pleasant / unpleasant*

considerado/a / desconsiderado/a	*considerate / inconsiderate*
cortés / descortés	*courteous / rude, discourteous*
honesto/a / deshonesto/a	*honest / dishonest*
organizado/a / desorganizado/a	*organized / disorganized*
Los niños **corteses** tienen buenos modales.	***Courteous** children have good manners.*
En cambio, **los descorteses** dejan mala impresión.	*On the other hand, **the rude ones** leave a bad impression.*

in-, im-

constante / inconstante	*constant, consistent / occasional*
conveniente / inconveniente	*convenient / inconvenient*
culto/a / inculto/a	*educated / uneducated*
disciplinado/a / indisciplinado/a	*disciplined / undisciplined*
fiel / infiel	*loyal / disloyal*
formal / informal	*formal / informal*
justo/a / injusto/a	*just / unjust*
paciente / impaciente	*patient / impatient*
prudente / imprudente	*prudent / imprudent*
seguro/a / inseguro/a	*sure / unsure*
tolerante / intolerante	*tolerant / intolerant*
Si perdonas, eres **tolerante**.	*If you forgive, you are **tolerant**.*
Si no aceptas a los demás, eres **intolerante**.	*If you do not accept others, you are **intolerant**.*

Remember that the form **im-** (not **in-**) precedes the consonants **p** and **b** in Spanish.

ir-

responsable / irresponsable	*responsible / irresponsible*
regular / irregular	*regular / irregular*
reparable / irreparable	*reparable / irreparable*
No sean **irresponsables**, hagan la tarea.	*Do not be **irresponsible**, do your homework.*

ex-

introvertido/a / extrovertido/a	*introverted / extroverted*

In some cases, the adverbs **mal**, **bien**, and **no** may precede adjectives:

educado/a / mal educado/a	*well-mannered / ill-mannered*
alcohólico/a / no alcohólico/a	*alcoholic / non-alcoholic*
bien intencionado/a / mal intencionado/a	*well-intentioned / ill-intentioned*
Las bebidas **no alcohólicas** no dañan el hígado.	***Non-alcoholic** beverages do not harm the liver.*

EJERCICIO 14·10

Definiciones. *¿Sabes cuál es el antónimo? Usa un prefijo para crear el antónimo.*

1. un joven que no es responsable: un joven _____

2. un auto que no se puede reparar: un auto _____

3. una chica que no tiene paciencia: una chica _____

4. una persona que no tiene disciplina: una persona _____

5. una ley que no es justa: una ley _____

6. una sociedad que no es tolerante: una sociedad _____

7. una situación que no es segura: una situación _____

8. una hora que no es conveniente: una hora _____

9. un niño que no es introvertido: un niño _____

10. un conductor que no es prudente: un conductor _____

Nouns and contrasts

Abstract nouns designate ideas and concepts that are not tangible.

Opposite nouns

The majority of contrasting nouns in Spanish are abstract nouns in the feminine singular. Some are masculine singular. Note that Spanish abstract nouns use the definite article (**el/la**), while English abstract nouns do not.

el amor / el odio	*love / hate*
el calor / el frío	*heat / cold*
el optimismo / el pesimismo	*optimism / pessimism*
el valor / la cobardía	*courage / cowardice*
la alegría / la tristeza	*happiness / sadness*
la apertura / la clausura	*opening / closing*
la arrogancia / la humildad	*arrogance / humility*
la belleza / la fealdad	*beauty / ugliness*
la bondad / la maldad	*goodness / evil*
la delicadeza / la rudeza	*delicacy / rudeness, roughness*
la esclavitud / la libertad	*slavery / freedom*
la fortaleza / la debilidad	*strength / weakness*
la inocencia / la malicia	*innocence / malice*
la locura / la cordura	*madness / sanity*
la rapidez / la lentitud	*speed, rapidity / slowness*
la riqueza / la pobreza	*richness, riches / poverty*
la soledad / la compañía	*solitude, loneliness / companionship*
la suavidad / la aspereza	*softness / roughness*
la verdad / la mentira	*the truth / a lie*
la vida / la muerte	*life / death*
la virtud / el vicio	*virtue / vice*

Definite articles and infinitives

The *neuter definite article* **lo**, followed by a masculine singular adjective form, functions as a noun. The English equivalent also uses a definite article (*the*).

lo + masculine singular adjective → noun

lo bueno / lo malo	*the good / the bad*
lo común / lo raro	*the common / the uncommon*

lo nuevo / lo viejo	the new / the old
lo posible / lo imposible	the possible / the impossible
lo positivo / lo negativo	the positive / the negative

A Spanish infinitive may be preceded by the masculine definite article **el**. This construction also functions as a noun. The English equivalent is usually a *gerund* (the *-ing* form), without an article.

el + infinitive → noun

el aterrizar / el despegar	*landing / taking off*
el comprar / el vender	*buying / selling*
el gastar / el ahorrar	*spending / saving*
el mentir / el decir la verdad	*lying / telling the truth*
el recordar / el olvidar	*remembering / forgetting*
El recordar los buenos tiempos me alegra.	***Remembering*** *good times cheers me up.*
El olvidar los malos tiempos es mi meta ahora.	***Forgetting*** *bad times is my goal now.*

Prefixes, antonyms, and contrasts

The negative opposite of a noun can also be formed with a prefix. Note that English and Spanish nouns may use a different prefix:

el empleo / el desempleo	*employment / unemployment*
la certidumbre / la incertidumbre	*certainty / uncertainty*
la esperanza / la desesperanza	*hope / despair*
la sensatez / la insensatez	*sense / lack of sense*
la tolerancia / la intolerancia	*tolerance / intolerance*
El desempleo ha aumentado recientemente.	***Unemployment*** *has risen recently.*

EJERCICIO
14·11

La filosofía de la vida. *Usa las formas apropiadas del verbo principal, los artículos y los adjetivos para crear las oraciones.*

MODELO   la amistad / ser / tesoro / incalculable

    La amistad es un tesoro incalculable.

1. la tolerancia / fortalecer / sociedades / compasivo (*compassionate*)

_____

2. la esperanza / aumentar / confianza / de las personas

_____

3. lo positivo / elevar / espíritu / y / mejorar / actitud / de los individuos

_____

4. el gastar / en exceso / crear / problemas económicos

_____

5. la verdad / triunfar / sobre / mentira siempre

_____

6. la incertidumbre / provocar / ansiedad / entre la población

_____

Verbs and antonyms

Here are several *verb* pairs that can be used to contrast actions and ideas:

abrir / cerrar	*to open / to close*
mentir / decir la verdad	*to lie / to tell the truth*
querer / odiar	*to love / to hate*
saber / ignorar	*to know / to be ignorant of*
subir / bajar	*to go up / to go down*

Prefixes and contrasts

Note the following prefixes used to create verbs of opposite meaning (antonym verbs):

agradar / desagradar	*to like, to please / to dislike, to displease*
conocer / desconocer	*to know / not to know*
pegar / despegar	*to attach / to detach*
preocuparse / despreocuparse	*to worry / to feel at ease*
Nos **agrada** el clima cálido y nos **desagrada** el frío.	*We **like** warm weather and **dislike** cold weather.*

Expressions for comparing and contrasting

There are fixed expressions that help establish comparisons and contrasts. When used effectively, they can strengthen your ability to write clearly.

Comparisons

These transition words and expressions establish similarities:

a la vez	*at the same time*
asimismo	*also*
del mismo modo	*in the same way*
igualmente	*equally*
La cocina mexicana es variada. **Del mismo modo**, la cocina de España es diversa.	*Mexican cuisine is varied. **In the same way**, Spain's cuisine is diverse.*

Contrasts

These transitional expressions point out differences and contrasts:

al contrario	*on the contrary*
de un lado	*on (the) one hand*
pero del otro lado	*on the other hand*
en cambio	*on the other hand*

mientras que	while
por el contrario	on the contrary
por un lado	on the one hand
pero por otro lado	on the other hand

Por un lado, Ada dice que me aprecia, pero **por otro lado**, no me trata bien.

On the one hand, *Ana says she appreciates me;* ***on the other hand***, *she does not treat me well.*

EJERCICIO 14·12

Te toca a ti. *Imagina que eres un(a) reportero/a de un periódico hispano en los EE.UU. Elige un tema y escribe una nota comparando los temas. Usa las frases para comunicar tu mensaje.*

¿Vacaciones en EE.UU. o en otro país? / La música popular o la ópera. / Las películas de horror o las películas cómicas.

Ambos/as _____

_____

Por un lado, _____

_____

Pero por otro lado, _____

_____

Son diferentes porque _____

_____

Igualmente, _____

_____

Por eso _____

_____

The passive voice

Verbs communicate the idea of *being* (*to be*) or *action* (*to start, to do*). Verbs and verb endings indicate time, mood, attitude, and voice. The *voice* of a verb is either *active* or *passive*. In the *active voice*, the subject of the verb is the "doer," who or which performs the action. In the active voice, the relationship between the action and the subject is clear and straightforward:

El cartero ha traído las cartas.	***The mail carrier*** *has delivered the letters.*
Los rosales florecen en la primavera.	***The rosebushes*** *flower in the spring.*

In the *passive voice* (**la voz pasiva**), the subject of the verb is acted upon by an *agent*, and it becomes a *passive subject*. Note the constructions in the following two sentences; the first one is in the *active voice*; the second is in the *passive voice*:

El cartero ha traído las cartas.	***The mail carrier*** *has delivered the letters.*
Las cartas **fueron traídas por el cartero**.	*The letters were delivered **by the mail carrier**.*

The agent of the previous example (**el cartero**) is not the subject of the sentence (**las cartas**). Note that a sentence in the passive voice does not always name the agent. Let's review the elements of the two examples that follow. In the first example below, you can identify the agent, **un arqueólogo**. In the second, the agent is not named.

La estatua **fue descubierta por un arqueólogo**.	*The statue **was discovered by an archeologist**.*
Los restos del cadáver **no han sido encontrados**.	*The remains of the body **have not been found**.*

The passive voice construction is similar in English and Spanish:

passive subject + a form of ser + past participle + por + agent

Las playas + son + afectadas + por + la polución.
The beaches are affected by pollution.

Remember the following:

◆ **Por** + *agent* does not appear in the sentence if the agent is not explicit or disclosed:

El componente secreto **fue descubierto**.   *The secret component **was discovered**.*

◆ In the Spanish passive construction, the past participle form (**-ado**, **-ido**) functions as an adjective and must agree with the passive subject in gender and number.

◆ You may wish to review the irregular past participles of frequently used verbs, such as:

romper	roto	*broken*
abrir	abierto	*opened*
escribir	escrito	*written*
hacer	hecho	*done*
imprimir	impreso	*printed*
morir	muerto	*dead*
volver	vuelto	*returned*
ver	visto	*seen*

EJERCICIO
15·1

Alerta: el último boletín del tiempo. *Cambia las oraciones de la voz activa a la voz pasiva. Recuerda colocar los elementos de la oración pasiva en el lugar apropiado.*

1. El huracán Alina ha afectado las costas de Texas.

_____

2. Los meteorólogos ya han emitido el último boletín del tiempo.

_____

3. A lo largo de la costa, los vientos huracanados han destruido muchos árboles.

_____

4. Los bomberos han asistido a un gran número de miembros de la población.

_____

5. Muchos ciudadanos no observaron las recomendaciones de las autoridades.

_____

6. En el futuro, la policía obligará a los habitantes a tomar medidas.

_____

7. Mañana, grupos de voluntarios iniciarán actividades de ayuda a los necesitados.

_____

8. Para evitar daños, el departamento de policía educará a la población.

_____

Decisiones en la empresa. *Contesta las preguntas. Usa los elementos que aparecen en la línea de la respuesta y la forma apropiada del verbo en la voz pasiva.*

1. ¿Enviaste los sobres por correo?

   No, _____ por la secretaria.

2. ¿Firmaste los contratos?

   No, _____ por el presidente.

3. ¿Fotocopiaste los documentos?

   No, _____ por mi asistente.

4. ¿Anunciaste la próxima reunión?

   No, _____ por el jefe del grupo.

5. ¿Redactaste el memorando?

   No, _____ por el grupo de publicidad.

6. ¿Has firmado la nómina (*payroll*)?

   No, _____ por el contable.

7. ¿Imprimiste la agenda?

   No, _____ por el voluntario.

8. ¿Divulgaste el nombre del futuro presidente de la compañía?

   No, _____ por su equipo de consejeros.

Passive construction with or without an explicit agent

The passive voice construction with **por** + *an explicit agent* emphasizes the agent who does the action:

La congregación fue recibida **por el Papa**.	*The congregation was greeted **by the Pope**.*
La propuesta fue abolida **por el superintendente**.	*The proposal was abolished **by the superintendent**.*

The passive voice without an explicit agent has a different purpose, and its message has a different effect. Read the following short paragraph divided into sentences; focus on the *active* and *passive voice* constructions:

Una comisión **ha iniciado** una investigación.	*A commission **has started** an investigation.*
Varios miembros del Congreso **serán interrogados**.	*Several members of Congress will **be interrogated**.*

| La comisión **fue creada** debido a protestas públicas. | *The commission **was created** due to public protests.* |
| Ya **han sido reveladas** acusaciones anónimas. | *Anonymous accusations **have been revealed**.* |

In the previous paragraph, the first sentence has an active voice verb, **ha iniciado**, with a subject that is a "doer": **una comisión**. The following example sentences are written in the passive construction, without the agent. This is one way the writer may avoid responsibility for or commitment to the information in the paragraph. This construction is typical of business-related statements, government briefings, or simply when the writer does not want to or need to say who is responsible for the actions.

Such passive constructions are often used in journalistic style. In that context, they often appear in the past or future tense. Note that this construction focuses on the person or thing acted upon:

La identidad de la acusada **no fue revelada**.   *The identity of the accused **was not revealed**.*

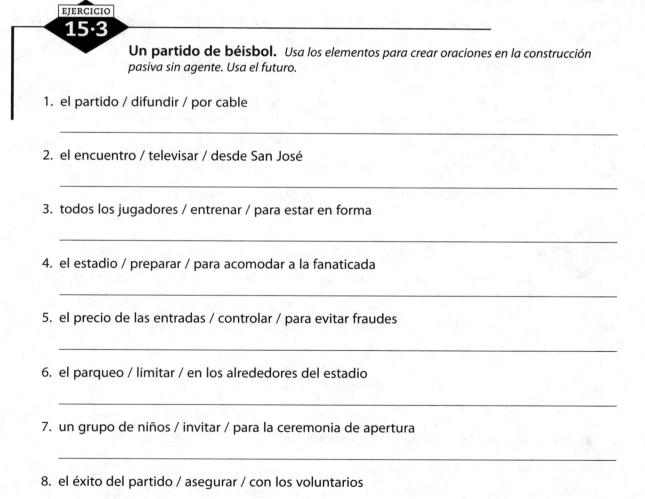

EJERCICIO
15·3

Un partido de béisbol. *Usa los elementos para crear oraciones en la construcción pasiva sin agente. Usa el futuro.*

1. el partido / difundir / por cable

2. el encuentro / televisar / desde San José

3. todos los jugadores / entrenar / para estar en forma

4. el estadio / preparar / para acomodar a la fanaticada

5. el precio de las entradas / controlar / para evitar fraudes

6. el parqueo / limitar / en los alrededores del estadio

7. un grupo de niños / invitar / para la ceremonia de apertura

8. el éxito del partido / asegurar / con los voluntarios

9. el himno nacional / interpretar / al comienzo del evento

_____

10. el encuentro / ver / en todo el país

_____

Other passive constructions

In Spanish, active voice constructions are more frequently used than passive constructions. Spanish also uses additional passive constructions, especially when the doer or agent is not explicit or implied.

The passive reflexive

The _passive reflexive_ is generally used when the subject is a _thing_ and the subject follows the verb. The reflexive pronoun **se** always precedes the verb.

se + verb in third person (singular or plural) + subject

Se + **vendió** + la empresa.	_The company **was sold**._
Se critican las reacciones de la oposición.	_The opposition's reactions **are being criticized**._
Se encontraron los tesoros en dos barcos.	_The treasures **were found** in two ships._
Aquí **se habla** alemán.	_German **is spoken** here._
Se venden autos usados.	_Used cars **are sold** / **for sale**._
Los autos **se venderán** mañana por la tarde.	_The cars **will be sold** tomorrow afternoon._

In this construction the passive subject may either precede or follow the verb.

EJERCICIO
15·4

Un poco de historia. _Construye las oraciones. Cambia la construcción pasiva a la pasiva refleja._

MODELO   La ciudad de Santo Domingo fue fundada en 1496.

La ciudad de Santo Domingo se fundó en 1496.

1. La ciudad de Santo Domingo fue trasladada en 1502.

_____

2. La ciudad fue declarada Patrimonio de la Humanidad.

_____

3. En Santo Domingo fueron creadas las primeras instituciones europeas en América.

_____

4. Durante la Colonia, fueron construidos grandes monumentos.

_____

5. Los monumentos han sido restaurados en época reciente.

_____

6. La restauración ha sido celebrada en el mundo entero.

_____

¿Qué se hace aquí? *Añade una explicación usando la forma pasiva refleja. Usa las palabras sugeridas.*

1. en una tintorería / lavar y planchar / ropa

_____

2. en una librería / vender libros / y tomar un café

_____

3. en un restaurante / cenar / y charlar con los amigos

_____

4. en una universidad / estudiar / y conocer a mucha gente

_____

5. en una tienda / vender artículos / y devolver mercancía

_____

6. en un teatro / escuchar conciertos / y aplaudir a los artistas

_____

7. en una playa / tomar el sol / y nadar

_____

8. en un casino / apostar dinero / y perder fortunas

_____

Te toca a ti. *Escribe tu receta favorita. Usa la forma de la pasiva refleja. Puedes usar los verbos sugeridos en la lista.*

lavar / cortar / preparar / freír / hornear / añadir / servir / acompañar con

Mi receta favorita.

_____

_____

_____

_____

_____

_____

_____

_____

The subjunctive mood

You have studied verb conjugations, verb tenses, and verb moods. A *conjugation* includes the forms and corresponding endings for each person: **yo**, **nosotros**, etc. A *tense* indicates the time frame or period of time of a verb: present, present perfect, imperfect, and others. The word *mood* indicates the *attitude* of the subject of the verb. The subject's attitude determines the mood.

> **subject's attitude → verb mood**

There are several verb moods in Spanish and other languages. The *indicative mood* conveys what the subject perceives as a reality or certainty; it states facts and convictions.

El precio del oro **sube**.	*The price of gold **is going up**.*
El boletín del tiempo **pronosticó** sol.	*The weather report **forecasted** sunshine.*

Some verbs that communicate facts, a sense of reality, or certainty are:

afirmar	*to declare, to sustain*
comunicar	*to communicate*
contar	*to tell*
decir	*to say*
establecer	*to establish*
explicar	*to explain*
indicar	*to indicate*
informar	*to inform, to tell*
mencionar	*to mention*
narrar	*to narrate*
reportar	*to report*
saber	*to know*

The verbs **pensar** (*to think*) and **creer** (*to believe*) do not convey certainty as strongly as **saber** (*to know*) or **afirmar** (*to state*); however, **pensar** and **creer** also require the *indicative* mood in the dependent clause. Note that in negative and interrogative forms, **pensar** and **creer** are often followed by the subjunctive.

The negative forms **no dudo que** (*I don't doubt that*) and **no niego que** (*I don't deny that*) indicate a degree of certainty or belief and may be followed by the indicative mood:

No dudo que Carlos viene.	*I **do not doubt** that Carlos is coming.*
No niego que soy lista.	*I **do not deny** that I am smart.*

Remember that the use of correct *verb tenses* and *moods* plays an important part in building sentences. In both the indicative and the subjunctive, your communication may refer to the past, the present, or an action or state in the future.

The subjunctive mood

The *subjunctive mood* communicates uncertainty, doubt, conjecture, wishes, desires, requests, orders, and other emotions. The subjunctive appears primarily in subordinate clauses. Remember that a *subordinate clause* does not convey a complete statement; it needs a *main clause* to communicate its meaning. Here are some verbs, used in the main clause, that require the subjunctive mood in the dependent clause:

WANT/DESIRE		FEELINGS/EMOTIONS		DOUBT/DENIAL	
amar	*to like, to love*	adorar	*to adore*	dudar	*to doubt*
desear	*to desire*	alegrarse	*to be glad*	negar	*to deny*
deplorar	*to deplore*	arrepentirse	*to regret*		
esperar	*to hope*	detestar	*to detest, to hate*		
exigir	*to demand*	lamentarse	*to complain*		
ordenar	*to order*	permitir	*to allow*		
pedir	*to ask*	querer	*to love*		
preferir	*to prefer*	sentir	*to be sorry*		
prohibir	*to forbid*	sorprenderse	*to be surprised*		
querer	*to wish, to want*	temer	*to fear*		
sugerir	*to suggest*	tener miedo	*to be afraid*		

The subjunctive is used far more frequently in Spanish than in English, where it has largely become a written form. Spanish has clear rules for the subjunctive, and its forms are distinctive:

Dudo que **llueva** hoy.
Quiere que la víctima **denuncie** al ladrón.

Les **pedimos** que **sean** puntuales.

***I doubt** it **will rain** today.*
*He wants that the victim **denounce** the robber (the victim to **denounce** the robber).*
***We ask** that you **be** punctual.*

EJERCICIO 16·1

¿Cierto o incierto? *Escribe* **C** *si el verbo de la proposición principal* (main clause) *indica certeza* (certainty). *Si no, escribe* **F**.

1. _____ Marcos y yo conocemos a la señora que vive en esa casa.

2. _____ Dudo que quiera vender esa casa.

3. _____ La gente cuenta que son un poco misteriosos.

4. _____ Su marido afirma que son felices en este barrio.

5. _____ Sus hijos dicen que no quieren mudarse tampoco.

6. _____ Pero mi marido niega que la señora diga la verdad.

7. _____ Te aseguro que la casa es preciosa.

8. _____ ¿Crees que vendan la casa?

The subjunctive and the subordinating conjunction que

In Unit 7 you studied *subordinating conjunctions*. In most of the examples in Unit 7, the verb in the main clause states a *fact* or a *certainty* in the *indicative mood*. There, you practiced writing sentences with a main clause, a subordinating conjunction, and a subordinate clause in the indicative.

Now you will build sentences using a main clause in the indicative that communicates *doubt*, *uncertainty*, or other *emotions*, followed by a subordinate clause that contains a form of the *subjunctive*. Most of the subordinate clauses are introduced by **que** (*that*), introducing a different (new) subject. Remember that the element **que** is never omitted in Spanish:

main clause + que + different subject + subjunctive in the subordinate clause

Yo quiero + **que** + **los ciudadanos** + **protejan** el medio ambiente.
*I want (that) citizens (to) **protect** the environment.*

Las autoridades **aconsejan que conservemos** energía.	*The authorities **advise (that)** we conserve energy.*
Los ambientalistas **exigen que** la población **ahorre** agua.	*The environmentalists **demand that** the public conserve water.*
Los voluntarios **esperan que** los esfuerzos **den** resultados.	*The volunteers **hope that** the efforts **will give** good results.*
Espero que la campaña **sea** un éxito.	*I hope that the campaign **succeeds**.*

Note that, in Spanish, the conjunction **que** can be omitted only if the subject of the main clause and the subordinate clause are the *same*. In that case, the infinitive, not the subjunctive, is used in the subordinate clause. In the following example, the subject expresses a desire (**quiere**). The same subject (**el presidente**) then completes the action (**contribuir**). You may wish to review the construction of *impersonal expressions* + *infinitive* in Unit 12.

El Presidente quiere contribuir a la campaña.	*The President wants to contribute to the campaign.*

EJERCICIO
16·2

¡Imagina! *Eres el/la reportero/a del periódico "El mundo" y escribes un artículo acerca de la situación política en Hispanoamérica. Usa el presente de indicativo o del subjuntivo del verbo entre paréntesis, según sea necesario.*

1. (confiar) El Presidente de Ecuador dice que _____ en el Proceso de paz.

2. (cumplir) El mandatario colombiano espera que Ecuador _____ su palabra.

3. (protestar) Muchos temen que los colombianos _____ en las calles de Bogotá.

4. (respetar) Los líderes piden que todos _____ las leyes internacionales.

5. (estar) El gobierno niega que el ejército _____ listo para invadir Ecuador.

6. (apoyar) Explica el ministro de defensa que Colombia _____ la paz.

7. (invadir) Las leyes internaciones prohíben que un país _____ otro país.

8. (perder) Un estudio reciente revela que los políticos _____ el apoyo de los ciudadanos.

The subjunctive mood   **155**

¡Usa tu imaginación! *Vas a expresar tus deseos, miedos, dudas, etc., en oraciones completas. Combina los elementos para crear tus oraciones. Incluye tus ideas después de los puntos suspensivos (...).*

MODELO   esperar / que mis amigos / cooperar...

    Espero que mis amigos cooperen con mi campaña.

1. desear / que mis amigos / respetar...

_____

2. dudar / que mis compañeros de trabajo / tener...

_____

3. tener miedo de / que mi jefe / descubrir que...

_____

4. sentir / que mi mejor amiga / necesitar hablar...

_____

5. preferir / que mis enemigos / decidir...

_____

6. no querer / que nadie / decir...

_____

7. detestar / que la gente / murmurar...

_____

8. proponer / que todos me / dejar...

_____

The subjunctive after impersonal expressions

Impersonal expressions do not have a specific subject or person; they always contain a verb in the third-person singular, usually **ser**, followed by a masculine singular adjective. In this unit you will use impersonal expressions to build sentences that require the subjunctive in the subordinate clause. Here is a list of frequently used impersonal expressions:

Es absurdo	*It is absurd*	Es indispensable	*It is indispensable*
Es aconsejable	*It is advisable*	Es (una) lástima	*It is a pity*
Es bueno	*It is good*	Es malo	*It is bad*
Es desalentador	*It is discouraging*	Es mejor	*It is better*
Es difícil	*It is unlikely*	Es menester	*It is necessary*
Es doloroso	*It hurts / is painful*	Es necesario	*It is necessary*

Es dudoso	*It is doubtful*	Es posible	*It is possible*
Es cómico	*It is funny*	Es preciso	*It is necessary*
Es extraño	*It is strange*	Es preferible	*It is better*
Es fácil	*It is likely*	Es preocupante	*It is disturbing*
Es fantástico	*It is fantastic*	Es probable	*It is likely*
Es importante	*It is important*	Es raro	*It is unlikely*
Es imposible	*It is impossible*	Es ridículo	*It is ridiculous*
Es improbable	*It is unlikely*	Es una pena	*It is a pity*
Es incierto	*It is uncertain*	Es terrible	*It is terrible*
Es increíble	*It is incredible*		

An adverb ending in -**mente** and other adverbs, such as **muy**, may be placed between the form of **ser** and the adjective, adding emphasis to the expression:

Fue absolutamente imprescindible	***It was absolutely*** *indispensable*
Es totalmente cierto	***It is absolutely*** *certain*
Es muy probable	***It is very*** *probable*

Impersonal expressions are followed by a subjunctive clause to convey a command or a suggestion, a possibility, a doubt, emotions, etc.:

impersonal expression + que + subjunctive

Es necesario + **que** + **termines**.	***It is necessary that you finish.***
Es terrible que hayas perdido tu billetera.	***It is terrible that you lost*** *your wallet.*

Other impersonal expressions are:

Más vale	*It is better that*
Mejor que	*It is better that*
Ojalá (que)	*I (Let's) hope that*
Conviene que	*It is advisable that*
Puede (ser) que	*It is possible that*
Conviene que **termines** ya.	***It is advisable*** *that* ***you finish.***
Era menester que **pagaras** los impuestos.	***It was necessary*** *that* ***you pay*** *your taxes.*
Será mejor que **te vayas**.	***It will be better*** *that* ***you go.***

Note that the main verb is in a different tense in each of the examples above: the present, the imperfect, and the future indicative, respectively.

The subjunctive is not used if the impersonal expression indicates *certainty*:

Es evidente que tu novio **es** guapo.	***It is obvious*** *that your boyfriend* ***is*** *handsome.*
¿**Es cierto** que Marcos **tiene** dieciocho años?	***Is it true*** *that Marcos* ***is*** *eighteen years old?*

Some other expressions that indicate *certainty* or *lack of doubt* are:

Es obvio	*It is obvious*
Es seguro	*It is certain*
Es verdad	*It's true*
No hay duda	*There is no doubt*

EJERCICIO
16·4

Un maratón. *Vas a preparar un grupo de amigos para correr en un maratón. Escribe una lista de las reglas que deben seguir. Construye tus oraciones combinando las expresiones impersonales + **que** + la forma del verbo en el presente de subjuntivo.*

MODELO   es preferible / dormir ocho horas

       Es preferible que duerman ocho horas.

1. es necesario / practicar ejercicios de calentamiento (*warm-up*)

   _____

2. es importante / mantener el peso (*weight*) ideal

   _____

3. es absolutamente indispensable / seguir una rutina de disciplina

   _____

4. es mejor / llevar una dieta saludable

   _____

5. es bueno / correr temprano por la mañana

   _____

6. no es absurdo / levantar pesas

   _____

7. es aconsejable / ser constantes

   _____

8. es ridículo / descansar solamente un día a la semana

   _____

EJERCICIO
16·5

Te toca a ti: ¿cómo será tu futuro? *Usa las expresiones impersonales para predecir tu futuro. Observa el modelo.*

MODELO   Es dudoso que

       Es dudoso que tenga cinco hijos.

1. Ojalá que

   _____

2. Es totalmente seguro que

   _____

3. Es casi improbable que

_____

4. Es indispensable que

_____

5. Puede ser que

_____

6. Es seguro que

_____

7. No es muy probable que

_____

Using the subjunctive with *if*-clauses in contrary-to-fact sentences

If-clauses can be used to communicate two types of situations. The first example that follows is a situation where a condition can be fulfilled, i.e., it can be realized. Note that the verb in both the main clause (**iremos**) and the verb in the subordinate clause (**llegas**) are in the indicative mood:

> **Iremos** al cine si **llegas** a tiempo.   *We will go to the movies if **you arrive** on time.*

In *contrary-to-fact* sentences, the *conditional* in the main clause allows us to express what *would* or *would not* happen if some other event *were* or *were not* to happen:

> —¿Qué **pasaría** si **vivieras** en China?   *—What **would happen** if **you lived** in China?*
> —**Aprendería** a hablar chino si **viviera** en China.   *—I **would learn** to speak Chinese if I **lived** in China.*

In the previous examples, the subordinating conjunction *if* introduces a clause stating something that is *not* a fact: *if you lived in China*, and it seems it will not be a reality. Thus, the verb in the subordinate clause is in the *imperfect subjunctive*. You need two elements to build this type of sentence:

> **resultant condition + *if* + contrary-to-fact condition**
>
> **Aprendería** a hablar chino + **si** + **viviera** en China.

Reversing the order of the clauses does not change the meaning of the sentence:

> Si **tuviéramos** experiencia, **trabajaríamos** más rápido.   *If **we had** experience, **we would work** faster.*
> Si Luisa **fuera** tú, lo **haría**.   *If Luisa **were you**, **she would do** it.*
> Y si yo **fuera** tú, también lo **haría**.   *And if I **were you**, **I would do** it too.*

Note that the *imperfect subjunctive* **-ra** form can also be used in the result clause instead of the conditional. In the second and third examples above, the English subjunctive form *were* is used, regardless of the subject.

> Si **tuviera** un millón de euros, **comprara** (**compraría**) un apartamento.   *If **I had** a million Euros, **I would buy** an apartment.*

Note that the *perfect conditional* is used to express what *would* or *would not have happened* if something else *had* or *had not happened*:

Si **hubiéramos tenido** tiempo, **habríamos visitado** Alemania.

*If **we had had** the time, **we would have visited** Germany.*

EJERCICIO
16·6

De la realidad a la hipótesis. *Las oraciones siguientes presentan la realidad. Cambia las oraciones a hipótesis no reales.*

MODELO   Si me visitas, verás mi nuevo apartamento.

          Si me visitaras, verías mi nuevo apartamento.

1. Si me llamas por teléfono, te doy las instrucciones para llegar a casa.

   _____

2. Si llegas antes de la ocho, conocerás a mi hermana.

   _____

3. Te preparo una paella de mariscos y un flan, si me lo pides.

   _____

4. Si quieres, alquilamos una película de Almodóvar.

   _____

5. Podemos ir al cine y tomar un café, si lo deseas.

   _____

6. Es una buena idea si traes tu nueva cámara digital.

   _____

7. Tomaremos fotos desde mi terraza si te gusta la vista.

   _____

8. Todo eso es posible, si tú quieres.

   _____

EJERCICIO
16·7

¿Que harías en las siguientes situaciones? *Escribe las oraciones con las sugerencias. Usa el imperfecto de subjuntivo.*

MODELO   Si me llamaran para una encuesta / colgar el teléfono

          Si me llamaran para una encuesta colgara (would hang up) *el teléfono.*

1. Si me mudara a Rusia / cambiar mi forma de vivir

_____

2. Si tuviera más tiempo / dedicarme a escribir mis memorias

_____

3. Si fuera más joven / probar otra profesión

_____

4. Si conociera al/a la presidente/a de los Estados Unidos / pedir su autógrafo

_____

5. Si viajara a Europa / visitar Coímbra y Praga

_____

6. Si pudiera lograr (*realize*) mi gran sueño / hacer muchos cambios en mi vida

_____

7. Si decidiera cambiar de vida / poder estudiar otra carrera

_____

8. Si ganara el premio grande de la lotería / comprar una casa para mis padres

_____

Subordinating conjunctions other than **que** + the subjunctive

See Unit 7 for a list of commonly used subordinating conjunctions. Subordinate clauses require the use of the subjunctive when the verb in the main clause expresses the usual message of *doubt*, *purpose*, *anticipation*, and *indefiniteness* that we have learned in the present unit.

Notice how the first two example sentences below convey different meanings. In the first example, with the subjunctive form **sea**, the challenge of learning Japanese does not come across as a real fact; in the second, with the indicative form **es**, the challenge is real; the person has already undertaken it:

Aprenderé japonés, **aunque sea** difícil.	*I will learn Japanese **although it may be** difficult.*
Aprenderé japonés, **aunque es** difícil.	*I will learn Japanese **although it is** difficult.*

Some of these clauses behave like adverbs, providing answers to questions such as **¿cuándo?**, **¿dónde?**, **¿cómo?**, etc. In these cases, they are called *adverbial clauses*:

Cuando pueda, **estudiaré** este capítulo.	*When I can, I will study this chapter.*
Descansaré **después de que termine** mi tarea.	*I will rest **after I am done** with my homework.*
Continuaré mis estudios, **a menos que me canse**.	*I will go on studying, **unless I get tired**.*

La comprarán, **aunque** el precio **sea** alto. *They will buy it **even though** the price **may be** high.*

Keep in mind the following sequence of tenses, which you will also review in Unit 17:

Hubiéramos comprado el pasaje **aunque habría sido** caro. *We would have bought the ticket even though it would have been expensive.*

Descansa unos minutos **cuando te sientas** cansado. *Rest a few minutes whenever you feel tired.*

Remember that the conjunction **que** is *omitted* when the subject of the main clause and the subordinate clause are the same. When the two subjects are the same, the infinitive, not the subjunctive, is used in the dependent clause:

Preparé un buen café para **disfrutar**lo. *I prepared good coffee to enjoy it (so that I could enjoy it).*

Toma la medicina para **curar**te. *Take your medicine so that you get better.*

EJERCICIO
16·8

Combina las dos cláusulas. De acuerdo al sentido de la oración, usa la conjunción apropiada de las dos que aparecen en cada paréntesis.

MODELO   (Cuando / Si)... salga el sol, iré a mi jardín.

Cuando salga el sol, iré a mi jardín.

1. (si / aunque) Tendré que trabajar en mi jardín... llueva mucho.

_____

2. (Aunque / Ya que)... tuviera unos guantes, no protegería mis manos.

_____

3. (Si / Después que)... me ponga los guantes, me pondré mi sombrero.

_____

4. (aunque / si) Tomaríamos limonada... tuvieras sed.

_____

5. (Cuando / Aunque)... empiece a trabajar en el jardín, rebajaré de peso.

_____

6. (Como / Si)... tuviera mucha paciencia, trabajaría lento, despacio.

_____

7. (si / aunque) Y... quisieras más limonada, cortaría los limones de mi jardín.

_____

EJERCICIO
16·9

Completa cada una de las oraciones siguientes con una frase original y apropiada. Observa la conjunción subrayada para escribir tu respuesta.

MODELO   Viajarán a la selva <u>aunque</u> ___*sea peligroso*___ .

1. Doce españoles quieren visitar el espacio <u>aunque</u> _____.

2. Una agencia de viajes prepara el viaje <u>porque</u> _____.

3. <u>Como</u> _____, hay mucho interés en este viaje.

4. <u>Aunque</u> la mayoría de los viajeros son ricos _____.

5. Los turistas espaciales preparan este viaje <u>de modo que</u> _____.

6. <u>Si</u> _____ puedes comprar tu billete por $150.000.

7. <u>Aunque</u> _____, esta aventura atrae a mucha gente.

8. <u>Si</u> has visto muchas películas del espacio, _____.

9. <u>Aunque</u> no hay fecha exacta de salida, _____.

10. _____, <u>si</u> quieres viajar a las estrellas.

The subjunctive in relative clauses

In Unit 8 you studied *relative pronouns* to build relative clauses that state certainty, using verbs in the *indicative* mood. In this unit, you will build sentences with relative clauses using the *subjunctive*. If the antecedent of the pronoun is *indefinite*, does not exist, or is not specific, the relative (subordinate) clause requires the subjunctive. The most frequently used indefinite pronouns are:

alguien	*someone*
algo	*something*
nadie	*nobody, no one*
nada	*nothing*
un/a, unos/as	*one, some*

Let us compare the following sentences and examine their clauses:

Tengo **unos** zapatos negros **que son** muy elegantes.	*I have **some** black shoes **that are** very elegant.*
Pero necesito **unos** zapatos **que sean** cómodos.	*But I need **some** shoes **that are** comfortable.*
¿Conoces **alguna** zapatería **que esté** cerca?	*Do you know **any** shoe store **that is** close by?*

The first example sentence above contains a relative clause starting with **que**, preceded by the antecedent **unos zapatos negros**. This pair of shoes is real, specific. In the second example, **necesito unos zapatos** refers to a *desired* pair of shoes. In the last example sentence, **alguna zapatería que esté** is *indefinite* and possibly nonexistent.

¿Indicativo o subjuntivo? *Lee cuidadosamente el contexto y decide qué forma del verbo necesitas.*

1. (ser) Tiene una novia que _____ feísima.

2. (poder) Necesita una peluquera que _____ hacerle un buen corte de pelo.

3. (querer) Conoce a una sicóloga que _____ ayudarla a ganar autoestima (*self-confidence*).

4. (tener) Eso sí, no hay nadie que _____ una novia tan fiel (*loyal*).

5. (comprender) Raúl no ha encontrado a nadie que lo _____ como ella.

6. (costar) Ayer ellos encontraron un apartamento que _____ poco.

7. (compartir) Raúl ha encontrado a alguien que _____ su filosofía de la vida.

8. (lograr) No hay nada que _____ separar a Raúl y su novia.

Te toca a ti. *Imagina que buscas tu casa ideal, tu trabajo ideal o tu pareja ideal. Elige el tema. Usa la lista de verbos siguientes para hacer tu trabajo.*

Mi _____ ideal.

1. buscar

_____

2. necesitar

_____

3. desear

_____

4. es necesario que yo...

_____

5. querer

_____

6. ¿conocer... ?

_____

The subjunctive mood and verb tenses

You have studied the use of the subjunctive in subordinate clauses when the verb in the main clause conveys uncertainty, doubt, conjecture, a wish or desire, a request or an order, and other emotions. With these rules in mind, we will focus on different *subjunctive tenses* to build your sentences.

Subjunctive mood and tenses

Both the indicative and the subjunctive moods have several *tenses*. A *verb tense* indicates the *time* the action or state takes place:

> verb tense → time

A tense may also indicate the *duration* of the action or state it denotes. Keep in mind that the tense of the verb in the main clause determines the tense of the subjunctive form in the subordinate clause.

Communicating in the present with the subjunctive

When communicating in the present, the first tense you must consider is the *present subjunctive* and when to use it. The verb in the main clause, which determines the present subjunctive in the subordinate clause, can be in one of three indicative tenses, or the imperative mood:

MAIN CLAUSE	SUBORDINATE CLAUSE
present indicative present perfect indicative future indicative command	→ present *or* present perfect subjunctive

Using the present subjunctive

The following examples all contain the *present subjunctive* in the subordinate clause:

El entrenador Sáenz **quiere que** su equipo **gane**.	*Coach Sáenz **wants** his team **to win**.*
Hoy **ha permitido que descansen**.	*Today he **has allowed them to rest**.*

| Pero mañana les **exigirá que practiquen** toda la tarde. | But tomorrow he **will demand that they practice** the whole afternoon. |
| **No dejes que** el Sr. Sáenz te **agote**. | **Do not let** Mr. Sáenz **wear** you **out**. |

Note that the main verbs in the above examples are in the *present*, *present perfect*, and *future* of the indicative, except for the last example above, where it is in the *imperative*. When the verb in the main clause is in any of these tenses, and requires the subjunctive, the verb in the subordinate clause is in the *present subjunctive*.

Remember that some main clause verbs do not require the use of the subjunctive. A main clause with a verb that states a fact, a certainty, or a good probability uses a form of the *indicative* mood in the subordinate clause:

| Mario **comenta que** tu libro **es** excelente. | Mario **mentioned that** your book **is** excellent. |
| Yo **sé que vendrás** mañana. | I **know you will come** tomorrow. |

EJERCICIO 17·1

¿Cuál es la respuesta correcta? *Subraya la forma apropiada del verbo.*

1. Es muy extraño que Luisa no (está / esté) en la oficina.

2. Es posible que Jacobo (llega / llegue) antes que ella hoy.

3. El jefe ha decidido que ellos dos (escriben / escriban) la carta para invitar a un líder de la comunidad.

4. El jefe les pedirá que (terminan / terminen) la carta antes del mediodía.

5. No le pidas a Luisa que te (ayuda / ayude) con tu proyecto.

6. Ella necesitará que tú (tienes / tengas) tu trabajo listo.

7. ¡Ah! Pedro dice que Luisa (llega / llegue) en media hora.

8. Luisa cree que (pueda / puede) terminar la carta ella sola.

EJERCICIO 17·2

Órdenes son órdenes. *Imagina que eres el gerente de una tienda y tienes que darles instrucciones a tus empleados. Escoge uno de los verbos de la lista y completa las oraciones con la forma apropiada del modo indicativo o imperativo.*

irse / dar / esperar / traer / insistir / tener / deber / envolver

1. José, dile a Mercedes que _____ los paquetes aquí.

2. Leila, no dejes que los clientes _____ mucho tiempo.

3. Carlos, no permitas que la Sra. Gómez _____ en llegar tarde.

4. Lucía, recuerda que los clientes _____ la razón.

5. Mara, pídele a Martín que _____ los paquetes de regalo.

6. Sra. López, no me pida que le _____ un aumento de sueldo (*raise*).

7. Franco, no olvides que _____ llegar a las ocho mañana.

8. Berta y Lana, no dejen que los clientes _____ sin comprar algo.

Using the present perfect subjunctive

Now let's consider when to use the *present perfect* subjunctive. The *present* subjunctive is used to refer to events that may occur *at the same time* or *later than* the action of the verb in the main clause; the *present perfect* subjunctive is used to refer to actions that occurred *before* the action of the main verb.

Remember that all compound verb tenses in Spanish are conjugated with the helping verb **haber** + *the past participle* of a verb. The present perfect subjunctive is formed with the *present subjunctive* of **haber** + *the past participle*: **haya salido, hayas salido, hayamos salido**, etc. Note the use of the *present* and the *present perfect* subjunctive in the following examples, and especially the tense of each verb in the main clause:

Es necesario que **Ud. salga** de aquí inmediatamente.	*It is necessary that you leave here immediately.*
Es posible que **hayas cometido** un error.	*It is possible that you have made a mistake.*
Dudamos que los chicos **hayan pedido** permiso.	*We doubt that the boys have asked permission.*

EJERCICIO
17·3

Práctica. *Subraya la respuesta correcta: ¿presente perfecto de indicativo o presente perfecto de subjuntivo?*

1. Es raro que los pilotos no (han llegado / hayan llegado) a la cabina.

2. Es posible que ellos (han volado / hayan volado) aquí desde otra ciudad.

3. ¡Ay! El mensaje en la pantalla dice que el vuelo se (ha retrasado / se haya retrasado).

4. Yo espero que el mal tiempo no (ha causado / haya causado) problemas.

5. ¿No es raro que los asistentes de vuelo (han subido / hayan subido) al avión hace unos minutos?

6. Bien, es obvio que las autoridades (han decidido / hayan decidido) la salida del vuelo.

7. Es posible que una falla mecánica (ha sido / haya sido) la causa del problema.

8. Estoy seguro de que mi esposa ya se (ha enterado / haya enterado) de este problema.

Tres situaciones. *Usa el presente perfecto de indicativo o el presente perfecto de subjuntivo de acuerdo al contexto.*

Alicia no se siente bien.

1. Es probable que _____ (comer) mucho.

2. Dudo que Alicia _____ (seguir) la dieta que le recomendó su doctor.

3. Es cierto que ella siempre _____ (preferir) la carne roja y el vino tinto.

4. Puede ser que anoche Alicia _____ (abusar) de la comida y la bebida.

Pedro y Sofía se casan hoy en Santiago.

5. Sabemos que ellos _____ (quererse) por mucho tiempo.

6. No creo que Pedro _____ (conocer) nunca a una mujer más extraordinaria.

7. Tampoco es extraño que Sofía _____ (enamorarse) de Pedro.

8. Hoy celebran la boda que ellos _____ (soñar) por mucho tiempo.

La Dra. Bernal tiene su consulta en la Avenida del Puerto.

9. La Dra. Bernal es la mejor dentista que (yo) _____ (tener).

10. No pienso que (tú) _____ (encontrar) un dentista mejor en esta ciudad.

11. Creo que yo nunca _____ (sufrir) una extracción con dolor.

12. Es curioso que ustedes no _____ (ir) a su consultorio antes.

Communicating in the past tense with the subjunctive

A verb in a *past tense* or in the *conditional* in the main clause, that communicates uncertainty, doubt, conjecture, a wish or desire, etc., requires a past tense of the subjunctive in the dependent (or subordinate) clause. Two possible tenses are the *imperfect* or the *pluperfect subjunctive.* You may wish to review the conjugation of these two tenses.

MAIN CLAUSE	SUBORDINATE CLAUSE
preterit indicative imperfect indicative pluperfect indicative conditional } →	imperfect subjunctive *or* pluperfect subjunctive

Using the imperfect subjunctive

Let's look at the *imperfect subjunctive.* Use this tense when the following three conditions are present: a.) the subjunctive is required in the subordinate clause because of what is stated in the main clause; b.) the verb in the main clause is in a past indicative tense (preterit, imperfect, pluperfect) or the conditional; and c.) the action of the verb in the subjunctive takes place at *the same time*, or *after* the action of the main verb.

Study the *imperfect subjunctive* in the subordinate clause in the following examples:

Ayer Alina me **pidió que** la **llevara** al dentista.	*Alina **asked** me **to take** her to the dentist.*
Ella no **quería que** el dentista le **sacara** la muela.	*She **did not want** the dentist **to pull out** her molar.*
Yo le **había pedido** a María **que** me **prestara** el auto.	*I **had asked** María **to lend** me her car.*
Lo **compraríamos** si **tuviéramos** el dinero.	*We **would buy** it if **we had** the money.*

In the examples above, the subjunctive forms in the subordinate clauses are in the imperfect subjunctive. Remember that the imperfect subjunctive has two different sets of endings, the **-ra** and the **-se** forms. The **-ra** form is currently the more widely used in the Spanish-speaking world.

EJERCICIO
17·5

En el circo. *Subraya la respuesta correcta: ¿un tiempo del indicativo o el imperfecto de subjuntivo?*

1. Era cómico que los monos (bailaban / bailaran) en la pista del circo.

2. Fue posible que ellos (salían / salieran) después de muchos aplausos.

3. Los niños querían que el domador de leones (se llevaba / se llevara) a las fieras (*wild animals*).

4. Yo esperaba que el espectáculo no (era / fuera) muy aburrido.

5. ¡Era cierto que los payasos (tenían / tuvieran) unos zapatos enormes!

6. Había muchas personas mayores que (se rieron / se rieran) más que los niños.

7. ¿No fue extraño que los trapecistas (*trapeze artists*) no (aparecieron / aparecieran)?

8. Yo observé que todo el mundo (se divirtió / se divirtiera) muchísimo.

EJERCICIO
17·6

Más situaciones. *Usa un tiempo del pasado del indicativo o el imperfecto de subjuntivo de acuerdo a la situación que presenta el contexto.*

El gabinete del abogado Fernández defiende a todo tipo de criminales.

1. Siempre dudábamos que Fernández _____ (ayudar) a la justicia.

2. Supimos que Fernández _____ (representar) al ladrón de los diamantes.

3. Estaba claro que Fernández _____ (querer) la libertad del ladrón.

4. Descubrieron que Fernández _____ (cobrar) una gran suma de dinero para la defensa.

5. El ladrón quería que su abogado _____ (ganar) fama y su libertad.

Los López, Mirta y Marcos, salieron de vacaciones a Hawai.

6. Ellos no estaban seguros de que _____ (hacer) buen tiempo durante las vacaciones.

7. Nunca creí que Mirta y su esposo _____ (visitar) las islas hawaianas.

8. Era preocupante que Marcos _____ (tener) tanto miedo a volar.

9. Seguramente Marcos _____ (consultarse) con un sicólogo.

10. Así fue posible que los López _____ (volar) miles de millas desde Nueva York a Hawai.

EJERCICIO
17·7

Te toca a ti. *Construye oraciones con el condicional y el imperfecto de subjuntivo y tus propias ideas. Usa la primera persona del plural,* **nosotros.**

MODELO tener / más éxito / si conservar...

Tendríamos más éxito si conserváramos más energía.

1. poder / cambiar el mundo / si trabajar...

_____

2. construir / una casa / si tener...

_____

3. visitar / Portugal / si saber...

_____

4. tener / más amigos / si poder...

_____

5. aprender / a escribir / si practicar...

_____

6. rebajar / de peso / si comer...

_____

7. ser / más tolerantes / si respetar...

_____

8. estar / más informados / si leer...

_____

Using the pluperfect subjunctive

Note that there are similarities in the situations that require the use of the *imperfect* (**hubiera**) and the *pluperfect* (**hubiera comprado**) tenses of the subjunctive, except for the last example below, which refers to the time frame of the tenses.

Use the *pluperfect subjunctive* when the following three elements are present: a.) the subjunctive is required in the subordinate clause because of what is stated in the main clause; b.) the verb in the main clause is in a past indicative tense (preterit, imperfect, pluperfect) or the conditional; and, c.) the action of the verb in the subjunctive has taken place *before* the action of the main verb.

Elías **dudó que** todos **hubieran aceptado** la invitación.	Elías **doubted that** everyone **had accepted** the invitation.
Marcia **deseaba que** nosotros **hubiéramos salido** temprano.	Marcia **wished** we **had left** early.
Alina **habría preferido que** la **hubieran dejado** ir a casa.	Alina **would have preferred** that **they let** her go home.
Tendrías ya la respuesta **si** te **hubieras comunicado** conmigo.	**You would** already **have** the answer **if you had communicated** with me.

In the previous sentences, the subjunctive forms (in the subordinate clauses) are in the *pluperfect subjunctive*. Keep in mind that the pluperfect subjunctive is a compound tense. The helping or auxiliary verb **haber** has two different forms (**-ra** and **-se**), **hubiera** and **hubiese**, followed by the past participles **-ado** or **-ido: yo hubiera sabido, nosotros hubiéramos sabido**, etc. The **-ra** form is the more widely used in the Spanish-speaking world.

EJERCICIO
17·8

*Ahora escribe las oraciones usando el pluscuamperfecto de subjuntivo en la oración según convenga. Usa las formas que terminan en **-ra**.*

1. Mónica había preferido / que tú / invitar / a su novio

   _____

2. no pensó / que yo / decir / nada / a nadie

   _____

3. negué / que mis padres / gastar / tanto dinero

   _____

4. no era posible / que ellos / comprar / un auto tan caro

   _____

5. preferían / que ustedes / decir / la verdad

   _____

6. no pensaban / que la fiesta / ser / un éxito

   _____

7. esperaba / que nosotros / entender / la carta

_____

8. no entendían / que yo / salir / de la oficina

_____

Punctuation and spelling

Correct punctuation and spelling are needed to communicate written messages effectively. Punctuation is an established system of standardized marks that separate structural units (sentences, quotes, paragraphs, etc.) and clarify the meaning of written language:

> **system of standardized marks → punctuation**

Spanish and English conventions regarding punctuation are similar, but they vary in detail. In writing, we must adhere to the punctuation rules specific to a given language.

In Unit 1, you wrote sentences based on their structures, word order, and punctuation. In other units you practiced other required punctuation symbols: commas, question marks, exclamation points, etc. In this unit we will review and expand details regarding punctuation, building sentences, and building paragraphs.

> **one or more sentences dealing with one topic → paragraph**

Punctuation marks

The following punctuation marks are used in both Spanish and English sentences:

la coma	*comma*
las comillas	*quotation marks*
dos puntos	*colon*
el paréntesis	*parenthesis*
el punto y coma	*semicolon*
el punto	*period*
el signo de admiración	*exclamation point*
el signo de exclamación	*exclamation point*
el signo de interrogación	*question mark*

The period

Use a period (.) to indicate the end of a declarative sentence (a sentence that makes a statement), an indirect question, or a command (imperative) sentence:

Pablo sabe la verdad.	*Pablo knows the truth.*
Ana no sabe quién toca a la puerta.	*Ana does not know who is knocking at the door.*
Firmen la carta antes de enviarla.	*Sign the letter before you mail it.*

A period separates sentences in a paragraph structure. The first letter of the word that follows a period is capitalized:

Esta noche vamos a observar un eclipse lunar. Los telescopios están listos. Los miembros del equipo nos enviarán los detalles.	*Tonight we will watch a lunar eclipse. **The** telescopes are ready. **The** members of the team will send us the details.*

Note that in typing or keying in text, you should leave a single space between a period and a new sentence. When you write paragraphs that are part of a longer piece, indent the first sentence or line of each paragraph:

El gobernador del Estado de Aragua pronunciará un discurso acerca de las necesidades de los ciudadanos. Dos de sus consejeros le comunicaron las preocupaciones de algunos de sus compatriotas.	*The governor of the State of Aragua will give a speech about the needs of the citizens. Two of his advisors told him about the concerns of some of his fellow citizens.*

Abbreviations

Periods are also used in abbreviations and some acronyms (**siglas**). Not all abbreviations have equivalents in both English and Spanish. Some abbreviations have been used for a very long time, while others have or may become obsolete, falling out of favor for various reasons. Here are some frequently used abbreviations in Spanish:

a. de J.C.	*B.C.*
a.C.	*B.C.*
d.C.	*A.D.*
Dr.	*Dr.*
Dra.	*Dr.*
Drs.	*Drs.*
etc.	*etc.*
ONU	*UN*
pág.	*p. (page)*
P.D.	*P.S.*
S.A.	*Inc.*
Sr.	*Mr.*
Sra.	*Mrs.*
Srta.	*Miss*
FUNDÉU (La Fundación del Español Urgente)	
UE	*EU (European Union)*
EE.UU.	*US or U.S.*
JJ.OO. (Juegos olímpicos)	*Olympic Games*

In Spanish, note the repetition of the initial letters of each component of abbreviations that consist of plural nouns such as **EE.UU.** Also, note that **FUNDÉU** has an accent mark to indicate the stressed syllable.

Encontraron evidencias de una civilización de alrededor del año **200 a. de J.C.**	*They found evidence of a civilization dated around **200 B.C.***
La petición va dirigida al **Dr.** E. Santos.	*The petition is addressed to **Dr**.E. Santos.*
El Consejo de Seguridad de la **ONU** tiene una sesión de emergencia.	*The **UN** Security Council has an emergency meeting.*

La abreviatura **P.D.** viene de la frase latina "postdata".

*The abbreviation **P.S.** comes from the Latin phrase "postscriptum."*

Los **EE.UU** ganaron más medallas en los **JJ.OO.** de 2008.

*The **US** won more medals in the 2008 **Olympic Games**.*

EJERCICIO 18·1

Construye un párrafo. *Hay cinco oraciones. Coloca los puntos y escribe las mayúsculas necesarias.*

juan Luis está cantando en el programa "La semana musical" ya ha cantado dos canciones viejas y una nueva que estrena hoy su grupo está compuesto de cinco músicos juan Luis ha cantado con ese grupo por más de veintitrés años él espera continuar ganando éxitos con su público

_____

_____

_____

_____

_____

_____

EJERCICIO 18·2

En español. *Cuidado con la puntuación.*

1. Mr. Jiménez travels to the U.S.

2. He found artifacts (*artefactos*) from 200 B.C.

3. Dr. Melissa Marcos is an expert in old civilizations.

4. Miss Marcos, her daughter, helps her mother.

5. They will give a lecture in the EU.

1. _____

2. _____

3. _____

4. _____

5. _____

Acronyms

Acronyms are words created with the initial letter or letters of each of the components of names of institutions, organizations, etc. Some are international. Periods are not usually used with acronyms:

OEA (Organización de Estados Americanos)	*OAS*
ONG (Organización no Gubernamental)	*NGO (Non-Governmental Organization)*
ONU	*UN*
OTAN (Organización del Tratado del Atlántico Norte)	*NATO*
OVNI (Objeto volador no identificado)	*UFO*
La **ONG** defiende los derechos de los niños.	*The **NGO** defends children's rights.*
Revelaron la presencia de **dos OVNI** en California.	*They revealed the presence of **two UFOs** in California.*

Note the Spanish spelling of the plural of **OVNI**, with no final **s**, in the example above.

Comma

A comma (,) indicates a brief pause in a sentence. In Spanish, use a comma to separate the elements of a series, except for the element immediately preceded by the conjunctions **y** and **o**. In English, *and* and *or* in such a series are often preceded by a comma.

Vamos a necesitar **lápices, papel y sobres**.	*We will need **pencils, paper, and envelopes**.*
Vimos a **los alumnos, los maestros, los ayudantes, los voluntarios, etc**.	*We saw **the students, the teachers, the aides, the volunteers, etc**.*

The series may consist of a series of nouns, adjectives that are part of a subject, or direct and indirect objects:

Viven en una casa **destartalada, descuidada y viejísima**.	*They live in a **ramshackle, rundown, very old** house.*
Cati, Rosa, María Luisa y Nina son hermanas.	***Cati, Rosa, María Luisa, and Nina** are sisters.*

Remember, the spelling of **y** (*and*) changes to **e** when preceded by a word that starts with **i-** or **hi-**:

Ana **e** Irene salieron.	*Ana **and** Irene left.*
En la cesta hay naranjas **e** higos.	*In the basket there are oranges **and** figs.*

Use the spelling **u** instead of **o** (*or*) when the word that follows the conjunction starts with **o-** or **ho-**:

Tiene siete **u** ocho millones de habitantes.	*It has seven **or** eight million people.*
Puedes freírlos **u** hornearlos.	*You can fry them **or** bake them.*

Vamos a revisar las oraciones. *Después, escribe las oraciones con la puntuación (puntos, comas) y los cambios apropiados de ortografía.*

1. Alicia Luisa y Irene son disciplinadas trabajadoras pacientes y eficientes

_____

2. Hacen ejercicios montan en bicicleta levantan pesas y corren siete ó ocho millas

_____

3. Estas chicas también hacen yoga trabajos comunitarios sirven a la comunidad

_____

4. Hacen campañas en EEUU para recoger (*raise*) fondos para niños y indigentes

_____

5. Han recibido premios certificados y innumerables homenajes de varias organizaciones

_____

6. Ellas demuestran que la rutina es esencial para ser disciplinado cumplir metas y triunfar

_____

Comma after vocatives, phrases, and transition words

A *vocative* is the person addressed in a message. In Unit 5 you studied imperative sentences, including nouns or vocatives used to address the person for whom the message is intended. A comma follows the vocative in English and Spanish:

Juan, abre la puerta para que tu hermano entre.

Juan, *open the door so that your brother may come in.*

A comma must be used to separate elements that introduce a sentence, such as infinitive phrases or phrases that express contrasts or similarities:

Al entrar en la tienda, encontré lo que buscaba.

Upon entering the store, *I found what I was looking for.*

En cambio, Alba es amable y generosa.

On the other hand, *Alba is pleasant and generous.*

Del mismo modo, Felipe coopera con todos sus colegas.

Likewise, *Felipe works well with all his colleagues.*

Commas are also used after *transition words or phrases*. You may wish to review Unit 11; most transition words are adverbs. They add a point or idea, illustrate examples, arrive at a conclusion, etc.

consecuentemente — *consequently*

de hecho — *in fact*

no obstante — *nevertheless*

por consiguiente	*therefore*
por eso	*therefore*
sin embargo	*however*
Llovió muchísimo esa tarde. **Consecuentemente,** las carreteras se inundaron.	*It rained a lot that afternoon. **Consequently,** the roads were flooded.*
La policía cerró varias carreteras. **Por consiguiente,** el tráfico estaba muy congestionado.	*The police closed a few roads. **Therefore,** the traffic was very congested.*

A comma separates *parenthetical phrases* such as relative clauses or adverbial clauses which include added information that may not be essential to the sentence:

Estudiaron el artículo de la profesora, **cuya obra se extiende por tres décadas,** para comprender sus teorías pedagógicas.	*They studied the professor's article, **whose work stretches over three decades,** in order to understand her pedagogical theories.*

Commas separate geographical names in Spanish, as they do in English:

La Habana, Cuba	*Havana, Cuba*
San Diego, California	*San Diego, California*

EJERCICIO
18·4

Construye oraciones con los elementos siguientes. Usa puntos y comas para indicar la puntuación apropiada.

1. a / las ocho / ven / esta / Carmen / noche

   _____

2. los / decidimos / al / escuchar / llegar / a casa / mensajes

   _____

3. de hecho / paciencia / mucho / no tienes / enojas / porque / mucho / te

   _____

4. una / recibieron / carta / San Antonio / de / Texas

   _____

5. tu / necesitaba / ayuda / amistad / tu / y / compañía / tu

   _____

6. dice / documento / eres / Lima / este / que / de / Perú

   _____

¡Atención, no hay comas! *Incluye las correcciones necesarias.*

Como ya sabemos los Juegos olímpicos competiciones de carácter deportivo se celebran cada cuatro años. Este evento internacional tiene lugar en una ciudad de un país diferente dentro de un continente diferente. Al decidir cuál será la ciudad anfitriona la cual es escogida por el Comité olímpico se inician los planes y las preparaciones para estar listos en cuatro años. Por un lado la ciudad debe proveer estadios e instalaciones para recibir a todos los deportistas que compiten sus entrenadores y los equipos médicos. Por otro lado la ciudad debe estar lista para los miles de personas que visitarán esa ciudad y ese país para disfrutar de los JJ.OO. Se supone que dentro del espíritu de esas competiciones las ganancias se deben dedicar a desarrollar el Movimiento Olímpico Internacional y el deporte.

Colons and semicolons

Colons (:) indicate a pause to call attention to what follows in a sentence. The colon may also introduce a list of elements:

> **Subastaron tres piezas: un cuadro de Picasso, una estatua italiana y un manuscrito del siglo XV.**
>
> *They auctioned three pieces: **a painting by Picasso, an Italian statue, and a fifteenth-century manuscript**.*

In Spanish, colons may bring a conclusion to an enumeration, which seems to reverse the order suggested in the previous examples:

> **Sanos, frescos y orgánicos:** así deben ser todos los ingredientes.
>
> *Healthy, fresh, and organic: that is how all the ingredients should be.*
>
> Claro, conciso, al grano: **has listado las cualidades de un buen discurso.**
>
> *Clear, concise, to the point: **you have listed the qualities of a good speech**.*

Another function of a colon is to introduce textual quotes. Remember to include quotation marks. A capital letter usually starts the quote:

> Lo decía el letrero: **"No fumar".**
>
> *The sign said: **"No smoking."***

Colons are used after a salutation in both formal and informal letters in Spanish:

> **Querida Anita:**
>
> *Dear Anita,*
>
> **Estimado Sr. Martínez:**
>
> *Dear Mr. Martínez:*

A semicolon (;) indicates a pause longer than one that uses a comma, but not as long as one indicated by a period. Usually, a semicolon separates elements of complex enumerations. Elements separated by semicolons sometimes have their own internal punctuation; each may have a subject-verb combination of its own.

> Las rosas necesitan el abono; los claveles, agua; las otras plantas, luz.
>
> *The roses need plant food; the carnations, water; the other plants, light.*

Parentheses and quotation marks

Parentheses and quotation marks have similar uses in both English and Spanish. Parentheses enclose incidental information or a clarification. Remember that elements inside parentheses are independent from the sentence; always follow appropriate spelling rules.

Salieron de Cuba **(diciembre, 1957)** antes de la Revolución.	*They left Cuba **(December 1957)** before the Revolution.*
Debido a la lluvia **(copiosa y persistente)** cancelaron el concierto.	*Due to the rainfall **(abundant and persistent)** they canceled the concert.*
Los delegados negaron **(¿acaso no lo sabían?)** la inocencia del acusado.	*The delegates denied **(perhaps they didn't know it?)** the innocence of the accused.*

At times, quotations get complicated. For sentences at this level, let's consider the most common uses of quotation marks. Quotation marks are used to show spoken language, to quote from a written or spoken source, and sometimes to refer to titles of poems, newspaper articles, etc.:

El vendedor dijo: **"Vaya a la caja, por favor"**.	*The salesman said: **"Go to the register, please."***
El artículo dice: **"El calentamiento global hace daño a todas las ballenas"**.	*The article states: **"Global warming is harming all the whales."***
El poema **"Sólo el amor"** está en esta colección.	*The poem **"Love Alone"** is in this collection.*

Note the use of the periods in the following Spanish examples. After quotation marks, a period ends the sentence; a complete sentence within parentheses ends with a period inside the end parenthesis:

Y dijimos lo siguiente: **"No vamos"**.	*And we said the following: **"We will not go."***
No respondía. **(Era obvio que estaba acompañado.)**	*He wasn't answering. **(It was obvious he had company.)***

Words or phrases used ironically, as well as words and phrases from another language, are usually set in quotations:

Él dijo que estaban muy **"ocupados"**.	*He said that they were very **"busy."***
Es como un **"déjà vu"**.	*It's like having a **"déjà vu."***

EJERCICIO 18·6

¿Coma (,)? ¿Punto y coma (;)? ¿Dos puntos (:)? *Usa la puntuación apropiada en las oraciones siguientes.*

1. Vamos a mudarnos a una casa más grande no tenemos suficiente espacio.

2. Los muebles de la sala los cuadros los platos de la cocina todo está listo.

3. Compramos cuatro aparatos nuevos una computadora un televisor HD un teléfono móvil y una aspiradora.

4. Cómoda amplia fresca y acogedora así es la casa nueva.

5. Una cocina debe ser lo mejor de una casa espaciosa bien equipada y llena de luz.

6. Ahora podemos quitar el letrero que dice Se vende casa.

Exclamation points and question marks

Review Units 3 and 4 for the use of question marks (¿?) and exclamation points (¡!) in questions and exclamatory sentences. Remember that with the appropriate punctuation, you can use declarative sentences, negative sentences, and questions to express an emphatic idea or extreme emotion. Don't forget that emphatic commands need exclamation points.

¡Las joyas desaparecieron!	*The jewels disappeared!*
¡No tenemos seguro!	*We do not have insurance!*
¡Pero dónde estás!	*But where are you!*
¡Levántate!	*Stand up!*

EJERCICIO 18·7

Ahora, necesitas añadir los signos de paréntesis ( ), dos puntos (:) o comillas (" ") donde sean necesarios.

1. El primer día del verano 21 de junio en el hemisferio norte nos trae alegría.

2. Mi madre mujer muy sabia siempre me hablaba de sus experiencias cuando era niña.

3. Uno de sus consejos era El tiempo es oro.

4. Pensaba que mi madre era invencible ¡qué ilusión! cuando yo era niño.

5. Todas las mañanas cantábamos una canción La cucaracha.

6. ¡Qué risa me da ahora han pasado tantos años porque mi madre era divertida!

7. Y le gustaba en especial un poema La rosa blanca.

8. Raras veces era dura, pero su amenaza siempre era ¡A la cama!

9. Cuando no estaba de buen humor, yo sabía que estaba ocupada.

10. Y puedo repetir las palabras que decía mi padre para recordarla Corazón de oro.

Some considerations about spelling

Spelling, the sequence of letters that compose a word, is a system of written conventions of a specific language. For example, the English spelling rule "i *before* e *except . . .* " does not apply to correct spelling in Spanish. In this unit, we will review some of the uses of *capital letters* in Spanish and their role in building sentences.

Capital letters (**las mayúsculas**) are needed in the following situations: the first letter of a sentence, the first letter of a proper noun, the first letter after a period or other end punctuation, and all letters of an acronym:

¿Alida es tu hermana? No sabíamos eso.	*Is Alida your sister? We did not know that.*
La **UNICEF** ayuda a los niños de muchos países.	*UNICEF helps children in many countries.*

Proper nouns

A *proper noun* designates a specific person, place, institution, or thing and is usually capitalized in both Spanish and English. Common nouns are not capitalized.

Veo a María.	*I see María.*
Estuvimos en Guadalajara.	*We were in Guadalajara.*
Trabajo en el Instituto Miguel de Cervantes.	*I work at the Miguel de Cervantes Institute.*
Los chicos irán con nosotras.	*The boys will go with us.*
Son los Gómez de siempre.	*They are the same Gomez family (the same Gomezes).*

Note above that in the plural, Spanish surnames referring to a family or a couple are preceded by the definite article **los**; do not add an **-s** or **-es** ending to the name itself.

EJERCICIO 18·8

La ortografía apropiada. *Subraya las palabras que deben llevar mayúsculas.*

en la universidad de sevilla, un grupo de estudiantes norteamericanos estudian un curso avanzado de literatura hispanoamericana contemporánea. en la lista de lecturas, hay dos novelas de mario vargas llosa, cuentos de isabel allende y obras de autoras mexicanas. al final del semestre y después del examen, los estudiantes van a celebrar el fin de curso en casa belisa, un restaurante popular cerca del río.

Proper names of geographical places

Nouns that refer to mountains, rivers, deserts, oceans, seas, and other geographical proper names are preceded by a definite article (**el/la/los/las**) which indicates the gender (masculine or feminine) and number (singular or plural) of that noun:

La papa es originaria de **los Andes**.	*Potatoes are originally from **the Andes**.*
de **las Rocosas**	*from **the Rocky Mountains***
Hacen rafting en **el Colorado**.	*They go rafting on **the Colorado** (River).*
El Sahara está en el norte de África.	***The Sahara** is in northern Africa.*
el Pacífico	***the Pacific** (Ocean)*
las Malvinas (en **el Atlántico**)	***the Falkland Islands** (in the Atlantic)*
la Bahía de Cochinos	***the Bay of Pigs***

A few proper names of regions, cities, and countries have "permanent" definite articles. In this case, the articles begin with a capital letter because they are part of the proper name:

La Habana	*Havana*
La Mancha	*La Mancha*
La Haya	*The Hague*
El Cairo	*Cairo*

For some countries, use of the definite article varies according to speech and local preferences; however, generally speaking, it is not often used:

Marcos nació **en Perú** pero vive **en la Argentina**.	*Marcos was born **in Peru** but lives **in Argentina**.*
En (el) Japón, la salsa es muy popular.	*In Japan, salsa is very popular.*

However, the definite article is always used when a phrase refers to a particular period of time in a country, continent, or region:

definite article + proper noun + complement(s)

la + **Rusia** + de los Zares	*the **Russia** of the Tzars*
la Salamanca del siglo XVI	*the **Salamanca** of the sixteenth century*
el México de Frida Kahlo	*Frida Kahlo's **Mexico***
la Cuba de ayer	*yesterday's **Cuba***

Keep in mind that nouns and adjectives that refer to the inhabitants of a country are *not* capitalized in Spanish:

Los venezolanos son amistosos.	***Venezuelans** are friendly.*
las chicas californianas	***California** girls*

EJERCICIO 18·9

Ortografía: ¿mayúscula o minúscula? *Si la letra inicial de alguna palabra es incorrecta, escribe la ortografía correcta.*

A mi amiga marcia le gusta escribir cuentos. Por eso, todos los Lunes escribe durante tres horas. Está escribiendo ahora dos cuentos sobre la california de principios del siglo XX. Ella es la mujer con más imaginación que conozco. Viajó por áfrica y otros lugares exóticos pero para Ella, el lugar más interesante es el Suroeste de los estados unidos.

_____

_____

Days of the week and months of the year

In Spanish, unlike English, names of the days of the week and months of the year are *common nouns*. Thus, they are not capitalized. In the examples below, note the articles and adjectives that precede those nouns:

No trabajo **los domingos**.	*I do not work **on Sundays**.*
El viernes es mi día favorito.	***Friday** is my favorite day.*
La conferencia es **este martes**.	*The conference is **this Tuesday**.*
Todos los lunes empiezo a las seis.	***Every Monday** I start at six o'clock.*

The names of the months are not preceded by articles unless they are accompanied by modifiers, and they are not capitalized:

Voy a Guatemala en **enero**.	*I travel to Guatemala in **January**.*
Me encanta **agosto**.	*I love **August**.*
Recuerdo **el julio** de mis vacaciones.	*I remember **the July** of my vacation.*

Constellations, stars, and planets

Names of constellations, stars, and planets are capitalized in Spanish:

el Sol	*the sun*
la Osa Mayor	*the Big Dipper (Bear)*
la Osa Menor	*the Little Dipper (Bear)*
la Vía Láctea	*the Milky Way*
la Luna	*the moon*
la Tierra	*Earth*
Júpiter	*Jupiter*
Marte	*Mars*
Plutón	*Pluto*
Saturno	*Saturn*
Urano	*Uranus*
Venus	*Venus*

Astrological signs

Astrological signs are capitalized in Spanish, but individuals who fall under the sign are not:

Aries	*Aries*
Tauro	*Taurus*
Géminis	*Gemini*
Cáncer	*Cancer*
Leo	*Leo*
Virgo	*Virgo*
Libra	*Libra*
Escorpio	*Scorpio*
Sagitario	*Sagittarius*
Capricornio	*Capricorn*
Acuario	*Aquarius*
Piscis	*Piscis*
Mi signo zodiacal es **Libra**.	*My sign is **Libra**.*
Soy un **piscis**.	*I am a **Piscis**.*

Cardinal points

Use capital letters only when you refer to the cardinal points themselves. Otherwise, use lower-case letters.

La Estrella Polar señala **el Norte**.	*The North Star points to **the North**.*
El sol sale por **el Este**.	*The sun rises in **the East**.*
Viajaremos al **sur**.	*We will travel **south**.*

EJERCICIO
18·10

Te toca a ti. *Contesta las preguntas en oraciones completas.*

1. ¿Qué día de la semana prefieres?

_____

2. ¿Cuándo vas de vacaciones? ¿En qué mes?

_____

3. ¿Qué día de la semana descansas?

_____

4. ¿En qué idioma escribes mejor?

_____

5. ¿Qué países te gustaría visitar?

_____

6. ¿Cuándo vas al cine?

_____

7. ¿Cuándo es tu cumpleaños, en marzo?

_____

8. Por último, ¿cuál es tu signo zodiacal?

_____

Letter writing

Some say writing letters is a lost art. In our busy lives, e-mailing and text messaging have replaced letter writing to a great extent. But the art is not all lost. We still receive hand-written, typed, and printed letters and need to master the written conventions needed to communicate effectively. Moreover, e-mails are often in the form of letters. You already know that spelling and punctuation rules are an essential part of written language. These rules apply to writing letters and many types of e-mail messages. Here are the terms used to identify the parts of a letter:

el encabezamiento	*heading*
la fecha	*date*
el/la destinatario/a	*addressee*
el saludo	*greeting*
la redacción de la carta	*body of the letter*
la despedida	*closing*
la firma	*signature*
la carta	*letter*

The heading includes the writer's contact information. In Spanish, greetings and closings are various formulas or set phrases used in different contexts.

Writing a letter

The formats of Spanish and English letters are somewhat similar, but there are some differences, especially in punctuation. When you write a letter in Spanish, in order to avoid misunderstandings, it is important to identify your reader, to choose formal (polite) or informal (familiar) verb forms, to select the corresponding letter format, and to follow the conventions of written language. First, let's consider formal letters.

Formal letters

Use the appropriate format for all letters. Formal letters include correspondence regarding legal matters, business, and trade. A letter addressed to a person who is not familiar to you, or to individuals you would normally address with polite verb forms, because of their position, age, or status, are also formal letters.

A business letter is usually written on letterhead paper which provides the sender's information: name, title, business department, address, etc. A personal letter is sometimes written on personalized stationery that provides the writer's contact information. If you use plain paper to write a formal letter, include your full name above your address at the top of the letter, or in the center, if you choose block style.

At the beginning of this unit, we listed the parts of a letter. You may wish to review them before you start the following exercise.

EJERCICIO
19·1

Una carta formal en español. *Debajo de cada número, escribe las palabras que designan las partes de una carta.*

1. _____

   _____

                                                                    2. _____

3. _____

   _____

   _____

4. _____:

5. _____

   _____

   _____

6. _____,

7. _____

Place and date

In the heading of the letter, the sender's city or town (usually at the top right) appears, separated from the date by a comma. Note the order of the date in Spanish: day, the preposition **de**, month, and year.

Quito, 12 de diciembre de 2010   *Quito, December 12, 2010*
Caracas, 15 de agosto de 2002   *Caracas, August 15, 2002*

Remember that names of the months of the year are not capitalized in Spanish. Note that, in Spanish, the ordinal number **primero** (*first*) is used to refer to the first day of the month.

Siempre celebramos el Año Nuevo **el**   *We always celebrate the New Year **on***
   primero de enero.   ***January first**.*

EJERCICIO
19·2

Las fechas de las cartas. *Escribe las fechas en español.*

1. Havana, November 13, 1988 _____

2. Santo Domingo, July 31, 2000 _____

3. Bogotá, January 1, 2012 _____

4. San Fernando, February 28, 2005 _____

5. Los Angeles, March 16, 2003 _____

6. Barcelona, April 23, 1995 _____

Formal greetings

In Spanish and in English, one difference between formal and informal greetings or salutations is the use of a title in formal letters. Good letter writing uses formal and informal salutation phrases and closing phrases appropriately. With a title you also use polite verb forms (**usted**, **ustedes**). Don't forget their abbreviations: **Ud.** and **Uds.**

The following greetings are used to address a formal letter to a person or persons you do not know, or to a person you must address with polite verb forms. The greeting may include only the addressee's last name, his or her full name, or no name, depending on how well you know the person:

Estimada Sra. López:	*Dear Mrs. López:*
Estimada Srta. Urrutia:	*Dear Miss Urrutia:*
Estimadas Sras. Lucía Aragón y Marta Felipe:	*Dear Mmes. Lucía Aragón and Marta Felipe:*
Estimado Sr. Bermúdez:	*Dear Mr. Bermúdez:*
Estimados Sres. Alberto Correa y Luis Correa:	*Dear Messrs. Alberto Correa and Luis Correa:*
Estimada señora:	*Dear Madam:*
Estimado señor:	*Dear Sir:*

The English abbreviation *Ms.* does not have a Spanish equivalent. Use **Sra.**, a title of courtesy, even if you do not know a woman's marital status. Note the Spanish punctuation for greetings. A colon (:) follows a formal salutation, both in English and Spanish.

Use the following salutations only to address a person you do not know:

Muy señor mío:	*Dear Sir:*
Muy señora mía:	*Dear Madam:*
Muy señores míos:	*Dear Sirs:*
Muy señoras mías:	*Dear Mesdames:*

With individuals who have a professional title, use the title if you know it:

Estimada señora Directora:	*Dear Director:*
Estimado Dr. Aranguren:	*Dear Dr. Aranguren:*
Estimada Dra. Bernal:	*Dear Dr. Bernal:*

Body of the letter

Here are a number of set phrases that appear frequently in the body of a formal letter:

A través de la presente	*The purpose of this letter*
De acuerdo con su solicitud	*In regard to your request*
Deseo comunicarle	*I would like to tell you*
He recibido su atenta carta	*I have received your letter*

Lamento informarle	*I am sorry to tell you*
Por medio de esta carta	*The purpose of this letter*
Tengo el gusto de comunicarle que	*I have the pleasure to inform you that*

Remember that the *conditional* and the *imperfect subjunctive* verb forms are used to indicate politeness:

Quisiera pedirle	***I would like*** *to request*
Nos gustaría recibir	***We would like*** *to receive*

Formal closings

In Spanish, formal closing formulas are often more elaborate than English closings and do not translate literally into English. Here are a few frequently used examples. Note that they are followed by a comma (,):

Atentamente,	*Respectfully yours,*
Con mi más cordial saludo,	*Sincerely,*
Con todo mi respeto,	*Yours truly,*
Cordialmente,	*Truly yours,*
Muy agradecido/a por su atención,	*With gratitude,*
Le saluda atentamente,	*Truly yours,*
Respetuosamente,	*Very truly yours,*
Su servidor,	*Yours truly,*
Un saludo afectuoso,	*Sincerely,*

Avoid using **sinceramente** at the end of a letter. It does *not* have the same meaning that it does in English.

The final closing of your letter is your signature. A postscript may be added. The abbreviation of the Latin phrase in English is *P.S.*, *postscriptum*. The corresponding phrase in Spanish is **P.D.**, **postdata**.

P.D. No olvide enviarme la cuenta.	**P.S.** *Do not forget to send me the bill.*

EJERCICIO
19·3

Práctica. *Usa la información que aparece a continuación y escribe la fecha, el saludo y una despedida para una carta formal.*

MODELO   Santiago de Compostela / March 12, 2002 / la presidenta de Asturias, S.A.

Santiago de Compostela, 12 de marzo de 2002

Estimada Sra. Presidenta:

Atentamente,

1. Madrid / May 3, 2001 / Doctor Blanco (tu médico)

_____

_____

_____

2. Guadalajara / July 19, 2009 / Berta Rodríguez (la abuela de uno de tus amigos)

_____

_____

_____

3. San Diego / January 13, 2010 / Pedro Vázquez (capitán de la policía)

_____

_____

_____

Informal letters

An informal letter is written to those familiar to you. A personal letter is sometimes written on personalized stationary that provides the writer's contact information.

Place and date

In an informal letter, the date may appear in numbers only. In Spanish, the first number refers to the day of the month. For a friendly letter, your address and the addressee's are not needed as part of the heading.

> Lima, 21-12-2002   _Lima, 12-21-2002_

Informal greetings

If you know the person to whom you are writing, use the correct form of the adjectives and nouns in the following formulas, with or without a first name. Note that a colon (:) is also used after an informal greeting in Spanish:

Querida amiga:	_Dear friend,_
Querida Ana:	_Dear Ana,_
Queridísimas hermanas:	_My dear sisters,_
Queridos Julio y Rosario:	_Dear Julio and Rosario,_

Informal closings

In English and in Spanish the closing of the letter will depend on the degree of intimacy between the intended reader and the person who writes the letter. Sometimes the closing is an entire sentence (ending with a period); sometimes it is just a phrase or a word (usually ending with a comma or an exclamation mark). These expressions cannot be translated literally. Note that many include the word **amistad** (_friendship_) or a reference to the relationship:

Abrazos y besos cariñosos,	_Hugs and kissses,_
Cariñosamente,	_Warm regards,_
Tu amigo/a,	_Your friend,_

The closing can be a full sentence in the first or third person, ending with a period:

Cuenta conmigo.	_You have all my support. (Count on me.)_
Te envío un abrazo cariñoso.	_My warmest regards,_
Te envío todo mi cariño.	_With all my love,_

Escribe la fecha en español. *Recuerda el orden de las palabras y la ortografía adecuada.*

1. 03-27-2000 _____

2. 05-05-1999 _____

3. 12-12-2008 _____

4. 08-08-2008 _____

5. 10-10-2003 _____

6. 02-10-1980 _____

Práctica. *Usa la información que aparece a continuación y escribe la fecha, el saludo y una despedida para una carta familiar.*

MODELO   Buenos Aires / March 25, 2001 / tu hermana Lucía

          Buenos Aires, 25 de marzo de 2001

          Mi querida (hermana) Lucía:

          Un abrazo,

1. Barcelona / May 10, 2001 / Anita (tu novia)

_____

_____

_____

2. Managua / June 9, 2002 / Úrsula Domínguez (tu tía)

_____

_____

_____

3. Guayaquil / August 3, 2003 / Pablo Duval (tu amigo de la infancia)

_____

_____

_____

Addressing an envelope

The following are the Spanish terms for addressing an envelope:

el/la remitente	*sender*
el/la destinatario/a	*addressee*
la dirección	*address*
el sobre	*the envelope*

When writing a person's address on an envelope, the lines follow a similar order in English and in Spanish. However, the order of the information in these lines varies. Your name and address appear at the top left corner of the envelope. The addressee's full name appears on the envelope. Courtesy titles may be used. Note the abbreviations; you may want to review the list under the section "Formal greetings," earlier in this chapter:

Sr. D. (Don)	*Mr.*
Sra. Dña. (Doña)	*Miss, Ms., Mrs.*

In many Spanish-speaking countries, addresses are longer; they may include numbers and letters that indicate streets and/or apartment numbers, even the floor numbers in a building, the name of a neighborhood within a city, and the zip code numbers (**distrito postal**). In some countries, the name of a province or state may also appear. Note that the name of the country must appear on international letters, as in the second example below:

Sr. Martín López Calvo
Calle Moratines, 25, 2° A
14225 Gijón, Asturias

Dr. A. López Iriarte
Calle de la Victoria, 30
Colonia "La Colmena"
Quito, Ecuador

Note that in Spanish-speaking countries, a street may be called **Callejón** (*alley*), **Camino** (*path*), or **Paseo** (*promenade*). Those names may be capitalized. The word **Avenida** (*avenue*) is usually abbreviated (**Ave.**):

Sra. María Pastor de González
Ave. de la Reina Victoria, 13, 4°, A
07882, Madrid

Note that the zip code consists of five digits and appears before the name of the town or city in most addresses throughout the Hispanic world.

When writing to a company, write the company's name on the first line, then the department and the name of the person (if applicable) on the second line, the street address on the third line, the zip code followed by the city on the fourth line, and the country on the fifth line. See the following example:

Aseguradora del Norte S.A.
Sra. Vallejo, Departamento de Reclamaciones
Avenida del Puerto, 118 Entresuelo
75009 Pontevedra (Galicia)

Escribe el sobre. *Usa la información para escribir el título y nombre del destinatario y su dirección en el orden apropiado. Usa la puntuación adecuada.*

MODELO   Una carta para tu abuela Margarita López-Rivas / Paseo de la Victoria / 27 / 1er Piso / Badajoz / 25667

    Sra. Margarita López

    Paseo de la Victoria, 27, Primer Piso

    25667 Badajoz

1. Una carta para tu amiga Lidia Gómez / Avenida del Norte / 27 / Barcelona / 00087

    _____

    _____

    _____

2. Una carta para el alcalde Raúl Benítez / Alcaldía de Pueblo Nuevo / 305 / Torreón / 27250 / México D.F.

    _____

    _____

    _____

3. Una carta para tus tíos Dolores y José Antonio Bermúdez / Calle C, 17111 / Apart. D / La Habana / 00891

    _____

    _____

    _____

Text messaging and e-mails

E-mail and text messaging have become the fastest ways to communicate all over the world. In Spanish, e-mail is most commonly called by an adaptation of its English name, **el email**, but it is also called **un correo**, **el correo electrónico**. The acronym **SMS** stands for both *Short Message Service* and **servicio de mensaje corto**. The acronym is used in text messaging, since it fits in a small screen.

Text messages use characters, letters, and numbers that can be read to reproduce sound (**bbr**, **beber** *to drink*) that imitates a word, abbreviations that reproduce sound to create a word (**bb**, **bebé** *baby*), and acronyms. It is a changing language, and there are variations throughout the Hispanic world. The following list is for your reference:

a2	adiós	*good-bye*	pco	poco	*a little*
ac	hace	*form of* hacer, *to do*	pf	por favor	*please*
aki	aquí	*here*	pq	porque	*because, why*
amr	amor	*love*	q	que	*that, what*
aora	ahora	*now*	q acs?	¿Qué haces?	*What are you doing?*
bb	bebé	*baby*	qand	cuando	*when*
bbr	beber	*to drink*	qdms	quedamos	*we're staying*
bs	besos	*kisses*	q qrs?	¿Qué quieres?	*What do you want?*
bye	adiós	*good-bye*	q risa!	¡Qué risa!	*What a laugh!*
chao	adiós	*good-bye*	q sea	qué sea	*whatever*
d2	dedos	*fingers*	q tal?	¿qué tal?	*What's happening?*
dfcl	difícil	*difficult*	sbs?	¿sabes?	*Do you know?*
dnd	dónde	*where*	salu2	saludos	*hello, good-bye*
exo	hecho	*act*	sms	mensaje	*message*
grrr	enfadado	*angry*	spro	espero	*I hope*
finde	fin de semana	*weekend*	tq	te quiero	*I love you*
hl	hasta luego	*see you later*	tqi	tengo que irme	*I have to leave*
k	que, qué	*that, what*	tb	también	*also*
kls	clase	*class*	tas OK?	¿Estás bien?	*Are you OK?*
KO	estoy muerto/a	*I'm in big trouble*	tqm	te quiero mucho	*I love you a lot*
msj	mensaje	*message*	tb	también	*also*
mxo	mucho	*a lot*	zzz	dormir	*sleeping*
npn	no pasa nada	*nothing's happening*			

E-mail messages are mostly used for informal communication. In the business world, though, they often must respect some of the formal conventions of the written language. A person's full name, business title, phone, and fax number appear at the bottom of the message. Accents are often avoided so as not to interfere with e-mail systems. No added dates are needed for e-mail messages.

Remember to use the appropriate format to write an e-mail to a friend: use an informal register for the greeting, the body of the message, and the closing. Use polite verb forms, a formal salutation, and a formal closing when sending a message to a person you do not know. Don't forget to use the appropriate punctuation.

EJERCICIO 19·7

Te toca a ti. *Vas a escribir dos correos electrónicos. Sigue las instrucciones para cada mensaje. ¡No olvides la puntuación apropiada!*

1. Escríbele un correo electrónico a un(a) amigo/a a.) salúdalo/la; b.) invítalo/la a tu fiesta el día de tu cumpleaños; c.) despídete.

_____

_____

_____

_____

2. Escríbele un correo electrónico al/la gobernador/a de tu estado o provincia a.) salúdalo/la; b.) felicítalo/la por su trabajo; c.) despídete.

_____

_____

_____

_____

Let's write!

Now it's time for you to become more independent in your writing. You've practiced writing different types of sentences. Learning to write effectively takes time and practice, especially in a second language. You are now aware of your weaknesses and, most of all, your strengths. You have studied and practiced how to convey ideas with both simple and complex sentences, strengthening your abilities to better communicate in Spanish.

We will start this unit with simple exercises and then move on to more complex sentences and paragraphs and more challenging activities. Study the model answers in each exercise. You will find examples of possible answers for most exercises in the Answer key.

EJERCICIO 20·1

Vamos a escribir oraciones. *Usa el tiempo verbal que indica cada paréntesis. Usa las formas apropiadas de los sustantivos, adjetivos o artículos de las palabras sugeridas para cada oración. ¡Usa la puntuación apropiada!*

MODELO   (*preterit*) mi / vecino / ir / a / el / Perú

        Mi vecino fue al Perú.

1. (*preterit*) mis / hermano / visitar / ese / región / vario / vez

   _____

2. (*preterit, passive voice*) el / idea / sugerir / por / la agencia / de viajes

   _____

3. (*imperfect*) el / proyecto / de / el / viaje / ser / interesante

   _____

4. (*preterit*) un / grupo / local / compartir / el / trayectoria / con / el / viajeros

   _____

5. (*preterit, passive voice*) el / turistas / recibir / por / un / banda / de música

   _____

6. (*imperfect*) el / cantante / no / cantar / en / español

_____

7. (*present*) ahora / hacer / planes / para / viajar / a / el / sur / de / Bolivia

_____

8. (*future*) el / próximo / vacaciones / mi / sobrinas / venir a / mi / casa

_____

EJERCICIO
20·2

Entrevistas cortas. *Usa las palabras interrogativas y escribe cinco preguntas acerca del tema de cada oración. Incluye los signos de interrogación.*

MODELO   Voy a ver una película.

¿qué? / ¿quién? / ¿por qué? / ¿dónde? / ¿cuándo? / ¿cómo?

¿Qué película quieres ver?

¿Quién es el protagonista?

¿Dónde filmaron la película?

¿Cuándo quieres ver la película?

¿Cómo es la película, corta o larga?

1. El vuelo Barcelona-Madrid tiene dos horas de retraso (*delay*).

¿por qué? / ¿quién?, ¿quiénes? / ¿dónde? / ¿cuándo? / ¿qué?

_____

_____

_____

_____

_____

2. Hoy es el aniversario de bodas de mis padres.

¿qué? / ¿quién?, ¿quiénes? / ¿dónde? / ¿cuándo? / ¿cómo?

_____

_____

_____

_____

_____

3. Vamos a cenar.

   ¿dónde? / ¿cuál? / ¿quién?, ¿quiénes? / ¿por qué? / ¿cuánto?

   _____

   _____

   _____

   _____

4. Mi amigo está en el hospital.

   ¿cómo? / ¿qué? / ¿quién?, ¿quiénes? / ¿dónde? / ¿cuándo?

   _____

   _____

   _____

   _____

5. Hay una venta especial en la tienda de productos electrónicos.

   ¿qué? / ¿dónde? / ¿cuánto/a?, ¿cuántos/as? / ¿cómo?

   _____

   _____

   _____

   _____

6. Hoy es mi cumpleaños.

   ¿cuántos?, ¿cuántas? / ¿qué? / ¿con quién?, ¿con quiénes? / ¿dónde? / ¿cómo?

   _____

   _____

   _____

   _____

Mis experiencias. *Escribe cada oración con las palabras sugeridas. Usa la persona* **yo** *del imperfecto de indicativo para los verbos entre paréntesis y las formas correspondientes de los sustantivos y adjetivos.*

MODELO   hace mucho tiempo (querer) escribir (vario) libros ya que (gustar) contar anécdotas

       Hace mucho tiempo, quería escribir varios libros ya que me gustaba contar anécdotas.

1. en otra época (ser) (más / menos) paciente porque (tener) (más / menos) tiempo.

    _____

2. a menudo (estudiar) español ya que (querer) hablar (claro) con mis amigos (mexicano)

    _____

3. con frecuencia (aprender) a escribir (mucho) tipos de oraciones más (complejo)

    _____

4. siempre (poder) contar con mi (bueno) amigo Pablito

    _____

5. a veces no (tener) la constancia (necesario) ni la disciplina (preciso) para estudiar

    _____

6. día tras día (ser) difícil escribir en dos idiomas (diferente) y a veces con palabras no (similar)

    _____

7. en ocasiones (ir) al cine para ver películas (mexicano) y (colombiano) y eran (divertido)

    _____

8. con frecuencia (reflexionar) sobre la (poco) capacidad de los seres humanos para ser (constante) y (dedicado)

    _____

Te toca a ti. *Vuelve al Ejercicio 20-3 (1-6) y* subraya *las frases adverbiales que indican la necesidad de usar el imperfecto. Ahora, usa* las frases subrayadas *y el verbo para escribir tus propias oraciones y narrar una anécdota tuya.*

MODELO   frase + tener

En otra época, yo tenía más tiempo para escribir cartas a mis amigos en varios estados de EE.UU.

1. frase + poder

_____

2. frase + querer

_____

3. frase + poder

_____

4. frase + ir

_____

5. frase + comprar

_____

6. frase + practicar

_____

Tus preferencias. *¿Te gusta la música? ¿El cine? ¿Te gustaba más leer cuando eras pequeño/a? Conecta tus ideas usando las conjunciones para escribir tus oraciones. Recuerda usar la puntuación apropiada.*

MODELO   No tolero _____ ni _____ .

No tolero la hipocresía, ni las personas que no dicen la verdad.

1. Me gustan _____ pero _____ .

_____

2. _____ y también _____ .

_____

3. En ocasiones _____ o _____ .

_____

4. _____ pero no puedo _____ .

_____

5. Detesto _____ , aunque _____ .

_____

6. No _____ , sino _____ .

_____

¿Cómo eres? El poder de las palabras. *Escribe un párrafo para describir quién y cómo eres: tu familia, tus costumbres, tus logros (achievements), tu educación y tus sueños. Piensa en los adjetivos, los adverbios y los tiempos verbales que necesitas para comunicar tus ideas.*

MODELO   *Me llamo Julián y tengo veintidós años. Soy alto, delgado y tengo el pelo rubio. Soy trabajador y quiero escribir bien en español.*

Así soy yo.

_____

_____

_____

_____

_____

_____

_____

Comparación y contraste. *Vas a escribir oraciones para comparar y contrastar ideas. Antes de escribir, repasa (review) las palabras y frases de comparación y contrastes y los tiempos del pasado, presente y futuro.*

MODELO   *La tecnología avanza muy rápido. Antes, los teléfonos celulares eran más grandes y caros. Ahora, son pequeños y más baratos.*

La tecnología y el futuro.

_____

_____

_____

_____

_____

_____

Los jóvenes. *Escribe un párrafo sobre los jóvenes de hoy. Incluye la voz pasiva y la pasiva refleja para no revelar tu identidad. Describe los jóvenes, la moda, las costumbres y los pasatiempos.*

MODELO   *Los jóvenes son la esperanza del mundo. Generalmente, son criticados por las personas mayores. Se dice que los jóvenes son egoístas, pero no siempre es verdad.*

Los jóvenes de hoy.

_____

_____

_____

_____

_____

_____

Si pudieras cambiar algo en tu vida, ¿qué harías? *Escribe un párrafo para explicar esta pregunta. Puedes usar el tiempo condicional o el subjuntivo.*

MODELO

    Si yo pudiera, no viviría en Estados Unidos por un año. Yo viviría en México para aprender español. Después, yo viajaría a Chile para conocer a los padres de mi amigo Felipe Cerdeña.

Si pudiera cambiar algo en mi vida,

_____

_____

_____

_____

_____

_____

Una carta. *Escríbele una carta a un(a) amigo/a. Cuéntale acerca de tu trabajo o tus estudios, del último libro que has leído y de tus planes para el futuro. Sigue el formato para una carta familiar. Incluye la puntuación apropiada.*

MODELO

                      Los Angeles, 25 de marzo de 2008

   Querida Martica:

       ¿Cómo estás? Quiero compartir contigo mis ideas.

Una carta a un(a) amigo/a:

                           _____

_____

_____

_____

_____

_____

_____

_____

_____

Review

·21·

This chapter offers a review of the structures presented throughout the whole book. Each exercise links to a specific chapter.

EJERCICIO
21·1

Chapter 1: Declarative sentences and word order. *Contesta cada pregunta en una oración completa. Usa la información entre paréntesis para la respuesta.*

1. ¿Dónde viven ustedes? (en ese edificio)

   _____

2. ¿Qué hizo el piloto? (aterrizar el avión)

   _____

3. ¿A qué hora van a salir tus amigos? (a las cuatro y media)

   _____

4. ¿A quién viste en el restaurante? (a Luisa)

   _____

5. ¿Cuándo recibió Ana el email? (anoche)

   _____

6. ¿Conoces a mi jefe? (no)

   _____

7. ¿Con qué frecuencia dice mentiras él? (siempre)

   _____

8. ¿Cuándo tiene tiempo libre Marta? (nunca)

   _____

9. ¿Viene alguien mañana? (no)

   _____

Chapter 2: Interrogative sentences. *Forma una pregunta para cada una de las respuestas a continuación.*

1. _____

Esperamos hasta las cinco.

2. _____

Sí, los estudiantes aprecian los comentarios de la profesora.

3. _____

No, no entregué el coche.

4. _____

No, señor. No tengo el boleto.

5. _____

Prefieren café.

6. _____

Ana va a dormir en la hamaca. No le gusta dormir en el sillón.

7. _____

Sí, es verdad.

8. _____

¡Claro que no!

EJERCICIO
21·3

Chapter 3: Questions and answers. I. *Contesta cada pregunta en una oración completa. Traduce las expresiones al español para las repuestas.*

1. ¿Adónde van tus amigos? (downtown)

_____

2. ¿Hasta cuándo vas a trabajar? (3 p.m.)

_____

3. ¿Dónde vive Isabel? (Salamanca)

_____

4. ¿Cómo están ustedes? (fine)

_____

II. *Forma una pregunta para cada respuesta. Empieza cada pregunta con <u>una palabra interrogativa</u>, por ejemplo, ¿Dónde?/¿Cuándo?/etc.*

1. _____

He visitado dieciséis países.

2. _____

El rojo y el amarillo son mis colores preferidos.

3. _____

Necesito cien dólares.

4. _____

Alex es inteligente, simpático y guapo.

5. _____

Sus padres van a comprar una casa, no un carro.

6. _____

Los regalos son para Lupita y su hermana.

7. _____

No vamos al concierto porque no tenemos el dinero para los boletos.

EJERCICIO
21·4

Chapter 4: Exclamatory sentences. I. *Reacciona a cada declaración con una frase exclamativa.*

1. Estos zapatos me costaron cien dólares.

_____

2. Mi sobrina va a tocar el violín esta noche.

_____

3. Vamos a invitar a treinta personas a cenar aquí en la casa.

_____

4. No podemos ir a la boda porque mi esposo está enfermo.

_____

5. Nos vemos aquí el jueves a las cuatro.

_____

II. *Escribe una oración o una pregunta para cada una de las siguientes reacciones.*

1. _____

   ¡Uf! Estoy cansadísima.

2. _____

   ¡Ojalá!

3. _____

   ¡Cómo miente ese chico!

4. _____

   ¡Pobre de ti!

5. _____

   ¡Menuda suerte que tienes!

EJERCICIO 21·5

Chapter 5: Imperatives. *Traduce al español las siguientes oraciones imperativas, usando las personas indicadas.*

1. Open the window. (tú)

   _____

2. Come in, please. (usted)

   _____

3. Buy the tickets yourselves! (vosotros)

   _____

4. Tell the truth! (tú)

   _____

5. Let's not invite so many people. (nosotros)

   _____

6. The game? Forget it! (vosotros)

   _____

7. Don't wait for me. (ustedes)

   _____

8. The homework? Just do it! (tú)

   _____

9. My keys? Find them! (ustedes)

_____

10. Don't call me! (tú)

_____

Chapter 6: Building sentences with coordinating conjunctions. *Combina cada par de oraciones con la conjunción más apropiada. Elije entre:*
o / pero / sino / ni / y

1. Juega bien al fútbol. Juega mejor al ténis.

_____

2. Vamos a México por dos semanas. Luego iremos a Guatemala.

_____

3. No fui al cine. Fui al teatro.

_____

4. No fui al cine. No fui al teatro.

_____

5. ¿Quieres helado? ¿Quieres un refresco?

_____

Chapter 7: Building sentences with subordinating conjunctions I. *Combina cada par de oraciones con una conjunción apropiada. En algunos casos, hay más de una posibilidad. Elije entre:*
porque / desde que / aunque / si / por más que / ya que / puesto que

1. No compré la blusa. Me gustaba mucho.

_____

2. Fui a ver esa película. La película recibió el premio Óscar el año pasado.

_____

3. Voy a mudarme a otra ciudad. Quisiera quedarme aquí con ustedes.

_____

4. Te ayudo con las matemáticas. Me ayudas con el español.

_____

5. Ya nos vamos. Todos estamos listos.

_____

6. Todos estamos contentos. Mi hermano ha vuelto a casa.

_____

II. *Escribe una pregunta para cada respuesta.*

1. _____

    No sé si Jaime va con nosotros hoy.

2. _____

    No sé dónde están mis padres.

3. _____

    Los zapatos cuestan $75.00.

4. _____

    Salí temprano porque estaba enojada.

5. _____

    Le mandamos la carta al director de la escuela.

6. _____

    El baile que me gusta más es el merengue.

EJERCICIO
21·8

Chapter 8: Relative pronouns. *Combina cada par de frases al usar el pronombre relativo más apropiado. Elije entre:*
que / quien / quienes / el que / lo que / los cuales / cuyo / lo cual

1. Cancelaron el examen. Me alivió.

_____

2. Mi hermana menor vive en California. Ella viene a visitarnos este verano.

_____

3. El profesor es un genio. Su libro explica todo de una forma sencilla.

_____

4. El verano pasado leí muchos libros. Algunos son muy interestantes.

_____

5. Mi amiga hace las cosas que quiere hacer. No hace las cosas que no quiere hacer.

_____

6. Voy a hablar con mi amiga. Ella escribió su tesis sobre este tópico.

_____

7. Ayer compré dos vestido nuevos. Me gusta más el rojo.

_____

8. Los estudiantes son de Argentina. Van a pasar un semestre en esta universidad.

_____

EJERCICIO
21·9

Chapter 9: Pronouns. *I. Subraya las respuestas más apropiadas. Underline the most appropriate answers.*

1. ¿Quién es esa chica?

   a. Ella es mi hermana.   b. Es mi hermana.

2. ¿Cuál de las chicas es la mexicana?

   a. Ella es la mexicana.   b. Es la mexicana.

3. ¿Quién ganó el premio?

   a. Él lo ganó.   b. Lo ganó.

4. ¿Han llegado los huéspedes?

   a. Sí, ellos han llegado.   b. Sí, han llegado.

II. Escribe cada oración de nuevo, sustituyendo los objetos directos e indirectos con los pronombres correspondientes.

1. Luisa conoce a Jacobo.

_____

2. Jorge le regaló la corbata a su hermano.

_____

3. María Isabel toca la guitarra.

_____

4. La señora me mostró las fotos de sus nietos.

_____

5. Ayer compramos los boletos para el concierto.

_____

III. *Contesta cada pregunta en una frase completa.*

1. ¿A qué hora te despiertas los sábados?

   _____

2. ¿Cuándo se ponen los abrigos los niños?

   _____

3. ¿De qué se preocupa tu mejor amigo?

   _____

4. ¿Qué comida te gusta más?

   _____

5. ¿A tu mejor amigo le gusta bailar?

   _____

6. ¿Qué tipo de libros les interesa a ti y a tus amigos?

   _____

7. ¿Qué regalos les agradan más a las mujeres? (en general)

   _____

8. ¿Qué personas te importan más en la vida?

   _____

EJERCICIO 21·10

Chapter 10: Using adjectives. *Traduce las siguientes oraciones al español.*

1. My sisters are tall, but I am short.

   _____

2. Yesterday I bought some interesting books.

   _____

3. Three of the books are great novels of the 20th century.

   _____

4. The author dedicated his book to his beloved wife, Margarita.

   _____

5. The poor girl got lost three times!

   _____

6. If you go through the open door, you will find the broken furniture.

_____

7. They have three girls, and the baby is their first boy.

_____

8. That gentleman sent you this red rose.

_____

Chapter 11: Using adverbs. *Traduce las siguientes oraciones al español.*

1. During the day, the children play outside.

_____

2. Afterwards, and with great pleasure, we went to the party.

_____

3. They behave badly in class, in general.

_____

4. Without a doubt, he earns very little.

_____

5. I'm not going to complain immediately, either.

_____

6. She always speaks slowly and carefully.

_____

7. The dresses are made by hand and are sold at a good price.

_____

8. Mario has already contacted me, but the others haven't called yet.

_____

9. He doesn't go anywhere at night.

_____

10. Of course, she talks incessantly.

_____

EJERCICIO
21·12

Chapter 12: Using infinitives. *Traduce las siguientes oraciones al español.*

1. I love to watch baseball!

   _____

2. Learning is fun.

   _____

3. Playing baseball instead of studying isn't always a good idea.

   _____

4. We prefer to relax after working all day.

   _____

5. She left without saying goodbye.

   _____

6. What do you want to do after you visit your grandmother?

   _____

7. I'm not afraid to start a new career.

   _____

8. Seeing is believing.

   _____

9. It's impossible to hear in this restaurant.

   _____

10. They're going to wash the dishes after they eat.

    _____

EJERCICIO
21·13

Chapter 13: Idioms and special phrases. *Expresa cada frase con un modismo que tenga más o menos el mismo sentido.*

1. No puede dormir.

   _____

2. Está lloviendo mucho.

   _____

Review   **213**

3. Ella está enferma y tiene que quedarse en cama.

_____

4. Van muy rapido.

_____

5. Vamos a caminar un poco.

_____

6. Quiero bailar.

_____

7. La niña tiene miedo a los perros.

_____

8. Los chicos no prestan atención a la profesora.

_____

9. No me importa nada.

_____

10. La chica siempre llega tarde.

_____

EJERCICIO
21·14

Chapter 14: Comparisons, contrasts, and antonyms. I. *Lee la información y escribe la conclusión, usando la forma del verbo **ser** en el presente.*

1. La casa en el campo cuesta un millón de dólares. La casa en la ciudad cuesta un millón de dólares. (caro)

_____

2. El bolso de Ana pesa cuatro libros; el de su hermana pesa tres. (pesado)

_____

3. Javier tiene cincuenta años, Roberto tiene veinticinco y Carlos tiene diecisiete. (mayor)

_____

4. La estudiante es muy, muy lista.

_____

5. Ricardo corre alrededor de la pista en cinco minutos. Álvaro corre alrededor de la pista en cuatro minutos, 30 segundos. (rápido)

_____

II. *Escribe los antónimos de las siguientes palabras.*

1. alegre _____

2. cariñoso _____

3. famoso _____

4. hábil _____

5. tacaño _____

6. callada _____

7. inculto _____

8. el desempleo _____

9. el despegar _____

10. la soledad _____

11. la pobreza _____

12. la mentira _____

13. la intolerancia _____

14. la locura _____

EJERCICIO 21·15

Chapter 15: The passive voice. I. *Cambia las oraciones de la voz activa a la voz pasiva.*

1. Las tormentas han destruido varias casas en el área.

_____

2. En general, la gente observó las recomendaciones de las autoridades.

_____

3. Las clínicas ofrecerán servicios de primer auxilio gratis a los heridos.

_____

II. *Cambia las construcciones en voz pasiva a voz pasiva refleja.*

1. El gobierno fue formado en 1963.

_____

2. Las nuevas leyes fueron aprobadas en seguida.

_____

3. Los líderes del antiguo gobierno fueron encarcelados.

____

4. Los libros de historia fueron quemados y la historia del país fue escrita de nuevo.

____

EJERCICIO
21·16

Chapter 16: The subjunctive mood. I. *Usa el presente del subjuntivo para traducir las siguientes oraciones al español.*

1. I want you to come to my party.

____

2. We request that you all arrive at 4 o'clock.

____

3. I doubt that it will rain.

____

4. It's incredible that you're turning (cumplir) thirty!

____

5. I hope to find a new dress that isn't very expensive.

____

II. *Usa el condicional y el imperfecto de subjuntivo para traducir las siguientes oraciones al español.*

1. I would buy a new car if I had more money.

____

2. We would speak better Spanish if we lived in Spain.

____

3. He would visit you in the hospital if he weren't sick himself.

____

4. They would come back home if they found work here in the city.

____

Chapter 17: The subjunctive mood and verb tenses. *Completa las siguientes oraciones usando las formas apropiadas del subjuntivo.*

1. Es necesario que todos (estudiar) _____ para el examen final.

2. Pídele a tu hermano que no (conducir) _____ tan rápido.

3. Estoy seguro que el profesor me dirá que (leer) _____ en voz alta.

4. ¿Van ustedes a exigir que (volver, nosotros) _____ a casa?

5. Espero que no (haber suspendido, tú) _____ el examen.

6. No creo que los chicos (haber salido) _____ todavía.

7. Era imprescindible que (ver, nosotros) _____ película.

8. Le sugerimos a Alba que (ayudar) _____ a su hermano.

9. Habríamos preferido que ella (comer) _____ lo que preparamos.

10. A mí me habría gustado que ellos (divertirse) _____ más.

Chapter 18: Punctuation and Spelling. *I. Combina las siguientes abreviaturas con sus equivalentes en inglés.*

1. a.C.   _____ Miss

2. EE.UU.   _____ Inc.

3. P.D.   _____ European Union (EU)

4. ONU   _____ The United Nations (UN)

5. S.A.   _____ Dr. (female)

6. Dra.   _____ P.S.

7. Srta.   _____ B.C.

8. UE   _____ The United States (USA / U.S.)

II. *Traduce la oración siguiente al español. Asegúrate de hacer caso a las diferencias formales en la escritura de las dos lenguas.*

It is very cold in parts of the U.S. in the months of December, January, and February.

_____

_____

Chapter 19: Letter writing. I. *Contesta las preguntas sobre las normas de una carta formal escrita en español.*

1. In a formal letter written in Spanish, where is the <u>heading</u> written?

   _____

2. What is included in the <u>heading</u>?

   _____

3. How is the date written?

   _____

4. How do you write the following:

   a. Dear Miss Sánchez: _____

   b. Dear Dr. Martínez: _____

   c. Dear Sir: _____

   d. Dear Sirs: _____

5. How could you express the following:

   a. I would like to inform you …   _____

   b. I would like to request …   _____

   c. Respectfully yours,   _____

   d. Sincerely,   _____

   e. sP.S.   _____

Answer key

1 Declarative sentences and word order

1·1 1. F 2. O 3. O 4. F 5. F 6. O

1·2 1. Mi hermano Marcos estuvo en Buenos Aires.; Mi hermano Marcos estará en Buenos Aires. 2. Él vivió en Argentina.; Él vivirá en Argentina. 3. Tuvo un apartamento en el centro de la ciudad.; Tendrá un apartamento en el centro de la ciudad. 4. Trabajó en una oficina del gobierno.; Trabajará en una oficina del gobierno. 5. Marcos viajó a Santiago también.; Marcos viajará a Santiago también.

1·3 1. Pedro Gómez vive en ese edificio. 2. Lucía es la esposa de Pedro. 3. Leímos la noticia de su boda en el periódico. 4. Tienen una casa en la playa. 5. Lucía y su esposo salieron de luna de miel. 6. Pedro y Lucía nacieron en Barcelona. 7. Mis hermanos estudiaron con ellos. 8. Recibimos un email de Pedro anoche.

1·4 *Some examples; other answers are possible:* 1. cuando necesito comunicarme 2. día tras día 3. cuando hago mucho ejercicio 4. en la piscina olímpica 5. en diez minutos 6. con sólo un billete 7. con frecuencia 8. en el autobús camino a casa

1·5 1. el cumpleaños de Laura 2. una fiesta 3. none 4. a Laura 5. la cena 6. mi guitarra 7. dos rancheras 8. none 9. su nombre

1·6 1. una reacción 2. un presidente 3. un problema 4. un recuento 5. una pregunta 6. una campaña 7. una solución

1·7 1. X 2. X 3. a 4. X 5. a 6. a 7. a 8. a

1·8 1. Melisa trabaja en la librería. 2. Ella ve a su jefe en la parada del autobús todas las mañanas. 3. Yo conozco a su jefe. 4. Él bebe cuatro tazas de café por la mañana. 5. Melisa prefiere el té. 6. Yo vi a su jefe la semana pasada. 7. Él lleva / usa ropas viejas. 8. El jefe de Melisa necesita una chaqueta nueva.

1·9 1. Paula alquiló un apartamento a su hermana Ana. 2. Ella tiene la llave del apartamento. 3. La hermana necesita ayuda. 4. Ana estudia inglés en la universidad. 5. Ella encontrará un trabajo mejor. 6. Ana y su hermana envían saludos a sus amigos. 7. Invitan a sus primos a su apartamento.

1·10 *Possible answers:* 1. Jamás digo mentiras. 2. Nunca falto a mi trabajo. 3. Nunca duermo hasta tarde. 4. Jamás termino el desayuno. 5. Tampoco ahorro agua. 6. Nunca gasto todo mi salario en la tienda. 7. Ni recibo un bono por Navidad.

1·11 1. Los políticos no mienten nunca.; Los políticos no mienten jamás. 2. Los periodistas no redactan noticias optimistas nunca.; Los periodistas no redactan noticias optimistas jamás. 3. Los vendedores no respaldan sus productos nunca.; Los vendedores no respaldan sus productos jamás. 4. Los camareros no sirven a los clientes con amabilidad nunca.; Los camareros no sirven a los clientes con amabilidad jamás. 5. Los maestros no asignan poca tarea a sus estudiantes nunca.; Los maestros no asignan poca tarea a sus estudiantes jamás. 6. Los marineros no tienen miedo al mar nunca.; Los marineros no tienen miedo al mar jamás.

1·12 1. Nunca 2. nada 3. no / nunca 4. nunca / jamás 5. nadie 6. nada

2 Interrogative sentences

2·1 1. ¿Llegas tarde? 2. ¿María ya está lista? 3. ¿Tiene poca paciencia? 4. ¿Esperamos hasta las cinco? 5. ¿Hay un taxi en la esquina? 6. ¿Hace calor en la calle? 7. ¿Lloverá esta noche? 8. ¿Llegaremos al cine a tiempo?

2·2 1. ¿No te gusta tu trabajo? 2. ¿Todavía no ganas mucho dinero? 3. ¿Ya no estudias en una universidad? 4. ¿No estás listo/a para un ascenso? 5. ¿Todavía no tienes novio/a? 6. ¿Ya no estás enamorado/a?

2·3 1. ¿Es ella tu profesora de matemáticas? 2. ¿Aprecian los alumnos los conocimientos de la profesora? 3. ¿Tiene ella un hermano en esta facultad? 4. ¿Eres su alumna preferida? 5. ¿Admira a sus colegas de otras disciplinas? 6. ¿Responde ella tus preguntas? 7. ¿Explicó la profesora la teoría?

2·4 1. ¿Uds. van de viaje a Barcelona? 2. ¿Los chicos visitarán a sus abuelos? 3. ¿Tus padres recibirán a mis amigos? 4. ¿Tú hablas catalán? 5. ¿Tu marido visitará a tus padres? 6. ¿Todos regresarán a mi casa?

2·5 1. ¿Necesita Ud. ayuda? 2. ¿Ven ustedes a los niños? 3. ¿Ya llegaron Uds.? / ¿Llegaron ya Uds.? 4. ¿Hizo Ud. una donación? 5. ¿Entregaron Uds. el auto? 6. ¿Quiere/Desea Ud. un asiento cerca de la ventana?

2·6 1. ¿Quiere/Desea Ud. este vestido? 2. ¿Prefiere Ud. este par de zapatos? 3. ¿Necesita Ud. lentes nuevos? 4. ¿Está Ud. cansado/a? 5. ¿Está Ud. listo/a para pagar? 6. ¿Pagó Ud. con una tarjeta de crédito?

2·7 1. ¿Prefieres un refresco de limón, una cola o una cerveza? 2. ¿Llegáis esta tarde o mañana? 3. ¿Desean ir a la playa o nadar en la piscina? 4. ¿Compramos la corbata, el sombrero o un libro? 5. ¿Quieren ver una película o cenar conmigo? 6. ¿Duerme en la hamaca o en el sillón? 7. ¿Vive en la ciudad o en el campo?

2·8 1. Lucía ve muchos programas dramáticos, ¿no? 2. Pedro prefiere los documentales del canal de cable, ¿no es verdad? 3. Carla y Marcos van a un concierto de un grupo mexicano, ¿no es cierto? 4. En el concierto venderán copias del último CD, ¿verdad? 5. Después del concierto irán a cenar todos juntos, ¿no es cierto? 6. Celebran la ocasión especial del cumpleaños de Lucía, ¿no es verdad?

2·9 *Possible answers:* 1. ¡Qué va! 2. ¡Qué va! 3. ¡Naturalmente! / ¡Claro que sí! 4. ¡Naturalmente! / ¡Claro que sí! 5. ¡Qué va!

3 Questions and answers

3·1 *Possible answers:* 1. ¿Cómo se llama? 2. ¿Dónde vive? 3. ¿Cuándo es su cumpleaños? 4. ¿Qué limpia / Qué hace Nora el viernes por la tarde? 5. ¿Qué estudia Nora? 6. ¿Dónde quiere trabajar Nora? 7. ¿Quiénes son sus amigas? 8. ¿Cuándo van de vacaciones?

3·2 1. Qué 2. Cuál 3. Cuáles 4. Cuál 5. Qué 6. Qué

3·3 1. ¿De dónde eres? 2. ¿Adónde vas? 3. ¿Desde cuándo estudias español? 4. ¿Cuándo vas a terminar / acabar este ejercicio? 5. ¿Hasta cuándo vas a esperar? 6. ¿A quién le escribes la mayoría de tus mensajes electrónicos? 7. ¿Quién toca a la puerta? 8. ¿Dónde estás (tú)?

3·4 1. ¿Cuántos países ha visitado? 2. ¿Cuándo decidió que quería ser cantante? 3. ¿Dónde será su próximo concierto? 4. ¿Cómo ensaya la voz para los conciertos? 5. ¿Por qué decidió dedicarse a la música? 6. ¿Cuáles son sus cantantes favoritos? 7. ¿Qué quiere hacer en el futuro? 8. ¿Cuándo serán sus próximas vacaciones?

3·5 1. ¿Cuántos años tiene Abel? 2. ¿A qué jugaba Abel? 3. ¿Quién lo llevaba? 4. ¿Qué quiere Abel? 5. ¿Dónde quiere jugar? 6. ¿Para qué equipo juega Abel? 7. ¿Cómo es Abel? 8. ¿Qué hace Abel para mantenerse en buena forma física? 9. ¿Qué será Abel? / ¿Quién será Abel? / ¿Cómo será Abel? 10. ¿Cuándo será famoso Abel?

3·6 1. Qué 2. Adónde 3. Cuándo 4. qué 5. qué 6. cuál 7. Qué 8. Qué / Cómo

4 Exclamatory sentences

4·1 1. ¡Hay una luna linda (bella)! 2. ¡Nosotras vamos a caminar por la playa! 3. ¡Hace mucho calor afuera! 4. ¡La limonada está fría! 5. ¡Lucy está muy cansada! 6. ¡Ahora nosotras estamos listas para descansar! 7. ¡No voy a dormir! 8. ¡Estoy de acuerdo!

4·3 1. ¡Cuánto cuestan estos zapatos!   2. ¡Qué largo es el vestido!   3. ¡Cómo ha subido el precio de la vida!   4. ¡Cuánto ganan!   5. ¡Qué amable es el camarero!   6. ¡Cuántas entradas vendieron para el concierto!   7. ¡Qué bien hacen la paella en este restaurante!   8. ¡Cuánta belleza hay en este lugar!

4·4 1. e   2. d   3. c   4. b   5. a

4·5 1. ¡Chitón, hay demasiado ruido!   2. ¡Cielos, la conferencia empieza a las ocho en punto!   3. ¡Pst / Chst / Eh, estamos aquí!   4. ¡Pobre de mí / Ay de mí, no tengo tiempo!   5. ¡Ojalá, necesito ganar!   6. ¡Ah, el reloj es bonito!

4·6 1. b / c   2. a   3. d   4. b / c   5. e

5 Imperatives

5·1 1. Trae el bolso / la cartera.   2. Lea la carta.   3. ¡Pase!   4. ¡Por favor, contesta el teléfono!   5. ¡Decide!   6. Escuchen, por favor.   7. ¡Crucen la calle ahora!   8. Ve a la estación de autobuses.

5·2 1. Escribe la carta ahora mismo.   2. Limpia el cuarto enseguida.   3. Haz la tarea de español.   4. Pon los papeles en la papelera.   5. Di la verdad.   6. Sal a la una de la tarde.   7. Ven a mi fiesta esta noche.   8. Ten paciencia.

5·3 1. Anita, llama al gerente.   2. Después, invita a los empleados.   3. No hagas más copias de estos documentos.   4. Lleva los modelos al Sr. Martínez.   5. Por favor, no revises las listas de clientes.   6. Y no ayudes al secretario.

5·4 2. Saque esa corbata de la vitrina, por favor.   5. Cargue la corbata a mi tarjeta de crédito.   6. Por favor, vaya a la otra caja.   7. Llame inmediatamente al gerente.   9. Guarde la corbata.

5·5 1. ¡Usemos el diccionario!   2. ¡Hagamos /Hagámosle preguntas a la maestra!   3. ¡Viajemos a México!   4. ¡Veamos telenovelas colombianas!   5. ¡Repasemos la gramática!   6. ¡Escuchemos las canciones españolas!

5·6 1. Preparen el salón.   2. Limpien las mesas.   3. Compren las bebidas.   4. Envíen las invitaciones.   5. Envuelvan los regalos.   6. Traigan las flores.

5·7 2. Corte la cebolla.   3. Abra la botella de aceite.   5. Sirva las cervezas a los invitados.

5·8 1. la; ¡Llámala!   2. los; ¡Recógelos!   3. nos; ¡Cómpranoslas!   4. me, lo; ¡Dímelo!   5. me, lo; ¡Léemelo!   6. me; ¡Espérame!

5·9 1. ¿La ventana? ¡Ciérrala ahora mismo!   2. ¿Tus zapatos? ¡No los tires al suelo!   3. ¿El perro? ¡No lo molestes!   4. ¿Tus amigos? ¡Llámalos a su casa!   5. ¿Las toallas? ¡Búscalas en el dormitorio!   6. ¿El auto? ¡Llévalo al mecánico!   7. ¿Las manzanas? ¡Lávalas antes de comerlas!   8. ¿Las luces? ¡No las apagues!   9. ¿Los vegetales? ¡Cómpralos en el mercado!   10. ¿Los ejercicios? ¡No los entregues!

5·10 1. Despiértense   2. Levántense   3. Prepárense   4. Lávense   5. Cepíllense   6. se desanimen   7. se miren   8. Pónganse   9. Siéntense   10. Quédense

6 Building sentences with coordinating conjunctions

6·1 1. Fui a casa de Laura y jugué con su perro.   2. Yo quería cenar con ella, pero Laura tenía una cita con el dentista.   3. Laura no faltará a la cita, pero no le gusta ir al dentista.   4. Laura no come de día ni duerme por la noche.   5. Va al dentista o tomará calmantes por mucho tiempo.   6. Tengo mucha paciencia pero Laura me enoja.   7. Es una linda persona pero es muy indecisa.   8. Regresé a casa y cené solo.

6·2 1. nosotras; Alicia y yo limpiamos la casa los sábados y los domingos cenamos con mis padres.   2. Yo, como; No como carne ni pollo.   3. prepara; Alicia prepara la ensalada de lechuga can aguacate y la limonada.   4. invitan; Mis padres invitan a mis primos o a sus amigos, los López.   5. nosotros; A veces, tomamos una copa de vino o bebemos un vaso de cerveza.   6. nos gusta; Nos gusta un café con el postre o un té de camomila.   7. ellos dan un paseo; Después, Alicia y su novio dan un paseo por la ciudad o por la playa.   8. son días; Los domingos no son días buenos ni malos.   9. yo; Los domingos ceno con mis padres pero prefiero una cena con mis primos.   10. van; Mis primos van al cine conmigo o al "Café Nostalgia".

6·3 1. La escritora llegó a la oficina y se sentó a escribir su novela.   2. Escribió el capítulo final pero no le gustó.   3. Escribió otro capítulo pero resultó muy aburrido.   4. O cambiaba el comienzo o el final sería imposible.   5. No tenía ideas y salió de la oficina.   6. No tenía ganas de escribir ni de buscar más ideas.   7. Salió de la oficina y fue a la librería.   8. Se sentó en una silla y tomó un café.   9. Observó a la gente a su alrededor e inició el capítulo.   10. La autora era inteligente y logró terminar el capítulo.

6·4   1. Bailas muy bien pero tocas la guitarra mejor.   2. No habla ni llora. / Ni habla ni llora.   3. Entras y sales. O entras o sales.   4. No eres amable con tus colegas ni tampoco eres cortés con tus amigos.   5. Es muy caro pero tengo dinero suficiente. / Es muy caro y tengo dinero suficiente.   6. No cerraron la tienda a las nueve sino a las diez. / No cerraron la tienda a las nueve ni a las diez.   7. Viajaremos por las montañas y luego por la costa.   8. Llévame al aeropuerto ahora o pierdo mi vuelo a Arizona.   9. Me gusta esta novela pero es muy larga.

6·5   1. Mi amiga y yo iremos al cine y compraremos las entradas.   2. No nos gustan las películas de horror ni (preferimos) las películas muy dramáticas.   3. No llueve mucho, pero date prisa.   4. Tenemos poco dinero, (tenemos) muchas deudas y nuestro apartamento es muy caro.   5. Ahorramos mucho, pero no somos tacaños.   6. O ganamos más dinero, pedimos un aumento de sueldo o buscamos otro trabajo.   7. No somos ambiciosos, sino cautelosos.   8. Somos jóvenes y tenemos el futuro por delante.

7   Building sentences with subordinating conjunctions

7·1   1. aunque / por más que   2. porque   3. después que   4. si   5. por más que / aunque   6. desde que   7. que   8. ya que

7·2   1. Necesito trabajar en mi jardín aunque llueve mucho.   2. Tengo unos guantes ya que quiero proteger mis manos.   3. Después que me pongo los guantes, me pongo mi sombrero.   4. Tomaremos una limonada si tienes sed.   5. Desde que empecé a trabajar en el jardín, he rebajado doce libras de peso.   6. Como tengo mucha paciencia, trabajo lento, despacio.   7. Puesto que quieres limonada, voy a cortar los limones de mi jardín.   8. Necesitamos hielo ya que quieres tomar la limonada fría.

7·4   1. ¡Dios mío! Se anuncia que habrá / va a haber una tormenta de nieve.   2. Mi esposo dice que ya había nevado mucho durante la noche.   3. Yo sé que en (el) invierno esto es posible.   4. Creo que podremos / vamos a poder subir la montaña en auto.   5. Pienso que será / va a ser un día magnífico para esquiar.   6. Ah, otro boletín de "El tiempo" dice que las condiciones del tiempo son ideales para los deportes de invierno.   7. Sabía que iba a ser un día bonito.   8. Mi marido sabe que soy optimista.   9. Lo cierto es que me encanta la nieve.   10. Me siento feliz cuando estoy en un lugar frío.

7·5   1. Ganaré mucho más dinero si trabajo más horas.   2. Terminaré mi máster si tomo dos cursos en línea este semestre.   3. Me casaré en agosto de este año si convenzo a mi novia.   4. Viajaré a Buenos Aires si gano el premio gordo.   5. Conseguiré mis metas si tengo claros mis objetivos.   6. Tendré el apoyo de mi familia si necesito ayuda en algún momento.   7. Compraré un apartamento si tengo un aumento de sueldo.   8. Visitaré a mis amigos si puedo conseguir un billete a buen precio.   9. Iré a Brasil si aprendo suficiente portugués para hablar con la gente.   10. Aumentaré mi fortuna si invierto mi dinero de manera sensata.

7·6   1. quién / cómo / por qué   2. cómo   3. por qué / cómo   4. si   5. qué   6. dónde   7. cuándo   8. quiénes

7·7   1. dónde están las joyas robadas   2. a qué hora llegarán los agentes   3. quién escribió la nota   4. adónde llevaron a la víctima   5. cuándo descubrieron el robo   6. por qué abandonaron la casa de la víctima   7. cómo se llama la sospechosa   8. a quiénes vamos a interrogar después   9. si asignaron un especialista a este caso   10. desde cuándo no hay un boletín de noticias

8   Relative pronouns

8·1   1. quien   2. que   3. que   4. quien / que   5. que   6. que   7. quienes   8. que   9. que   10. quien

8·2   1. la invitación que recibí   2. la persona que me envió la invitación   3. la respuesta que escribí   4. las estampillas que compré   5. los regalos que escogí   6. la persona que / a quien conocí en la fiesta   7. la música que tocaron   8. el traje que llevé

8·4   1. los que; Los que llegan temprano y están listos no tienen que hacer cola.   2. la que; La que compró el billete en la Internet fue más lista.   3. el que; El que factura el equipaje está dispuesto a perderlo.   4. los; Los que no tienen asientos están anotados en la lista de espera.   5. las; Las que no siguen las órdenes del capitán no son disciplinadas.   6. los / las que; Los / Las que están ya en la cabina deben tomar asiento.

8·5   1. El hombre cuyo hermano llegó es mi jefe.   2. Luli, cuyo esposo no está aquí, quiere comprar un auto de lujo.   3. La dama, cuya bolsa es horrible, cree que es elegante.   4. ¡Esta chica, cuyo novio es muy bien parecido, es tan aburrida!   5. ¿Te gusta *La sombra del viento*, cuyo autor es español?   6. Miranda, cuyos padres no viven aquí, es demasiado joven para manejar sola.

8·6 1. No tenemos entradas para el concierto, lo cual me enfurece.   2. Quiero sentarme con Carla y Lupe, las cuales son fanáticas del rap.   3. Hay que hacer cola con Juan, cuya paciencia es corta.   4. Podemos darle una propina a Mario, lo cual me parece lógico.   5. Mario hace la cola, que es muy larga.   6. Así, nos vamos al café con Marcos, que tiene el auto aquí mismo.   7. Mario vio a Rolando Villazón, a quien escuchó en el concierto ayer.   8. Detesto esta situación en que me encuentro aquí ahora.

8·7 1. La prensa publica la reacción del Presidente, la cual no está clara para mí.   2. Según el Presidente, quien fue elegido por voto popular, no hay crisis económica.   3. El Presidente mencionó entre otras cosas una crisis económica, la cual es real.   4. El pueblo, que / el cual está muy bien informado, necesita confiar en su gobierno.   5. La crisis internacional, que / la cual afecta a muchas naciones, es una prioridad.   6. Un líder necesita comunicar claramente, lo cual es muy importante.   7. El discurso del Presidente, cuyas palabras estoy leyendo ahora, no aclara la situación.   8. El partido de la oposición, que / el cual espera ganar las próximas elecciones, no ha comentado.

8·8 1. que   2. la que   3. el que   4. el que   5. el cual   6. que   7. lo cual   8. la que

9   Using pronouns

9·1 1. Marcos, él es el hermano de Marta.   2. Trabaja con Marta.   3. Él es el chef, no Marta.   4. Conozco bien a Marta.   5. Yo quiero al cine esta noche; no Marta.   6. ¿Quieres ir al cine?

9·2 1. usted   2. usted   3. tú   4. usted   5. usted   6. ustedes   7. ustedes   8. tú

9·3 1. Ellos querían comer.   2. Tú cantas pero ella toca la guitarra.   3. ¡Ellas pueden terminar la tarea!   4. Ustedes empezaron a las diez pero nosotros terminamos temprano.   5. Ahora, tú descansas mientras yo lavo la ropa.

9·4 1. lo; La policía lo encontró.   2. la; La llevaron al hospital.   3. lo; La víctima no lo reveló.   4. le; El médico le diagnosticó un trauma leve.   5. le (se), lo; La enfermera se lo llevó.   6. le (se), lo; El noticiero local se lo comunicó.   7. los; Al día siguiente la policía los investigó.   8. la; El criminal la recibirá.

9·5 1. Le di una nota a ella.   2. Le pedimos un favor a su hermano.   3. Nos trajeron una computadora nueva a nosotros.   4. Luis y Ana le pidieron un aumento a su jefe.   5. Marcela les mandó flores a ellos / ellas.   6. Tú nos preparaste la recepción a nosotros.   7. Cindy le dijo varios chistes a mi hermano.   8. Roberto les anunció su jubilación a sus amigos.

9·6 1. Los clientes le devolvieron los zapatos   2. El empleado les mostró otro modelo   3. Le compraron ese par de zapatos.   4. La tienda les dio un descuento   5. Los clientes gastaron más dinero.   6. El jefe le dio una comisión   7. Los clientes les agradecieron la amabilidad

9·7 *Possible answers:*   1. ¿Le gusta el té?   2. ¿Les gusta la comida mexicana?   3. ¿Le gusta correr por la playa?   4. ¿Les gusta nadar en la piscina?   5. ¿Le gustan los programas cómicos o dramáticos?   6. ¿Les ha gustado esta encuesta?

9·8 1. Me fascinan las novelas de misterio.   2. No me interesan las biografías, son aburridas.   3. Me duele la cabeza y tomo una aspirina.   4. Me hace falta dinero y voy al banco.   5. Me basta con poco, soy modesto/a.   6. Me cae mal Carolina; es antipática.   7. Me cae bien Nina porque es agradable.   8. Me faltan diez dólares.   9. Me toca descansar porque he terminado el ejercicio.   10. Me encanta estudiar español.

9·9 1. se   2. nos   3. se   4. se   5. me   6. te   7. os   8. me

9·10 Eduardo Benítez dirige una agencia de publicidad. Eduardo la dirige con éxito. El año pasado dobló las ganancias. Y las logró con su esfuerzo. Los inversionistas le agradecen su perseverancia. Eduardo les asegura que al año próximo doblará las ganancias: más dinero. Y van a ganarlo / lo van a ganar porque hay una gran demanda en el mercado internacional. Eduardo lo conoce muy bien.

9·11 1. Estoy admirándola.   2. Van a encontrarlas.   3. Vas a pedirlo.   4. No va a tenerla.   5. ¿Quieren dejarlo?   6. Vamos a terminarlo.

10   Using adjectives

10·1 famosos, bellas, elevadas, africanas, vegetarianos, compleja, jóvenes, ágiles, curiosa, inteligentes, simpáticos, enormes, tropicales

10·2   1. fieles; incapacitadas   2. habladoras   3. tropicales   4. agresivos; inteligentes   5. cariñosa; simpática   6. humanas   7. rápidas   8. anfibio

10·4   1. f; largo pelo   2. a; bellas flores   3. d; dulce bebida   4. b; fuerte dolor   5. e; destructivo huracán   6. c; suave piel

10·6   1. buen   2. algún   3. gran   4. mal   5. ningún   6. primer   7. tercer   8. cien

10·7   1. Ayer mi hermano fue a visitar a su viejo amigo Mario.   2. Mario mismo me dijo que admira a mi padre.   3. Él cree que nuestro padre es una gran influencia en su propia vida.   4. El padre de Mario es muy viejo y está enfermo.   5. El padre de Mario vivía en una casa vieja en Guatemala.   6. Un día decidió mudarse a Nuevo México.   7. La familia de Mario no era pobre.   8. Una vieja amiga mía conoció a Mario y a su padre, Don Julián.   9. Pobre Don Julián, está demasiado enfermo para regresar a Guatemala.

10·8   1. abiertas   2. muertas   3. desechos   4. desenvueltos   5. impreso   6. reescrito   7. revuelta   8. rotas

11 Using adverbs

11·1   *Possible answers; there may be others:*   1. hoy   2. lejos / cerca   3. Mientras / Cuando; mucho / bastante / poco   4. nunca / jamás   5. Siempre   6. siempre / incluso / también   7. Aquí / Allí / Allá   8. muy / bastante

11·2   1. discretamente   2. pacientemente   3. puntualmente   4. delicadamente   5. frecuentemente   6. respetuosamente   7. rápidamente   8. tranquilamente

11·3   1. g; luchar valientemente   2. c; conducir cuidadosamente   3. h; respirar profundamente   4. e; vestirse elegantemente   5. a; hacer ejercicios frecuentemente   6. f; meditar silenciosamente   7. b; oler agradablemente   8. d.; tratar cortésmente

11·5   *Some examples; other answers are possible:*   1. en voz baja   2. con los brazos abiertos   3. a buen precio   4. por todas partes   5. en ninguna parte   6. de buena gana   7. en voz alta   8. en voz baja

11·6   1. Actualmente, todos los productos ecológicos son populares.   2. Por consiguiente, construir una casa ecológica, tiene sentido.   3. En general, a la gente le gusta una casa hermosa en un barrio bueno.   4. Es importante buscar un buen lugar, en particular bien orientado para ahorrar energía.   5. El viento puede ayudar a consumir menos electricidad, especialmente en el verano.   6. Los ecologistas reciben con gusto las noticias de los avances de la tecnología verde.   7. Sin duda, hay más demanda de casas ecológicas.   8. Es extremadamente importante considerar todas las posibilidades, en particular plantas dentro de la casa para reducir la contaminación.

11·7   *Possible answers:*   1. Por fin / Entonces   2. completamente / absolutamente   3. realmente   4. En seguida / Seguidamente   5. Al cabo de   6. dificultosamente   7. con rapidez / velozmente / sin demora   8. claramente / indiscutiblemente / con toda seguridad   9. en todo lugar / por toda la casa   10. Finalmente / Por último   11. Arriba de / Sobre   12. dentro del agua   13. En seguida / Inmediatamente / Rápidamente   14. por fortuna / felizmente / dichosamente / por dicha

12 Using infinitives

12·1   1. Caminar es saludable.   2. Nadar abre el apetito.   3. Correr quema muchas calorías.   4. Jugar al golf es muy relajante.   5. Remar puede ser difícil.   6. Subir una montaña no es mi actividad preferida.   7. Bailar es casi un deporte.   8. Pero dormir es mi actividad favorita.

12·2   1. Comer y beber en exceso no mejora la salud.   2. Asistir a un concierto de música clásica inspira a muchas personas.   3. Compartir mensajes por email nos comunica con nuestros amigos.   4. Invertir dinero en la bolsa puede aumentar una fortuna.   5. Contribuir a una campaña electoral satisface a los ciudadanos.   6. Ayudar a los desamparados tiene mérito.

12·3   1. el leer   2. el dormir   3. el trabajar   4. el perder   5. el ahorrar   6. el comer y charlar

12·4   1. Al despertarse, mi hermana llamó por teléfono a su amiga Loli.   2. En vez de preparar el desayuno, perdió mucho tiempo.   3. Antes de salir a su trabajo, no apagó la cafetera.   4. En lugar de ayudar en la casa, complicó mi situación.   5. Sin despedirse de mí, salió de casa.   6. Después de llegar a la oficina, llamó a mi madre.

12·7   *Possible answers:*   1. ¿Qué prefiere hacer al salir del trabajo?   2. ¿A qué hora necesita llegar al aeropuerto?   3. ¿Dónde quiere hacer escala?   4. ¿Qué necesita facturar?   5. ¿Adónde le gustaría ir?   6. ¿Con quién preferiría viajar la próxima vez?

12·8   1. Vi el avión aterrizar.   2. Escuchamos al agente (de vuelo) saludar a los pasajeros.   3. Mary empezó a prepararse para recibir a su familia.   4. Ella fue a pedir una silla de ruedas.   5. Luis empezó a buscar las maletas.   6. Los niños se pusieron a llorar cuando se despertaron.   7. Entonces Luis oyó sonar su celular.   8. Escuchó hablar una voz familiar.   9. Entonces vio venir a su hermana.   10. Por fin, todos fueron a buscar el auto.

12·9   1. no dejó escapar al criminal   2. mandó hacer una investigación   3. permitió visitar a la víctima en el hospital   4. prohibieron llegar a los periodistas al salón   5. no dejaron revelar el nombre de la víctima   6. nos impidió llegar a recepción en el hospital

12·11   *Possible answers:*   1. Seguramente van a salir de compras a Nueva York el año que viene.   2. Tal vez Miranda y Alejandro van a querer acompañar a sus padres la próxima vez.   3. Afortunadamente mis sobrinos van a competir en el torneo de golf este año.   4. Con toda certeza, Cati y Luisa no se van a entrenar para participar en los Juegos Panamericanos en el futuro.   5. Desgraciadamente mis hermanos no van a asistir a la Fiesta de San Fermín nunca más.   6. Desde ahora, tú y yo nos vamos a comunicar por email con más frecuencia.

13 Idioms and special phrases

13·1   1. k; El detective llevó a cabo un excelente trabajo.   2. e; Pasó la noche en blanco.   3. b; Afuera, llovía a cántaros.   4. a; Ató cabos.   5. f; No quería dejar pasar la ocasión.   6. c; Sacó una foto del sospechoso.   7. g; Para el detective, el caso valía la pena.   8. i; El sospechoso guardaba cama.   9. j; Pero el sospechoso era hombre muerto.   10. d; El detective iba a salirse con la suya.   11. g; El trabajo valió la pena.

13·2   1. Carlos se da prisa.   2. Felipe da una mano a Mario. Felipe le da una mano a Mario.   3. Ahora, Ana se da cuenta de mi problema.   4. Luisa me da gracias por mis consejos.   5. Cuando entramos, Ana nos da la mano.   6. Benita da a conocer los secretos de todos.   7. Berta y Alina dan ánimo a sus amigos.   8. A todos nos encanta dar una vuelta.

13·4   1. hace el papel de   2. hace preguntas   3. hace favores   4. hace daño   5. hace caso   6. hace la vida imposible

13·5   1. c; Habla con mucha claridad, pone los puntos sobre las íes.   2. g; No gasta mucho dinero, no tira la casa por la ventana.   3. a; Es convincente, se sale con la suya.   4. b; No es puntual, no llega a tiempo, pierde el tren.   5. f; Cuida sus intereses, no pierde nada de vista.   6. e; No discute ni pelea con sus hermanos, se pone de acuerdo.   7. d; Acepta las explicaciones de sus amigos, no pone nada en duda.

13·6   1. tiene sueño   2. tengo prisa   3. tienen éxito   4. tenía frío   5. tenía dolor de cabeza   6. tienen ganas   7. tenemos paciencia   8. no tengo suerte / tengo mala suerte   9. no tiene razón   10. tienes la culpa

13·7   1. El saber no ocupa lugar.   2. Cuando una puerta se cierra, cien se abren. / Quien espera, desespera. / Persevera y triunfarás.   3. Ojos que no ven, corazón que no siente.   4. Peor es nada.   5. Más vale tarde que nunca.   6. Amigo en la adversidad es un amigo de verdad.   7. El tiempo lo cura todo. / Lo pasado, pasado está. / Borrón y cuenta nueva.   8. El que la hace, la paga. / Quien mal anda, mal acaba.

13·8   1. bajo siete llaves   2. loco como una cabra   3. blanco como un papel   4. ¡Como que dos y dos son cuatro!   5. desternillarme de la risa   6. te vas a meter en un lío   7. no vienen al caso   8. te llegó la hora

13·9   *Some examples; other answers are possible:*   1. Vale la pena.   2. Dime con quién andas y te diré quién eres.   3. Cada oveja con su pareja.   4. No viene al caso.   5. Nunca es tarde si la dicha es buena.   6. La casa está patas arriba.   7. Para chuparse los dedos.   8. Es un ladrillo.

14 Comparisons, contrasts, and antonyms

14·1   1. D   2. S   3. S   4. D   5. S

14·3   1. China es el país más poblado del mundo.   2. Nueva York es la ciudad más atractiva de los EE.UU.   3. Los perros son los animales más fieles al hombre.   4. Los zafiros son las piedras más caras de la colección.   5. El fútbol es el deporte más popular entre los jóvenes ecuatorianos.   6. San Agustín es la población más antigua de la Florida.   7. Las carreras de caballos son los eventos más populares de la temporada.   8. El flamenco es la música española más conocida en el mundo.

14·4   1. El paquete rojo es el más pesado y el paquete verde es el menos pesado de los tres.   2. Alicia es la más alta y Rosalba es la menos alta de las tres.   3. El bolso de cocodrilo es el más caro y el bolso de tela es el menos caro de los tres.   4. Santo Domingo es la más antigua y San Agustín es la menos antigua de las tres.   5. El artículo es el más largo y la carta es la menos larga de los tres.   6. El bañador de Marta es el más grande y el de Lidia es el más pequeño.

14·5   1. La novela *La casa verde* es muy larga. Es larguísima.   2. El tren de alta velocidad es muy veloz. Es velocísimo.   3. El tango es muy popular en toda la América hispana. Es popularísimo.   4. Margarita es muy fuerte. Es fuertísima.   5. Las pinturas del museo del Prado son muy valiosas. Son valiosísimas.   6. Los romanos crearon obras arquitectónicas muy importantes. Son importantísimas.   7. Los bienes raíces en Nueva York son muy costosos. Son costosísimos.   8. Los tesoros en el fondo del mar Caribe son muy ricos. Son riquísimos.

14·6   1. La familia de Marcos es muy rica / riquísima.   2. Son muy generosos / generosísimos con la comunidad.   3. Ellos tenían una mansión muy grande /grandísima.   4. El padre de Marcos vendió la mansión por una cantidad muy alta / altísima.   5. La familia dio una cantidad muy notable / notabilísima a obras de caridad.   6. Marcos donó una colección de monedas muy valiosa / valiosísima.

14·7   1. Los atletas estadounidenses son más jóvenes que los mexicanos.   2. El hermano de Julián es el ganador más joven.   3. El mejor gimnasta del equipo estadounidense no ganó una medalla.   4. Este es un grupo más grande de fanáticos.   5. El público dijo que este partido de tenis fue peor que el de ayer.   6. El estadio más grande de Canadá estará listo para las competencias.

14·9   1. complicado 2. oscuro 3. rápido 4. frío 5. listo / inteligente 6. delgado 7. áspera 8. fuerte

14·10   1. irresponsable 2. irreparable 3. impaciente 4. indisciplinada 5. injusta 6. intolerante 7. insegura 8. inconveniente 9. extrovertido 10. imprudente

14·11   1. La tolerancia fortalece las sociedades compasivas.   2. La esperanza aumenta la confianza de las personas.   3. Lo positivo eleva el espíritu y mejora la actitud de los individuos.   4. El gastar en exceso crea problemas económicos.   5. La verdad triunfa sobre la mentira siempre.   6. La incertidumbre provoca ansiedad entre la población.

15 The passive voice

15·1   1. Las costas de Texas han sido afectadas por el huracán Alina.   2. El último boletín del tiempo ya ha sido emitido por los meteorólogos.   3. A lo largo de la costa, muchos árboles han sido destruidos por los vientos huracanados.   4. Un gran número de miembros de la población han sido (fueron) asistidos por los bomberos.   5. Las recomendaciones de las autoridades no fueron observadas por muchos ciudadanos.   6. En el futuro los habitantes serán obligados por la policía a tomar medidas.   7. Mañana, las actividades de ayuda a los necesitados serán iniciadas por grupos de voluntarios.   8. Para evitar daños, la población será educada por el departamento de policía.

15·2   1. fueron enviados 2. fueron firmados 3. fueron fotocopiados 4. fue anunciada 5. fue redactado 6. fue firmada 7. fue impresa 8. fue divulgado

15·3   1. El partido será difundido por cable.   2. El encuentro será televisado desde San José.   3. Todos los jugadores serán entrenados para estar en forma.   4. El estadio será preparado para acomodar a la fanaticada.   5. El precio de las entradas será controlado para evitar fraudes.   6. El parqueo será limitado en los alrededores del estadio.   7. Un grupo de niños será invitado para la ceremonia de apertura.   8. El éxito del partido será asegurado con los voluntarios.   9. El himno nacional será interpretado al comienzo del evento.   10. El encuentro será visto en todo el país.

15·4   1. La ciudad de Santo Domingo se trasladó en 1502. 2. La ciudad se declaró Patrimonio de la Humanidad.   3. En Santo Domingo se crearon las primeras instituciones europeas en América.   4. Durante la Colonia, se construyeron grandes monumentos.   5. Los monumentos se restauraron en época reciente.   6. La restauración se celebró en el mundo entero.

15·5   1. En una tintorería se lava y se plancha ropa.   2. En una librería se venden libros y se toma un café.   3. En un restaurante se cena y se charla con los amigos.   4. En una universidad se estudia y se conoce a mucha gente.   5. En una tienda se venden artículos y se devuelve mercancía.   6. En un teatro se escuchan conciertos y se aplauden a los artistas.   7. En una playa se toma el sol y se nada.   8. En un casino se apuesta dinero y se pierden fortunas.

16 The subjunctive mood

16·1   1. C 2. F 3. C 4. C 5. C 6. F 7. C 8. F

16·2   1. confía 2. cumpla 3. protesten 4. respeten 5. esté 6. apoya 7. invada 8. pierden

16·3 1. Deseo que mis amigos respeten... 2. Dudo que mis compañeros de trabajo tengan... 3. Tengo miedo de que mi jefe descubra que... 4. Siento que mi mejor amiga necesite hablar... 5. Prefiero que mis enemigos decidan... 6. No quiero que nadie diga... 7. Detesto que la gente murmure... 8. Propongo que todos me dejen...

16·4 1. Es necesario que practiquen ejercicios de calentamiento. 2. Es importante que mantengan el peso ideal. 3. Es absolutamente indispensable que sigan una rutina de disciplina. 4. Es mejor que lleven una dieta saludable. 5. Es bueno que corran temprano por la mañana. 6. No es absurdo que levanten pesas. 7. Es aconsejable que sean constantes. 8. Es ridículo que descansen solamente un día a la semana.

16·6 1. Si me llamaras por teléfono, te daría las instrucciones para llegar a casa. 2. Si llegaras antes de la ocho, conocerías a mi hermana. 3. Te prepararía una paella de mariscos y un flan, si me lo pidieras. 4. Si quisieras, alquilaríamos una película de Almodóvar. 5. Podríamos ir al cine y tomar un café, si lo desearas. 6. Sería una buena idea si trajeras tu nueva cámara digital. 7. Tomaríamos fotos desde mi terraza si te gustara la vista. 8. Todo eso sería posible, si tú quisieras.

16·7 1. Si me mudara a Rusia, cambiara mi forma de vivir. 2. Si tuviera más tiempo, me dedicara a escribir mis memorias. 3. Si fuera más joven, probara otra profesión. 4. Si conociera al/a la presidente/a de Estados Unidos, le pidiera su autógrafo. 5. Si viajara a Europa, visitara Coímbra y Praga. 6. Si pudiera lograr mi gran sueño, hiciera muchos cambios en mi vida. 7. Si decidiera cambiar de vida, pudiera estudiar otra carrera. 8. Si ganara el premio grande de la lotería, comprara una casa para mis padres.

16·8 1. Tendré que trabajar en mi jardín aunque llueva mucho. 2. Aunque tuviera unos guantes, no protegería mis manos. 3. Después que me ponga los guantes, me pondré mi sombrero. 4. Tomaríamos limonada si tuvieras sed. 5. Cuando empiece a trabajar en el jardín, rebajaré de peso. 6. Si tuviera mucha paciencia, trabajaría lento, despacio. 7. Y si quisieras más limonada, cortaría los limones de mi jardín.

16·10 1. es 2. pueda 3. quiere 4. tenga 5. comprenda 6. cuesta 7. comparte 8. logre

17 The subjunctive mood and verb tenses

17·1 1. esté 2. llegue 3. escriban 4. terminen 5. ayude 6. tengas 7. llega 8. puede

17·2 1. traiga 2. esperen 3. insista 4. tienen 5. envuelva 6. dé 7. debes 8. se vayan

17·3 1. hayan llegado 2. hayan volado 3. ha retrasado 4. haya causado 5. hayan subido 6. han decidido 7. haya sido 8. ha enterado

17·4 1. haya comido 2. haya seguido 3. ha preferido 4. haya abusado 5. se han querido 6. haya conocido 7. se haya enamorado 8. han soñado 9. he tenido 10. hayas encontrado 11. he sufrido 12. hayan ido

17·5 1. bailaran 2. salieran 3. se llevara 4. fuera 5. tenían 6. se rieron 7. aparecieran 8. se divirtió

17·6 1. ayudara 2. representó / representaba / había representado 3. quería / había querido 4. cobró / cobraba / había cobrado 5. ganara 6. hiciera 7. visitaran 8. tuviera 9. se consultó / se había consultado 10. volaran

17·7 *Answers include verb forms only.* 1. Podríamos, trabajáramos 2. Construiríamos, tuviéramos 3. Visitaríamos, supiéramos 4. Tendríamos, pudiéramos 5. Aprenderíamos, practicáramos 6. Rebajaríamos, comiéramos 7. Seríamos, respetáramos 8. Estaríamos, leyéramos

17·8 1. Mónica había preferido que tú hubieras invitado a su novio. 2. No pensó que yo hubiera dicho nada a nadie. 3. Negué que mis padres hubieran gastado tanto dinero. 4. No era posible que ellos hubieran comprado un auto tan caro. 5. Preferían que ustedes hubieran dicho la verdad. 6. No pensaban que la fiesta hubiera sido un éxito. 7. Esperaba que nosotros hubiéramos entendido la carta. 8. No entendían que yo hubiera salido de la oficina.

18 Punctuation and spelling

18·1 Juan Luis está cantando en el programa "La semana musical". Ya ha cantado dos canciones viejas y una nueva que estrena hoy. Su grupo está compuesto de cinco músicos. Juan Luis ha cantado con ese grupo por más de veintitrés años. Él espera continuar ganando éxitos con su público.

18·2 1. El Sr. Jiménez viaja a los EE.UU. 2. Encontró artefactos del 200 a.C. 3. La Dra. Melissa Marcos es una experta en civilizaciones antiguas. 4. La Srta. Marcos, su hija, ayuda a su madre. 5. Darán una conferencia en la UE.

18·3 1. Alicia, Luisa e Irene son disciplinadas, trabajadoras, pacientes y eficientes. 2. Hacen ejercicios, montan en bicicleta, levantan pesas y corren siete u ocho millas. 3. Estas chicas también hacen yoga, trabajos comunitarios y sirven a la comunidad. 4. Hacen campañas en EE.UU. para recoger fondos para niños e indigentes. 5. Han recibido premios, certificados e innumerables homenajes de varias organizaciones. 6. Ellas demuestran que la rutina es esencial para ser disciplinado, cumplir metas y triunfar.

18·4 1. Carmen, ven esta noche a las ocho. Ven esta noche a las ocho, Carmen. 2. Al llegar a casa, decidimos escuchar los mensajes. Decidimos escuchar los mensajes al llegar a la casa. 3. De hecho, no tienes paciencia porque te enojas mucho. 4. Recibieron una carta de San Antonio, Texas. 5. Necesitaba tu ayuda, tu amistad y tu compañía. 6. Este documento dice que eres de Lima, Perú.

18·5 Como ya sabemos, los Juegos Olímpicos, competiciones de carácter deportivo, se celebran cada cuatro años. Este evento internacional tiene lugar en una ciudad de un país diferente, dentro de un continente diferente. Al decidir cuál será la ciudad anfitriona, la cual es escogida por el Comité Olímpico, se inician los planes y las preparaciones para estar listos en cuatro años. Por un lado, la ciudad debe proveer estadios e instalaciones para recibir a todos los deportistas que compiten, sus entrenadores y los equipos médicos. Por otro lado, la ciudad debe estar lista para los miles de personas que visitarán esa ciudad y ese país para disfrutar de los JJ.OO. Se supone que dentro del espíritu de esas competiciones, las ganancias se deben dedicar a desarrollar el Movimiento Olímpico Internacional y el deporte.

18·6 1. Vamos a mudarnos a una casa más grande; no tenemos suficiente espacio. 2. Los muebles de la sala, los cuadros, los platos de la cocina: todo está listo. 3. Compramos cuatro aparatos nuevos: una computadora, un televisor HD, un teléfono móvil y una aspiradora. 4. Cómoda, amplia, fresca y acogedora: así es la casa nueva. 5. Una cocina debe ser lo mejor de una casa: espaciosa, bien equipada y llena de luz. 6. Ahora podemos quitar el letrero que dice: "Se vende casa".

18·7 1. El primer día del verano (21 de junio en el hemisferio norte) nos trae alegría. 2. Mi madre (mujer muy sabia) siempre me hablaba de sus experiencias cuando era niña. 3. Uno de sus consejos era: "El tiempo es oro". 4. Pensaba que mi madre era invencible (¡qué ilusión!) cuando yo era niño. 5. Todas las mañanas cantábamos una canción: "La cucaracha". 6. ¡Qué risa me da ahora (han pasado tantos años) porque mi madre era divertida! 7. Y le gustaba en especial un poema: "La rosa blanca". 8. Raras veces era dura, pero su amenaza siempre era: "¡A la cama!". 9. Cuando no estaba de buen humor, yo sabía que estaba ocupada. 10. Y puedo repetir las palabras que decía mi padre para recordarla: "Corazón de oro".

18·8 En, Universidad, Sevilla, En, Mario Vargas Llosa, Isabel Allende, Al, Casa Belisa

18·9 Marcia, lunes, California, África, ella, suroeste, Estados Unidos

19 Letter writing

19·1 1. el encabezamiento 2. la fecha 3. el destinatario 4. el saludo 5. la redacción de la carta 6. la despedida 7. la firma

19·2 1. La Habana, 13 de noviembre de 1988 2. Santo Domingo, 31 de julio de 2000 3. Bogotá, 1 de enero de 2012 4. San Fernando, 28 de febrero de 2005 5. Los Ángeles, 16 de marzo de 2003 6. Barcelona, 23 de abril de 1995

19·3 *There may be other possible closing formulas.*

1. Madrid, 3 de mayo de 2001
   Estimado Dr. Blanco:
   Atentamente,
2. Guadalajara, 19 de julio de 2009
   Querida Sra. Rodríguez:
   Le saluda cordialmente,
3. San Diego, 13 de enero de 2010
   Estimado Capitán Vázquez:
   Con todo mi respeto,

19·4 1. 27 de marzo de 2000 2. 5 de mayo de 1999 3. 12 de diciembre de 2008 4. 8 de agosto de 2008 5. 10 de octubre de 2003 6. 10 de febrero de 1980

19·5 1. Barcelona, 10 de mayo de 2001
   Mi queridísima Anita:
   Con todo mi amor,

2. Managua, 9 de junio de 2002
   Mi querida tía Úrsula:
   Con todo mi cariño,
3. Guayaquil, 3 de agosto de 2003
   Mi querido amigo:
   Un abrazo cariñoso,

19·6 1. Sra. Lidia Gómez
   Avenida del Norte, 27
   00087 Barcelona
2. Sr. Alcalde Raúl Benítez
   Alcaldía de Pueblo Nuevo
   Torreón, 305
   27250 México D.F.
3. Sres. Dolores y Antonio Bermúdez
   Calle C, 17111, Apart. D
   00891 La Habana

20 Let's write!

20·1 1. Mis hermanos visitaron esa región varias veces.   2. La idea fue sugerida por la agencia de viajes   3. El proyecto del viaje era interesante.   4. Un grupo local compartió la trayectoria con los viajeros.   5. Los turistas fueron recibidos por una banda de música.   6. El cantante no cantaba en español.   7. Ahora hacen planes para viajar al sur de Bolivia.   8. Las próximas vacaciones, mis sobrinas vendrán a mi casa.

20·2 *Some examples; other answers are possible.*   1. ¿Por qué vas a Madrid? ¿Quiénes van a Madrid contigo? ¿Dónde está tu pasaporte? ¿Cuándo regresas a Barcelona? ¿Qué vas a hacer en Madrid mañana?   2. ¿Qué regalo has comprado? ¿Quiénes van a celebrar el aniversario? ¿Dónde van a celebrar el aniversario? ¿Cuándo se casaron tus padres? ¿Cómo van a celebrar el aniversario?   3. ¿Dónde quieres cenar? ¿Cuál es tu plato favorito? ¿Quiénes van a cenar? ¿Por qué no invitas a tus amigos? ¿Cuánto cuesta la cena?   4. ¿Cómo está tu amigo? ¿Qué le pasa a tu amigo? ¿Quién es el médico de tu amigo? ¿Dónde está el hospital? ¿Cuándo vas a visitar a tu amigo?   5. ¿Qué productos quieres comprar? ¿Dónde está la tienda? ¿Cuánto dinero vas a gastar? ¿Cuántas veces has ido a esa tienda? ¿Cómo vas a pagar, con tarjeta de crédito?   6. ¿Cuántos años cumples? ¿Qué regalos quieres recibir? ¿Con quién vas a celebrar tu cumpleaños? ¿Dónde va a ser la fiesta? ¿Cómo quieres celebrar tu cumpleaños?

20·3 1. En otra época, era más paciente porque tenía más tiempo.   2. A menudo estudiaba español, ya que quería hablar claro con mis amigos mexicanos.   3. Con frecuencia, aprendía a escribir muchos tipos de oraciones más complejas.   4. Siempre podía contar con mi buen amigo Pablito.   5. A veces, no tenía la constancia necesaria ni la disciplina precisa para estudiar.   6. Día tras día, era difícil escribir en dos idiomas diferentes y a veces con palabras no similares.   7. En ocasiones, iba al cine para ver películas mexicanas y colombianas y eran divertidas.   8. Con frecuencia reflexionaba sobre la poca capacidad de los seres humanos para ser constantes y dedicados.

20·4 1. En otra época, yo podía...   2. A menudo quería...   3. Con frecuencia podía...   4. Siempre iba...   5. A veces compraba...   6. Día tras día practicaba...

20·5 *Some examples; other answers are possible:*   1. Me gustan las películas españolas, pero prefiero las italianas.   2. Cuando puedo, voy a un concierto, y también al teatro.   3. En ocasiones olvido las palabras en español o tengo que usar un diccionario.   4. Quiero escribir mejor en español, pero no puedo practicar todos los días porque trabajo mucho.   5. Detesto hacer ejercicios en el gimnasio, aunque mis amigos van todos los días.   6. No tengo ganas de trabajar ahora, sino de comer papas fritas, beber un refresco y ver la tele.

20·6 *Some examples; other answers are possible:*   Me llamo Julián y tengo veintidós años. Soy alto, delgado y tengo el pelo rubio. Soy trabajador: me levanto a las seis de la mañana y siempre llego a tiempo a mi trabajo. Mi familia es muy cariñosa y siempre me ayuda en mis momentos difíciles. Me llaman por teléfono los fines de semana. He aprendido a hablar y escribir en francés y puedo hablar ruso con mis vecinos. Eso para mí es un gran logro. Ahora quiero terminar mis estudios universitarios y ser meteorólogo. Estudié en Los Ángeles y voy a continuar estudiando cursos en línea (*online*).

20·7 *Sample answer:*   La tecnología avanza muy rápido. Antes, los teléfonos celulares eran más grandes y caros. Ahora, son pequeños y más baratos. Las computadoras también son más rápidas. Hoy usamos el ratón para hacer un clic y escribir un documento. O hacemos un clic para entrar en una página de la Internet. En cambio, en el futuro, no necesitaremos el ratón. Solamente usaremos un dedo para tocar la pantalla.

20·8   *Sample answer:*   Los jóvenes de hoy. Los jóvenes son la esperanza del mundo. Generalmente, son criticados por las personas mayores. Se dice que los jóvenes son egoístas, pero no siempre es verdad. Muchos ayudan a las personas mayores. Los jóvenes siguen la moda. Les gustan la ropa y los zapatos que otros jóvenes usan. También, quieren tener todos los avances tecnológicos.

20·9   *Sample answer:*   Si yo pudiera, no viviría en Estados Unidos por un año. Yo viviría en México para aprender español. Después, yo viajaría a Chile para conocer a los padres de mi amigo Felipe Cerdeña. Quisiera visitar la costa chilena y compararla con la costa de California. Me gustaría ser ingeniero civil y construir puentes. Si pudiera conseguir una beca, podría ir a una buena universidad y cambiar mi vida.

20·10   *Sample answer:*

San Juan, 25 de marzo de 2008

Querida Martica:

    ¿Cómo estás? Quería saludarte y decirte que tengo un nuevo trabajo. Ayer comencé a trabajar en la Clínica del Puerto, una clínica dental en Oviedo. La clínica se especializa en la ortodoncia y en los tratamientos para blanquear (bleach) los dientes. Ahora soy la recepcionista. Este verano voy a terminar mi entrenamiento como asistenta dental, y luego el semestre que viene, como higienista.

    ¿Has terminado tus estudios? Cuando termine mi entrenamiento visitaré a mi familia en Miami. Quiero verte entonces. Podemos hacer planes para cenar una noche, ¿no crees?

Con un saludo cariñoso,

Felicia

21   Review

21·1   1. Vivimos en ese edificio.   2. Aterrizó el avión.   3. Van a salir a las cuatro y media.   4. Vi a Luisa.   5. Recibió el email anoche./Lo recibió anoche.   6. No, no lo conozco.   7. Siempre dice mentiras.   8. Nunca tiene tiempo libre.   9. No, no viene nadie mañana.

21·2   1. ¿Hasta cuando esperaron/esperan ustedes?   2. ¿Aprecian los estudiantes los comentarios de la profesora?   3. ¿Entregaste/Entregó usted el coche?   4. ¿Tienes/Tiene usted el boleto?   5. ¿Qué prefieren ellos?   6. ¿Dónde va a dormir Ana? ¿Por qué?   7. ¿Es verdad que [*Answers will vary*] / [*Answers will vary*], ¿verdad?   8. *Answers will vary.*

21·3   I.   1. Van al centro.   2. Voy a trabajar hasta las 3 de la tarde.   3. Vive en Salamanca.   4. Estamos bien, gracias.   II.   1. ¿Cuántos países has visitado?   2. ¿Cuáles son tus colores preferidos?   3. ¿Cuánto dinero necesitas?   4. ¿Cómo es Alex?   5. Sus padres van a comprar una casa, ¿verdad?   6. ¿Para quiénes son los regalos?   7. ¿Por qué no van al concierto?

21·4   I.   1. ¡Vaya!/¡Qué caros son!   2. ¡Qué bien/mal toca la niña!   3. ¡Caray!/¡Caramba!/¡Caracoles!/¿Estás loca?   4. ¡Pobrecito! /Lo siento mucho./¡Qué pena!   5. De acuerdo./Bien./¡Hasta pronto!   II.   *Answers will vary. The following are suggestions*   1. ¿Quieres ir a bailar esta noche?   2. Vamos a ganar la lotería con este billete.   3. Juan dice que eres su novia.   4. Saqué un 65 por ciento en el examen de matemáticas.   5. ¡Mira! ¡He encontrado $50!

21·5   1. Abre la ventana.   2. Pase, por favor.   3. Comprad los boletos vosotros mismos.   4. Di la verdad.   5. No invitemos a tantas personas.   6. ¿El partido? ¡Olvidadlo!   7. No me esperen.   8. ¿La tarea? Hazla.   9. ¿Mis llaves? Encuéntrenlas.   10. No me llames.

21·6   1. Juega bien al fútbol, pero juega mejor al ténis.   2. Vamos a México por dos semanas, y luego iremos a Guatemala.   3. No fui al cine, sino al teatro.   4. No fui ni al cine ni al teatro.   5. ¿Quieres helado o un refresco?

21·7   I.   1. No compré la blusa, aunque me gustaba mucho.   2. Fui a ver esa película puesto que/ya que/porque recibió el premio Óscar el año pasado.   3. Voy a mudarme a otra ciudad, aunque/por más que quisiera quedarme aquí con ustedes.   4. Te ayudo con las matemáticas si me ayudas con el español.   5. Ya nos vamos, ya que todos estamos listos.   6. Todos estamos contentos, ya que/puesto que/porque mi hermano ha vuelto a casa.   II.   1. ¿Va Jaime con nosotros?   2. ¿Dónde están tus padres?   3. ¿Cuánto cuestan los zapatos?   4. ¿Por qué saliste temprano?   5. ¿A quién le mandaron la carta?   6. ¿Qué baile te gusta más?

21·8   1. Cancelaron el examen, lo cual me alivió.   2. Mi hermana menor, quien/que vive en California, viene a visitarnos este verano.   3. El profesor, cuyo libro lo explica todo de una forma sencilla, es un genio.   4. El verano pasado leí muchos libros, algunos de los cuales son muy interesantes.   5. Mi amiga sólo hace lo que quiere hacer.   6. Voy a hablar con mi amiga, quien/que escribió su tesis sobre este tópico.   7. Ayer compré dos vestidos, de los cuales me gusta más el rojo.   8. Los estudiantes que van a pasar un semestre en esta universidad son de Argentina.

21·9   I.   1. b   2. a   3. a   4. b   II.   1. Luisa lo conoce.   2. Jorge se la regaló (a su hermano).   3. María Isabel la toca.   4. La señora me las mostró.   5. Ayer los compramos.   III. 1. Me despierto a las dos [*answers will vary*]   2. Se los ponen antes de salir/en el invierno/cuando tienen frío.   3. Se preocupa de sus niños [*answers will vary*]   4. Me gusta más la cocina mexicana. [*answers will vary*]   5. Sí, le gusta./No, no le gusta (bailar).   6. Nos interesan los libros de ciencia ficción. [*answers will vary*]   7. A las mujeres les/nos agradan más las flores / los chocolates. [*answers will vary*]   8. Las personas que me importan más son mis padres/mis hijos. [*answers will vary*]

21·10   1. Mis hermanas son altas, pero yo soy bajo/baja.   2. Ayer compré unos libros interesantes.   3. Tres de estos libros son grandes novelas del Siglo XIX.   4. El autor dedicó su libro a su amada esposa, Margarita.   5. ¡La pobrecita/La pobre chica/La pobre se perdió tres veces!   6. Si pasas por la puerta abierta, encontrarás los muebles rotos.   7. Tienen tres hijas, y el bebé es su primer hijo/barón.   8. Aquel caballero le mandó esta rosa roja.

21·11   1. Durante el día, los niños juegan afuera.   2. Luego/Después, y con gusto, fuimos a la fiesta.   3. Se portan mal en clase, en general.   4. Sin duda, gana muy poco.   5. Tampoco voy a quejarme en seguida.   6. Ella siempre habla lenta y cuidadosamente.   7. Los vestidos son hechos a mano y son vendidos a buen precio.   8. Mario ya me ha contactado, pero los otros no han llamado todavía.   9. Él no va a ninguna parte de noche.   10. Claro, habla sin cesar.

21·12   1. Me encanta ver al béisbol.   2. El aprender/Aprender es divertido.   3. Jugar al béisbol en vez de estudiar no es siempre una buena idea.   4. Preferimos relajarnos después de trabajar todo el día.   5. Salió sin despedirse.   6. ¿Qué quieres hacer después de visitar a tu abuela?   7. No temo empezar una carrera nueva.   8. Ver es creer.   9. Es imposible escuchar en este restaurante.   10. Van a lavar los platos después de comer.

21·13   1. Pasé la noche en blanco.   2. Está lloviendo a cántaros.   3. Ella tiene que guardar cama.   4. Van a toda vela.   5. Vamos a dar un paseo.   6. Tengo ganas de bailar.   7. Los perros le dan miedo a la niña.   8. Los chicos no le hacen caso a la profesora.   9. Me importa un pepino.   10. Más vale tarde que nunca.

21·14   I.   1. La casa en el campo es tan cara como la casa en la ciudad.   2. El bolso de Ana es más pesado que el de su hermana.   3. Roberto es mayor que Carlos; Javier es el mayor de los tres.   4. La estudiante es listísima.   5. Ricardo corre más rápido/rápidamente que Álvaro.   II.   1. triste   2. frío   3. desconocido   4. incompetente   5. generoso   6. habladora   7. inculto   8. el empleo   9. el aterrizar   10. la compañía   11. la riqueza   12. la verdad   13. la tolerancia   14. la cordura

21·15   I.   1. Varias casas en el área han sido destruidas.   2. En general, las recomendaciones de las autoridades fueron observadas.   3. Servicios de primer auxilio gratis serán ofrecidos .   II.   1. Se formó el gobierno en 1963.   2. Se aprobaron las nuevas leyes en seguida.   3. Se encarcelaron los líderes del antiguo gobierno.   4. Se quemaron los libros de historia y se escribió la historia del país de nuevo.

21·16   I.   1. Quiero que vengas a mi fiesta.   2. Les pedimos que lleguen a las cuatro.   3. Dudo que llueva.   4. ¡Es increíble que cumplas treinta años!   5. Espero encontrar un vestido nuevo que no sea muy caro.   II.   1. Compraría un carro nuevo si tuviera más dinero.   2. Hablaríamos mejor español si viviéramos en España.   3. Te visitaría en el hospital si no estuviera enfermo él mismo.   4. Volverían a casa si encontraran trabajo aquí en la ciudad.

21·17   1. estudiemos/estudien   2. conduzca   3. lea   4. volvamos   5. hayas suspendido   6. hayan salido   7. viéramos   8. ayudara   9. comiera   10. se hubieran divertido

21·18   I.   1. B.C.   2. USA/U.S.   3. P.S.   4. UN   5. Inc.   6. Dr.   7. Miss   8. EU   II.   Hace mucho frío en partes de los Estados Unidos (EE.UU.) en los meses de diciembre, enero y febrero.

21·19   1. In the upper right hand corner   2. The city and the date   3. número del día + de + mes + del + año (29 de mayo del 2017)   4. a. Estimada Srta. Sánchez: b. Estimado Dr. Martínez: c. Estimado señor: d. Estimados señores: 5. a. Deseo comunicarle   b. Quisiera pedirle   c. Atentamente,   d. Un saludo afectuoso/Con mi más cordial saludo,   e. P.D.

Put Your Spanish Language into Practice!

At busuu, you can practice your Spanish skills through graded courses and a broad range of engaging activities. And as you study, busuu encourages direct interaction with native speakers through video and audio chat.

With busuu, you can:

- Practice with exercises that hone all four skills (reading, writing, speaking, listening).
- Enjoy flexible language learning—anytime, anywhere—to fit into your busy schedule.
- Receive personalized feedback on your exercises, talk with native speakers via an integrated chat, and get to know people from all over the world.

With over 55 million registered users, busuu is the largest social network for language learning in the world!

Special Offer: 20% off Premium membership

McGraw-Hill Education has partnered with busuu to provide an exclusive discount on busuu's award-winning Premium service.

Discount: 20% off any plan
Access code: BUSUUSPA20
Code expiry date: June 30, 2018

Or Try A New Language!

busuu offers courses in eleven other languages, specially designed by educational experts. With programs ranging from Beginning to Upper Intermediate, you'll quickly find the level that works for you!

Sign up or log in on **www.busuu.com** and enter your discount code on the payment page to get your exclusive discount!